The Southern Baptists

Ellen M. Rosenberg

The Southern Baptists

A Subculture in Transition

The University of Tennessee Press   KNOXVILLE

Frontispiece: Baptism, rural Louisiana, 1920s.
Photograph courtesy of the E. C. Dargan Research Library,
Sunday School Board, Southern Baptist Convention.

Library of Congress Cataloging-in-Publication Data

Rosenberg, Ellen MacGilvra, 1929–
    The Southern Baptists : a subculture in transition /
    Ellen M. Rosenberg.—1st ed.
        p.   cm.
    Bibliography: p.
    Includes index.
    ISBN 0–87049–598–4 (cloth: alk. paper) :
    1. Southern Baptist Convention. 2. Sociology, Christian (Baptist)
3. Baptists—United States. 4. Southern States—Religious life and
customs. 5. Southern States—Social conditions. I. Title.
BX6462.7.R66 1989
305.6'61—dc19   88–31610 CIP

Contents

List of Illustrations   vii

Preface   ix

1   **The Hyper-Americans**   1
Southern Baptists as Southerners   1
The Class That Did Not Struggle   6
An Anthropological Perspective on Religion   10
The Texas Connection   14

2   **A Social History of
the Southern Baptists**   20
From the Beginnings to the New World   20
Post-Revolutionary Expansion and Pre-War Schism   23
Landmarkism   32
That War and Its Aftermath   35
The First "New South"   39
Between the World Wars   43
Boom, Quake, and Aftershock   47

3   **The Southern Baptist Polity:
Denominational Structure and
Financing**   51
Obsession with Bureaucracy   51
The Corporate Structure   54
The Annual Meeting and the Presidency   59
Central Mission Organizations   68

The Sunday School Board   75
The Seminaries   78
The Lay Organizations   86
The Social Concerns Agencies   91
Miscellaneous Denominational Agencies   93
The State Level of Organization   95
District Associations   99

4   **Congregations, Pastors, and Families**   101
The Church as a Total Institution   101
A New Rationale for Church Segregation   109
Privatized Families in Homogeneous Churches   115
The Pastor as Role Model and Rule-Maker   119
Family Ministry and Church Discipline   127

5   **Ideology: Theological, Social,
and Aesthetic Dimensions**   133
"Theology" and Ecclesiology   133
Exclusivity and Anti-Ecumenism   149
Social Ethics   153
Liturgy and Aesthetics   168
Is There a Southern Baptist Mind?
Jimmy Carter as Exemplar   175

6   **Southern Baptists, the New Religious
Political Right, and the South**   180
The Southern Context
of the New Religious Political Right   180
The Southern Strategy, the New Religious
Political Right, and the Capture of
the Southern Baptist Convention   184
Internal Implications for the Southern Baptists   204
Southern Baptist Identity in the Newest South   211

References   215

Index   231

List of Illustrations

Baptism, rural Louisiana, 1920s.   *frontispiece*

The Rev. Victor I. Masters   xii

First Baptist Church, Austin, Texas   4

First Baptist Church, Nashville, Tennessee,
   1837–1884   33

Bethlehem Baptist Church,
   Clarksville, Georgia   45

Hendricks Avenue Baptist Church,
   Jacksonville, Florida   48

First Baptist Church, Quincy, California   49

Sunday School Board display,
   annual meeting, 1950   60

Coffee break, annual meeting, 1948   61

Prayer time, annual meeting, 1986   61

Missionary and child, Virginia, 1983   72

Missionary and child, Ethiopia, 1986   73

Woman's Missionary Union leaders, 1950   88

Baptist Student Union booth,
   Louisiana Tech, 1939   97

Senior Baptist Young People's Union,
   Spanish-American church,
   East Las Vegas, New Mexico, 1920s   110

Family night, First Baptist Church,
   Meridian, Mississippi, 1960   116–17

Sunday School class, First Baptist Church,
  Tallahassee, Florida, 1960   120
Fundraising, University Baptist Church,
  Abilene, Texas   128
The Lord's Supper   144
Baptism   145
Southern Baptists against the death penalty,
  1977   162
President and Mrs. Jimmy Carter,
  Baptist Men's meeting, 1978   176
SBC moderates at the Alamo, 1988   203
Pat Robertson recruiters at the Southern Baptist
  Convention annual meeting, 1987   211
Presidents of the Southern Baptist Convention,
  1987   213

Preface

This kind of ethnography is like making a formal portrait of a large moving object while trying to climb inside it without being sure what direction it's going or whether it makes any difference.

In 1981, I started to do a classic anthropological study of the Southern Baptist subculture. After all, anthropologists had done good work on Hutterites and Hare Krishna. Here was the largest Protestant denomination in the United States, fourteen and a half million people, geographically concentrated, largely undescribed. Most work on southern religion combined all the evangelicals—Baptists and Methodists and Presbyterians—or generalized to include both black and white Baptists, obliterating the differences between them. Surely Southern Baptists deserved a spotlight of their own. Behind and beyond this were questions as to the place of the denomination in the power structure of the South, its response to the changes in the southern caste system since desegregation, its role in fostering Bible Belt sexual conservatism, and its possible connection with the gathering movement known as the New Religious Right.

In my earliest conversations with Southern Baptists there were reports of a conservative (fundamentalist) assault on the denominational structure. One prescient pastor announced in early 1982 that the fundamentalists had won—it was all over but the real estate, he said. But the majority downplayed the importance of the threat. Most of the religious press, echoing the fundamentalist leaders, insisted that the differences were theological. But I knew that theology was largely ideological, that religious groups select for emphasis those aspects of their tradition which are congruent with their class interests, express their prejudices, reinforce their identity, or at the very least support their claims to authority.

With the massive changes that had taken place in the South in the last thirty years, it was logical to assume that the controversy might reflect these changes in this most southern of institutions. And that is indeed the way it seems to me now, when the Southern Baptist Convention is cracking apart in reaction to the changes in the southern caste system. Each side accuses the other of betraying Baptist tradition, and each side is half right, since the "Baptist tradition" has contained the crucial contradiction since the beginning. Interpretative freedom for each individual was always posed against Biblical authority; as diversity of interpretation increased among the moderates, the fundamentalists came to insist on conformity to their own (highly selective) literalist view. The competition between them had its own dynamic—of conspiracy, exploitation, manipulation, anger, and bitterness.

So it was like trying to do a biography of a person of long and complex history who was struggling with a life-threatening disease. It was difficult, but necessary, to try to do justice to the whole person without neglecting the way the struggle itself highlighted aspects of character, unexpected strengths, unrevealed weaknesses, unacknowledged contradictions, and was changing the person in its course. My subtitled term "transition" is weak because it is noncommittal, but no one can predict the outcome. The expected polarization, a movement away from the possibility of compromise, continues to occur. The nature of the denominational structure, however, makes a clear split less probable than in a more centralized, less diffuse, organization.

A terminological note: I do not use the term "race" or any of its derivatives, although I cannot help but quote others who do. Carl Degler (1977: 89) claims that "the South was unique. No other society in the New World in which Negro slavery was established found it necessary to defend slavery on racial grounds to the extent that the American South did . . . a biological defense of slavery set the South apart." Gunnar Myrdal recognized the value of avoiding the term: "We believe the term 'caste'—with its socially static connotations—is less dangerous and inaccurate than the term 'race'—with its biologically static connotation" (1944: 1223). American anthropology, presumed to be expert, has shamefully failed to straighten out the rest of the world on this matter.

Encountering the Southern Baptists was like meeting the Rock of Gibraltar: it was there on the map but the size and looming strength had to be met first-hand. The vast bulk of the publishing enterprise and the variety of open meetings and conferences were daunting but invaluable as source material. It turned out that Southern Baptists talked about themselves with remarkable freedom, eagerness to explain, yet some wariness on the part of some Southern Baptist bureaucrats, a term used here without prejudice. As the fundamentalist assault proceeded, this wariness was matched by outpourings of frankness from the unhappy moderates eager to say obliquely what they often dared not directly.

Being a Southern Baptist was, Faulkner said, "an emotional condition that has nothing to do with God or politics or anything else" (1965: 189). The tragicomic stereotypes abound. But then a Southern Baptist woman, employed as a counselor at a denominational institution, said that her "spiritual development" was heavily influenced by Roman Catholic mysticism and replied to a question, "Well, you have to think of it dialectically." And a senior pastor, fiercely loyal to the Southern Baptist Convention, described his members' ability to tolerate contradictions by "narcotizing themselves with their own self-delusions." This diversity, complexity, and capacity for self-perception were totally unexpected and point up the immense and humbling difficulties in doing ethnographic justice to such a huge subculture.

One special source deserves special mention: the Rev. Victor Masters. A preacher-writer, he was editor of the *Western Recorder*, the Kentucky Southern Baptist newspaper, for over twenty years, 1921–1942, a little like being the editor of *L'Osservatore Romano*, since the premier Southern Baptist seminary is in Louisville. During his tenure as publicity director for the domestic missions agency, he published six books of commentary and history, and one of these, *Country Church in the South* (1917), received wide public attention. The books and his newspaper editorials turned out to be both reflectors and shapers of Southern Baptist thought expressed in vivid language during a critical thirty-odd year period.

Born in Anderson, South Carolina, in 1867, Masters earned a B.A. degree from Furman in 1888 and an A.M. the following year. (In 1888 there were 12,562 bachelors' degrees granted to American males; the proportion did not reach 2 percent until 1920.) Masters must have come from an elite background, but as usual with Southern Baptist individuals, it is almost impossible to infer much about class. He was ordained in 1889 and pastored several small churches in South Carolina while he was at Southern Seminary in Louisville, from which he received the Th.M. degree in 1893. His editorial career started with weekly state papers, twelve years at the Home Mission Board and then the long tenure in Kentucky until his retirement in 1942. He died in Florida in 1954, his wife and two sons having predeceased him.

Masters believed in equal justice and a kind of paternalistic religious

Author-editor Rev. Victor I. Masters at work on *Country Church in the South,* c. 1916. (Photograph courtesy of the E. C. Dargan Research Library, Sunday School Board, Southern Baptist Convention.)

uplift for blacks, but abhorred the prospect of social equality with them. He was anti-Semitic; while condemning prejudice, he could write that Americans were "getting weary of those Jews, who get themselves placed sympathetically before a long-suffering public as interpreters-in-chief of tolerance, by the urban press of America that profits largely by Jewish business advertisements—to tell American Christians just what is religious prejudice and how they must avoid it" (Kelsey 1973: 254–55). He was also anti-Catholic, defending legislation to require a literacy qualification for immigrants: "just a bill as that . . . evidently would not have been vetoed by two successive Presidents, without very strong pressure having been brought to bear from some source . . . if the people have the question raised in their minds and should go on the search and find certain Romanist 'influences' at work to defeat the will of the country, it would put the hierarchy in bad order. True it already smells to high heaven for its insolent priestly meddlesomeness in affairs of state" (1916: 25).

Masters was militaristic, attacking "anti-war propaganda between the World Wars as a product of international Communism" (Kelsey 1973: 113). Southern Baptist social historian John Lee Eighmy (1969: 368n) feels Masters was "among Southern Baptists, the most persistent critic of social Christianity," writing that "social gospel ends could best be achieved as the natural fruit of individual regeneration," leading the opposition to a proposed Twentieth Amendment to regulate child labor in a typical pre-millennial expression. He was, all in all, a "highly respected author, editor, and publicist," Southern Baptist historian James J. Thompson, Jr. (1982: 37) concludes, and a model example of educated Southern Baptist leadership over that long period. Masters' words have contributed a special kind of authenticity to this study.

My primary debt, however, is owed to the several hundred living Southern Baptists who so openly shared their thoughts, memories, opinions, and feelings. All requests for confidence have been honored, and every effort made to keep unidentifiable the sources whom it might be hurtful to specify.

Thanks go especially to friends and colleagues Don Boyer, Dave Detzer, Russ Fryer, and Herb Janick, who listened and read and made helpful suggestions. Though they improved the result, they are not in any way responsible for it.

Thanks are also due to the Southeastern Baptist Theological Seminary, the Dargan-Carver Library of the Southern Baptist Convention, the Harvard and Yale Divinity Schools, and the Wilson Library of the University of North Carolina for their research facilities. Special appreciation goes to Mary Kohn and Rosemary Hughes, in charge of Interlibrary Loan at the Haas Library of Western Connecticut State University, to Rebecca Torstrick for special field work, and to Pat McShea and Bill Karnoscak, who did much more than produce clean copy from chaotic typescript.

Gratitude is also due to the Western Connecticut State University for a sabbatical year 1981–1982 and a research grant in the summer of 1986. Portions of this material were presented in very different form in October 1984 to the Society for the Scientific Study of Religion in Chicago, and in December 1985 to the American Anthropological Association in Washington.

A paper, grounded in this work but including much additional research, appears as "'Serving Jesus in the South:' Southern Baptist Women under Assault from the New Right," in *Women in the South*, Southern Anthropological Society Proceedings, no. 22, *ed.* Holly Mathews (Athens: Univ. of Georgia Press: 1989), 122–35.

The Southern Baptists

I   The Hyper-Americans

> The Southern Baptist emotional condition . . . came from
> times of hardship in the South where there was little or no
> food for the human spirit – where there were no books, no
> theatre, no music, and life was pretty hard and a lot of it
> happened out in the sun, for very little reward and that
> was the only escape they had. I think that is the human
> spirit aspiring toward something. Of course, it got warped
> and twisted in the process.
>
> — William Faulkner, 20 May 1957
> (Gwynn and Blotner 1965: 189–90)

Southern Baptists as Southerners

The United States is supposed to be the most religious country
in the developed world, and the least class-ridden. But religion in America,
while serving as one of the mechanisms that blur class consciousness, is
at the same time a vehicle for the most exquisite nuances of class difference
and the most blatant claims of class prejudice and class identity. Much of
this takes place among denominations in most American communities, as
people switch faith commitments to match their movement in the class
structure. The Southern Baptists, almost uniquely because of their huge
bulk and geographical concentration, have been able to express class-based
allegiance within their own denomination. Their peculiar history has made
them the vehicle of white solidarity in the South. But it doesn't work any-
more: just as the Southern Baptists were being accepted into the mainstream of American religious culture, they have been led into a backwater
and firmly moored there, possibly for good.

There are twenty-odd Baptist groups in this country, Protestantism containing the seeds of further protest, and the groups tend to splinter over doctrine or style or personality or property. They total thirty million Americans, the Southern Baptists (SBs) by far the largest group with fourteen and a half million members. Although there are now SB churches in all fifty states, 75 percent of the membership and the sources of about 80 percent of the four billion dollars in annual financial contributions are concentrated still in the eleven states of the Old Confederacy. The Convention has consistently refused to change its name to anything less regional; the reasons for this have changed through time, but it has profound cultural meaning. Every time SBs have made this decision they have said something very important about who they want to be as well as who they are.

Many Southern Baptists refer to themselves simply as Baptists but then get upset if they are confused with other Baptist groups. Geography is a partial explanation; in the Deep South the so-and-so Baptist Church can usually be assumed to be Southern Baptist, since the other groups will specify "Missionary" or "Free Will" or "Independent." Around the fringe of the South all the Baptist churches will be specific, the SBs putting their full name in the title, or lettering "S.B.C." below the name on the sign. In the North and West, "affiliated with the Southern Baptist Convention" is likely to be spelled out.

Because of their rural past and associated educational deficiencies, only 6 percent of Southern Baptists are college graduates, compared to 12 percent for Methodists and Roman Catholics, or 34 percent for Episcopalians (Roof and McKinney 1987: 112–13). Southern Baptists have been resultantly underrepresented in national leadership, although some of the greatest and most powerful Southern politicians have belonged to the fold: the conservative John McClellan and the liberal Brooks Hays of Arkansas; the Talmadges of Georgia, father Gene and son Herman; the late Carl Perkins of Kentucky; Wright Patman and Otto Passman in the House, and the late Gillis Long, Huey's cousin, Theodore Bilbo in the Senate, all of Louisiana; and Lester Maddox of Georgia. The present towering figures are not few – Jesse Helms of North Carolina, Strom Thurmond of South Carolina, West Virginia's Robert Byrd, Tennessee's Albert Gore, Jr., Bennett Johnston of Louisiana and Thad Cochran of Mississippi, all of the Senate. Trent Lott of Mississippi, Newt Gingrich of Georgia, Claude Pepper of Florida, and Dick Gephardt of Missouri, star among many others in the House. Mark White and Martha Layne Collins have recently occupied the governors' mansions of Texas and Kentucky. Harry Truman was a Southern Baptist, although he never used the full term in his autobiography, and, unforgettably, Jimmy Carter, and Barbara Jordan of Texas, one of the relative handful of blacks. Preacher-author Will Campbell and TV personality Anita Bryant are SBs, as are evangelists Billy Graham and Pat Robertson. John Birch himself, and composer Virgil Thompson, behavioral psychologist J.B. Watson, sociobiologist Edward O. Wilson, cartoonist Doug Marlette of *Kudzu*, journalists Bill Moyers and Jody Powell, and Jesse James grew up that way.

But Jesse Jackson and Jerry Falwell, though Baptists, are not Southern Baptists, and neither is Mark Hatfield, senator from Oregon, who may attend a Southern Baptist church in Washington but started out in the Conservative Baptists, a 1947 split from the northern branch. John D. Rockefeller was a Northern Baptist, refusing to join the Episcopalians in the 1890s when everyone else was, and Harry Emerson Fosdick of Riverside Church, and now Harvey Cox of *The Secular City* and Harvard Divinity School.

The power of the Southern Baptists in the South is profound and pervasive, like that formerly exercised by the Democratic Party, but it is partially masked because denominational agencies are dispersed and the center, the SB Vatican, is in Nashville. In the big cities, Southern Baptist power is often symboled by the proximity of the First Baptist Church to the capitol building itself. In Jackson, Mississippi, it's right across the street, although it looks like Barchester, complete with vicarage garden. "It gazes on the seat of government in something of the same way that Westminster Abbey gazes on the House of Commons. Twenty years ago a handful of powerful families in its pews dominated Mississippi," wrote *New York Times* reporter Roy Reed (1983: B14).

Erskine Caldwell states, "The First Baptist church in a typical Southern city almost invariably has the largest membership, the most imposing edifice architecturally, and the greatest amount of weekly gross income of any Protestant church in town. After it, in descending order come, with few exceptions, the Second Baptist, the Methodist and the Presbyterian churches" (1968: 79–80). Winfred Moore, leader of the moderates in the contemporary split, who pastors at the First Baptist Church in Amarillo ("by far the biggest and wealthiest game in town," says Michael S. Farrell) believes "The free enterprise system is under God" (Farrell 1986: 10). Marshall Frady points up the Baptist advantage in politics: "For an aspiring politician to have been born a Baptist is considered one of those providential blessings like being born with a grits-and-gravy drawl; if he was born any-

First Baptist Church, Austin, Texas. (Photograph courtesy of the E. C. Dargan Research Library, Sunday School Board, Southern Baptist Convention.)

thing else, even Methodist or Presbyterian, he simply doesn't talk about it much – the political import of the other denominations ranges from irrelevant to ominous" (1967: 39). And Caldwell does the same for business, quoting a young Atlanta stockbroker: "There's something about religion, when you grow up with it in the Baptist church and get to know it like I did, that makes a sort of brotherhood and you don't have to break down doors or get a formal introduction no matter how rich the prospect is. It's like knowing the same language or being an Elk or something like that" (1968: 129).

"It's not straining a point to say that the moral aspects of Southern culture have by and large been provided by Southern Baptists," wrote social historian George Kelsey (1972: v), and religious historian Martin Marty concluded, "In the South you still have an Empire ('There are more Baptists than people')" (1974: 215). A senior Southern Baptist pastor confided, "If you understand the Southern Baptists, you'll have a key . . . to understanding the South."

The South is incomprehensible without consideration of the black factor, not just the slave system but more the ideology that developed after its unacknowledged military defeat. Perhaps only 95 percent of the differences between North and South are due to the color-coded caste system, but that isn't the story put out by the South. The extent of the mythmaking is all too similar to that in colonial Africa and India and Brazil, not to speak of Quebec and Ireland. One version came in a 1981 radio program from the National Humanities Center in Raleigh. Ancient Rome and the modern South were alike, the professors said, since they shared the same values and traditions—closeness to land, sense of family, sense of religious awe, sense of hierarchy. But all of these in the South, the professors did not say, stem obviously from the black-white coexistence or, more subtly, from the resultant retarded urbanization, the cynical preservation of rural life in order to control economic development. The religious institutions play an overwhelmingly ideological role, focusing attention and energy on intangible futures and masking the reality of present human miseries, themselves maintained in classic authoritarian ways. Deference patterns and religious awe remain; they reinforce here-and-now power.

To be southern is to be hyper-American: hyper-rural, because of the late industrialization; hyper-patriotic, with its chauvinistic and authoritarian connotations; hyper- also in indifference to history and anti-intellectualism with consequent vulnerability to mass culture (athletic contests and beauty pageants, differentially southern), and hyper-racist and -sexist, these two related organically in the southern psyche. The sense of separateness, reflecting and reinforcing these intensities, has also had an ideological function which has served the archaic social structure well. All the romantic stuff about the South—the mysterious differences, its rescue of regional cultures, its Alamo role against creeping materialism and homogenization—are unthinkable without the presence of the black caste and the social mechanisms of closeness and distance, confession and denial, adopted by both black and white to deal with their sharing of the same space.

With all the change that has occurred, the South and particularly Southern Baptists are still subject to those myths as they hide from themselves, and from the rest of the world, the racist underbelly of neo-fundamentalism and the New Religious Political Right (NRPR), in Samuel Hill and Dennis Owen's term (1982). Indeed, the factors that continue to make the South different from the rest of the United States—the extent of poverty, the inequality of income, the disparity in educational resources and the stinginess of social services, the tolerance of violence and the death penalty, and the sexual prudery—are exactly those factors which distinguish the United States from the rest of the developed world. The South, because of its commitment to its caste system, has been able to exercise a veto over the social maturation of the country as a whole, and southern religious institutions have been crucial to this success. The United States is unique in this huge, regionally dominant, in every sense conservative working-class religious movement forged in the struggle to keep its status in coexistence with a black underclass.

The differences continue. Political scientists Earl and Merle Black point out that the modern Southern Republicans have adopted the old messages: "There are . . . carefully calibrated and relatively subtle racial appeals" (1987: 271). More scathing is Roger Wilkins, Senior Fellow of the Institute of Policy Studies: "Ronald Reagan's dirty little secret is that he has found a way to make racism palatable and politically potent again" (1984: 437). Senator Jesse Helms can slide over the overt bigotry of his old radio shows and talk instead of opposition to the Martin Luther King holiday, and support for the anti-black side of U.S. foreign policy in South Africa; voters in North Carolina will be reassured. The so-called "social" issues, which almost always have economic implications, can be coded to mask their underlying truth. Political writer Johnny Greene points out, "The regional issue of race baiting would be conveniently replaced with a national issue disguised as pro-family morality . . . Blacks were no longer lynched; they were simply nonproductive recipients of a welfare system that should be terminated" (1981: 119). Concern over crime-in-the-streets becomes another coded, loaded, issue.

The Class That Did Not Struggle

The modern Southern Baptists were the product of a bargain, the Great Race Settlement, struck during the 1890s. Southern poor whites were persuaded to abandon class-based Populist politics if their edge over blacks could be maintained, through segregation in social institutions, public accommodations, and the workplace, and denial of voting and other civil rights. The Southern Baptist Convention (SBC) formed the largest institution of this class of poor whites, yet economic development and social change continually threatened their solidarity. The few affluent and educated Southern Baptists would start to pull the denomination into the mainstream and bring class-based issues again to the fore. To check this tendency, the SBC pursued a long agenda of contradictory goals and objectives in the effort to be at the same time Baptist, successful, and cohesive.

These are the dilemmas of white solidarity, played out in religious terms – basic Baptist beliefs in the primacy of the individual conscience, local church autonomy, democracy, and the individual response to a direct call from God, yet bureaucratic organization for denominational promotion, power and success, bigness, missions and expansion; power and success, yet denial of their own past powerlessness (i.e., of their own place in the class structure); ministry educated for leadership inside and outside the denomination, yet a basic distrust of biblical scholarship; urban affluence and political influence, yet rural purity and rejection of materialism; universal evangelism, yet local church homogeneity of class and color; congregational dependence on the ideal of intact nuclear families under paternal authority, yet age grading and sex segregation for more effective denominational socialization; desire to win in competition, yet fear of comparison leading to exclusivity and anti-ecumenism; a certain aloofness from the public policy arena, yet ferocious lobbying on selected issues.

There were different permutations and combinations of these objectives at different times, resulting in a shifting series of dilemmas. For example, the seminaries wanted the prestige of educated faculty members but required them to sign creedal statements; the direct calling from God could lead women everywhere but into positions where they might exercise authority over men. Most of these simmer unresolved, for they cannot be clarified or even discussed openly since the inconsistencies would be too obvious. This evasion pushes attempts at resolution down to the local level. Occasionally these dilemmas, in theological coloration, have surfaced nationally and threatened to split the denomination (and thus the class it represents). The archetypal case is the evolution controversy of the mid-1920s, a question of Biblical literalism, in which an anti-evolution exhortation was adopted but a creedal statement was also developed, supposed to be signed by all agencies but with no sanction against those who declined. The result was continued unity, yet paralysis in theological discussion and political effectiveness for thirty years. As Walter B. Shurden comments, "Denominational unity is more important to most Southern Baptists than arguments about the Bible" (1978: 225).

Maurice Godelier has pointed out the utility of this behavior for social groups at different levels of cultural complexity. A system reproduces itself, he states, under conditions in which "contradictions are *regulated* and this regulation maintains a *provisional* unity" (trans. and quoted by Lee 1979: 5).

For the Southern Baptists, the purpose of the exercise was the holding together of the poor white class through the years of the Solid South, keeping
their part of the bargain. It was a gigantic balancing act—the tightropes
that bind. Since the Second World War, as their center of gravity moved
into the middle class, the Southern Baptists were again, and more mas-
sively, trying to move into the mainstream. In their unique way, they were
reinforcing other time-honored SB themes: anti-Catholicism, a highly selective literalism about Scripture, and a positively foolish inconsistency about
church-state issues. Sexual bigotry was there, too, and a somewhat faddish
concern for family solidarity for reasons about which they were not entirely
candid. Stirrings of functional cooperation with other religious groups,
and a real if somewhat distanced compassion for unfortunate people everywhere, softened the edges of the old hard lines. So did the very American
enthusiasm and energy and responses to emergency appeals.

They had, in other words, come a long way. But these internal changes,
the growing sophistication of some professors, the increasing breadth of
ethical emphases in some of the agencies, brought into question what Southern Baptist identity was. This occurred at just the time, and for some of
the same reasons, that conservative Southern Protestants generally were being mobilized for political action, and the Southern Baptist Convention
was a huge prize. A reactionary theological and social-ethical movement
became co-opted and merged with a national reactionary political one and
has resulted in a fundamentalist takeover of the Convention. The ostensible
rallying cry, just as it had been in the 1920s, was Biblical inerrancy, but
this didn't arise as an issue, or a code word for one, until there was a substantial group of people to whom the concept was uncomfortable, if not
irrelevant.

The people in charge of the Southern Baptists are men (the term is used
here in the exclusive sense, because there aren't any women among them)
born in the Depression who benefited from the economic expansion and
development of the 1950s and 1960s rolling over the southern social landscape like a thick but patchy fog. They speak for a subculture only recently
powerful in its place, but now they are unsure of the boundaries of their
landscape and their ability to plan, plant, and prune it to their own purposes. They were poised for a ruling role, as dominant rather than dominated, as neo-Bourbons rather than poor whites. Hegemony over southern
culture was their right and their destiny, and they were cheated of their
inheritance by the Supreme Court.

The Brown decision of 1954 broke faith with the Great Race Settlement.

The government could no longer ensure segregation in the crucial institution of public education – the place where family authority meets ideas of cultural appropriateness, vocational or preprofessional preparation to fulfill various class expectations, and young people's social environment (the arena for mate selection and new family formation). The subsequent Civil Rights efforts, and the very large economic changes which then ensued, have transformed the region. Anthony F.C. Wallace's concept of revitalization – "any conscious, organized effort . . . to construct a more satisfying culture" (1966: 30) – helps to explain southern reaction. Stephen A. Smith's analysis of the new southern mythology is also helpful: "The death of a mythic vision leaves a society consciously seeking definitions of appropriate behavior and unconsciously struggling to find or create a new mythology, to generate new symbols, and to define new goals" (1985: 59).

This search, and this latest challenge to SBC unity, is much more frontal, sharply defined, and well-organized. It takes its inspiration and strength from the larger coalition (the NRPR) which has had a very specific public policy agenda and a certain indifference to democratic practices and traditional American values like tolerance and openness. Its victory is possible because the Solid South – and the need to maintain it – is no longer there. The class structure and political alignments of the South have shattered and the SBC has shattered with it. All of them are in the process of reformation: what happens to the one will affect what happens to the other – they are in reciprocal relationship – but the larger socioeconomic forces have infinitely greater strength.

In their frustration and outrage, the fundamentalist Southern Baptists are striking back, using religious language (the only tongue in which they are truly at home) because it is important to them that religion itself be strengthened, since it has been the source of what strength they themselves possess. And of their own concept of religion, too. After mainstream and liberal involvement in the civil rights, anti-Vietnam, and nuclear freeze movements, hunger and homelessness, they cry, "that's not what religion is," or "that's not all that religion should stand for – what about *us*?" Just as "New World slavery provided Protestant Christianity with an epic stage for vindicating itself as the most liberal and progressive force in human history," David Brion Davis (1984: 129) wrote, so the "social issues" of the 1980s provide the fundamentalists with a means of proclaiming that their old-time religion has not lost its power.

Prayer in the schools is an important concern of this group, but the principal battleground is sex and family, particularly the issues of abortion, homosexuality, and pornography. Significantly, on these issues the NRPR can form close alliances in national politics with many Roman Catholics, Mormons, Missouri Synod Lutherans, and Orthodox Jews, and even link arms with a few feminists. This complex of issues has other advantages. In all groups it cross-cuts divisions of class, region, and color. It also focuses in time-honored fashion on private morality rather than the structure of social systems, on interior sin rather than public injustices, on aspects of behavior which appeal to the prudery and prurience that, for widely different historical reasons, are part of all of those traditions.

The battle has been seen almost totally as an internal one, founded on theology or in intra-denominational politics, and the personal involvements of the fundamentalist leaders with the national NRPR have been dealt with mostly by indirection. The genius of the fundamentalist leadership is to realize how well the focus on sex and family, and Biblical literalism, go together. The leaders can court the masses of inerrantists and simultaneously appeal to political ultra-rights without saying so, because they are the same people. The goals of the NRPR can be furthered (through Sunday School curricula, missions programs, Marriage Enrichment retreats, sermons and publicity-resolutions passed at annual meetings, not to speak of petitions circulated in the pews, lobbying at state capitols, and voter registration drives) with judicious emphasis on the ever-present Biblical themes of sin and vice. The Old Testament provides a tribal model of male religion and male control of family life; the New adds Pauline prudery and skittishness about the reputation of the nascent Christian communities, selectively filtered through misogynistic mistranslations. As religious sociologist James Davison Hunter says, "the family may prove to be a final battleground in conservative Protestantism's century-long battle with modernity" (1983: 70). And if "the family" is the last arena of white male authority, why not increase its importance, and the area of its control?

An Anthropological Perspective on Religion

Without claiming for a moment that all anthropologists would agree, here is one possible approach. It tries to make universal statements that apply to all places and all periods, and also is very sensitive to stages of cultural evolution and the implications of their differences for generalizations about human nature. It enters into an analysis of religion in any society determined not to limit the inquiry to churches and gods. Following Anthony

Wallace's pathbreaking work, it is attuned to ritual—stereotyped sequences of behavior—and refuses to take for granted, for example, the singing of "The Star-Spangled Banner" before a college basketball game, or the fact that many Southern Baptists bring their Bibles to church but don't open them there. It uses the classic sociological institutional categories—economics, politics, family, religion, education, social stratification—for analytic purposes but is not baffled if human behavior refuses to stay in those pigeonholes. The challenge, and the most sense, come from looking at the connections among them.

From this perspective, religion is expected to have political, economic, and educational functions at all levels of cultural development, and in complex societies to form one of the most important mechanisms for status placement, group identity, and social control. It knows that all the world's great religions (but not the religions of pre-state societies) have a great deal to say about sexual and reproductive behavior and family structure, and it knows some of the reasons (demography has profound economic consequences). It is aware of the process of institutionalization and its potential impact on the original prophetic vision (the difference, for example, between the radical egalitarianism of Jesus and the almost bureaucratic caution displayed by Paul). It sees theology as a product of a particular group of a particular time, using as raw material a mix of vision, history and tradition, legend, myth, and the need for continuity. Then, as the theology develops, the ideas become a statement of ideology, a system of belief in support of a system of power.

Peter Berger's ideas of "social religion" are appropriate in this connection. He writes, appositely, "There may at first be something bewildering in the spectacle of Negro Baptist ministers acting as NAACP secretaries and white Baptist preachers heading White Citizens Councils. If we understand religion *on both sides* as reflecting the outlook and interests of the respective social constituencies, there will be no more bewilderment . . . In *both* cases it is operating as social religion in the service of a particular group" (1961: 85). This is inevitable; as Wallace points out, religions, always specific to a place, time, and group, develop value systems that will help them to adapt to their particular circumstances—instrumental values. Beyond these, religions can provide "identity values" that "define . . . the boundaries of loyalty, assert that outsiders are outsiders, and insist upon the distinctive virtues of one's own kind . . . It is not surprising, therefore, to find that religion is frequently a way of asserting an ethnic or class or racial identity in a situation of intergroup conflict, and resistance to change in religion may be based more on grounds of identity than on reluctance to adopt instrumental values more appropriate to the new circumstances of society" (1966: 26).

Religious institutions (usually) sacralize their value system and their source of authority (even when that is their own individual consciences), and this supernatural validation tends to lead to difficulty and delay in value change. Carl Degler suggests that southern devotion to biblical literalism developed this way: "Since a literal interpretation of the Bible gave little or no support to an abolitionist position, it is not surprising that anti-slavery people in order to use Christianity *against* slavery resorted to an interpretative or metaphorical exegesis of the Bible. It is not accidental, therefore, that southerners should become increasingly fond of literal interpretation of the Bible, just as they found a narrow construction of the Constitution useful in defending slavery" (1977: 61).

The doyen of American sociologists of religion, Robert Bellah, has sketched an evolutionary trajectory for the orientation of religious ideas (1964). After a long period of primitive this-world religious thinking, focused on important problems like how to help your baby get well and where the fish are biting, the world's great religions (as self-styled by their own historians) emerged from the matrix of the church-state symbioses of the Old World agrarian societies. Without exception they focused the attention of their followers on *the next world* (or the next incarnation,) providing a motivation for resignation and submission to authority in this life, essential to state power. With modernization, religious orientation has increasingly returned to *this world*, a process some blame on science, or, tautologically, on secularism, as the promise of heaven or the threat of hell lost its literal meaning.

But this last shift needs elaboration. Uniquely in human history, Europe "modernized," industrialized, and developed a market economy. Theocracies and capitalism are arguably incompatible because theocratic imperatives to regulate every aspect of behavior interfere with market freedom. The Reformation effected the absolutely necessary break between church and state (in the northern countries which were those that became capitalist—the British and Scandinavian Establishments have long lost their authority to intrude in economic life). Capital itself became subject to the rules of the market, and land made the same switch at the same time in the same process of change.

What is less well recognized is the Reformation's religious contribution to the creation of a free market in labor. Minimal "nuclear" families, with the fathers as heads and agents, had to be freed from ties to manor, parish, or corporate kin group to go where the jobs were. This vast game of musical chairs led to religiously plural nations, and pluralism, the choice of religious affiliation, led inevitably to loss of any institutional commitment for some – and what looked like secularization, including loss of religious control over sexual morality and reproductive ethics. Religion, in societies where the process has gone the farthest, has become a private matter; control over sex and family has been relinquished first by the church (forced out by the state) and then by the state itself.

One of the most interesting aspects of the end-of-the-twentieth-century world is that there are entire countries at different stages in the progression, and there are also, within most countries, class-based groups at various points. There are also people, usually religious leaders, who deplore the progression itself and quixotically resolve to arrest or repeal it, for their own membership or for the entire society if they can achieve control. Those people are usually called fundamentalists, and there are lots of them in Iran, Pakistan, Saudi Arabia and Mauritania, in the Punjab and in Sri Lanka, in Israel, in Rome, in Salt Lake City, and in Nashville.

That there is probably no nation that is Christian fundamentalist is no accident, for the developed world is primarily the Christian world, where the market process has gone the farthest. Poland and the Irish Republic are anomalies, incompletely developed and sharing an identification of a Christian community with frustrated nationalism. The competitive context in which a given religious institution operates can hasten its journey down the road toward modernity or retard it as it drags its heels in contradistinction to those around it. It may pick up an identification with the feudal Establishment, as Lutheranism did in Germany, where it is then not hard to see how Roman Catholicism later became involved with the labor movement in the Rhineland. The Shah of Iran seized the mullahs' lands and, in his drive to Westernize, had to repudiate their puritanism; it is not hard to see how resistance to the Shah on all grounds would be led by the mullahs and use religious language. In Connecticut, the Roman Catholic leadership has close friends in the state capitol and many communicants in corporate boardrooms, and little motivation for ecumenism; in North Carolina the Roman Catholics are the only religious group paying much attention to the material needs of migrant agricultural workers, and they belong to the Council of Churches.

Southern Baptists were the institutional voice of the common southern folk. Differentiating themselves from the better educated Methodists and

Presbyterians, and certainly from the repudiated Episcopalians, they then split from the northern Baptists over slavery and were free to develop within the context of an increasingly defensive southern distinctiveness. In a Jim Crow South, Southern Baptists became the voice of white solidarity, in contradistinction to all the forces above and below them in the class structure, and in middle-class triumphalist respectability dissociated from the black Baptists with whom they shared so much history they wished to deny.

Now the southern context has changed. White solidarity is shattered, not least because most blacks vote and there are thousands of aggressive, affluent in-migrants, who have little patience with the old comfortable traditions. Southern Baptists are reacting by reexamining their identity and their place in the new social structure of the South, albeit in an unpleasant and perhaps self-defeating manner. The motives which have brought them to this point are not going to go away.

Nor is religion going to disappear under the assault of scientific fact or the specter of secularism, civil religion, or "a secular communications environment that is, at bottom, hostile to any genuine religious witness," as *Christian Century* editor James Wall complained (1985: 459). Religion, instead, is the inevitable product of human ability to use language, the symbolic capacity people will always find a way to exercise. Religious institutions will be around, too, but they will not be necessarily the same ones, and their relationship to other aspects of the social world can be expected to change, and change, and change again.

The Texas Connection

Many Southern Baptists, whether moderate, fundamentalist, or neutral, believe that their South is divided into four regions with a predictable range of views. The South Atlantic region (Virginia and the Carolinas) is the most "liberal," a word seldom used in any other connotation. Then the Deep South, Georgia, Alabama, and Mississippi (northern Florida may be anomalous). Then Kentucky and Tennessee, special because of the seminary in Louisville and the denominational headquarters in Nashville, as well as a long history of religious controversy. Finally, the extremely conservative "Southwest," Arkansas, northern Louisiana, Oklahoma and Texas, which breaks the record for everything, including the Southern Baptists. The primary locus of support for the fundamentalists, James L. Guth states

(1983: 177) is in small and medium-sized working-class churches in the South and Southwest.

Texas, *Newsweek* said, is "where Southern Baptists have literally inherited the earth and faith is as partisan as football." And more Texans read the *Baptist Standard* every week than read *Newsweek* or any other publication. The 2.3 million SBs are not evenly distributed throughout the state, being concentrated in the northern and eastern sections, where there are fewer Germans, Hispanics, and, for that matter, cows. These southerners came in after the Mexican War with a dream of extending the area of cotton, slavery, and the rest of southern culture, and thousands more followed at the end of the Civil War. By 1901 the SB Home Mission Board reported to the annual meeting that "the portion of Texas which has been settled is, perhaps, the strongest Baptist ground in all the Territory of the Southern Baptist Convention" (*Annual* 1901: 142). This is still true: in 1986 one-third of all the new SB churches were in Texas, which contributed one-sixth of the total central funding. The state has great wealth but great extremes in its distribution, making minimal effort to tax its people for public purposes – not just typical cowboy capitalism but the designer of the type. The poverty level, below which families of four become eligible for public help with medical bills, was defined in Texas as $2,500 when the federal standard was $10,200.

The nuances of difference in Texas style might be summarized in the contrast between the equally famous Southern Baptist preachers of the inter-war period, Frank Norris of Fort Worth and George Washington Truett of Dallas. The two cities, thirty-odd miles apart, have ever been competitive, and the two famous men had their own version of the conflict, Norris sending Truett a telegram on a Sunday morning with the message, "How can a man like you occupy a Baptist pulpit?" Norris, a leader of the then Fundamentalists, was flamboyant, sensationalist, involved in suspicion of arson on more than one occasion and in a murder charge of which he was acquitted on grounds of self-defense. For his style and the swirls of controversy surrounding him he was declared persona non grata by the Baptist General Convention of Texas in 1924, although by that time he had built the Fort Worth First Baptist Church into the largest church in the denomination. He criticized the SBC's embryonic centralized fund-raising efforts and refused to use the denomination's own Sunday School materials, agitating for decentralization and local missions.

He preached a great deal against various kinds of sin and vice. Drinking, dancing, and gambling were the principal objects of his activist crusades, and he led the denominational fight for doctrinal purity and against evolution, instigating investigations of its teaching at Texas colleges and accusing other ministers of preaching heresy.

Strikingly, he also explicitly believed in a cross-class church, combining his sensationalism with "a warm folksiness," bringing poor kids into the sanctuary deliberately to spill ice cream on the carpet. He "wanted churches in which the lowliest Baptist could mix with college graduates and not feel resented, where the congregation comprised 'one big happy family' with 'sweet and beautiful fellowship'" (Thompson 1982: 160).

Truett, on the other hand, was much closer to the modern "liberal" Southern Baptist, although, as was common in his time, not seminary-trained. He was no less devoted to the Bible than Norris but saw it as "home base but not the sole province of wide-ranging wisdom" (Reavis 1984: 19). He preached on topics like Christian charity, familial duty, and missionary work, and was much more interested than Norris in common human problems, social conditions, and non-sectarian charity. A much-beloved figure, Truett occupied the pulpit of the First Baptist Church, Dallas, for 47 years.

After his death his place was taken by W. A. Criswell, now in his forty-second year there. Criswell has been called the "ayatollah" of the contemporary SB fundamentalists, is the subject of a joke that St. Peter has him listed under Real Estate rather than Religion, and in a sense recombines both Texas traditions. He was somewhat magically picked out of youthful obscurity to fill Truett's place, in what has now grown by his efforts to be by far the largest SB church in the world, with over 25,000 members and an annual budget of $12 million. It advertises itself, however, as "the largest country church in the world," even as it raised $1.85 million in one Sunday collection for upkeep on the real estate. "But," Dr. Criswell says of his gigantic institution, "we do not have a whole lot of diversity within our congregation. They won't come. *You can't get them to come.* You just can't mix in a democratic congregation the utterly poor and the affluent. The poor feel intimidated" (Parmley 1985: 46). Nonetheless, the church as a whole is "multi-racial," in SB nomenclature: "though the Sunday morning crowd . . . is largely upper class and white as snow," there are separate "chapels" for Cambodians, Laotians, Hispanics, Koreans, Japanese, and Chinese—as well as "poor people," evidently a Dallas gloss for blacks.

The fundamentalist junta has its headquarters in Texas, indeed, as some

SB observers dare to suggest, in Dallas at this very church. The brilliant Trinidadian writer, V. S. Naipaul, who somehow covered the 1984 Republican Convention for *The New York Review of Books*, knew he had to go hear Dr. Criswell preach there to make any sense of his Dallas adventure. "American endeavor and success were contained within old American faith and pieties. Karl Marx and homosexuality were on the other side . . . and could be lumped together," he found. Criswell's church was an obligatory shrine for any Southern Baptist pilgrimage.

Dallas, June 1984
   Downtown Dallas at six o'clock on a Wednesday evening realized Jane Jacobs' worst nightmares and would give pause to the proponents of the neutron bomb. Nobody was on the streets, nobody, and the Martians could have landed— maybe they had. Inside the enormous hotels there were ghostly shadows of life, but the gigantic office buildings seemed void, looming over the concrete emptiness below. It was 97 degrees Fahrenheit: the temperature would go down twenty degrees during the night but be back up in the nineties by eleven the next morning. The Dallas First Baptist Church is a brick Gothic pile, near-cubic in configuration, with pale stone and black glass outbuildings, five acres in all, including a Christian academy and a Bible Institute where preachers are trained. Outside the sanctuary is an 1871 Historical Marker which states "the first building on this site was a one-room structure, which members financed by weaving rugs, making hominy, preserves and cheese to sell at fairs near Dallas, then a frontier town of 2,500."
   Just inside the door was a water fountain, and one could come in off the street just to get a drink, a blessedly welcome public service in that socially barren landscape. The sanctuary had probably been all golden oak at one time, but much of the old-fashioned wood has been covered with paint the color of whipped cream. As cool as it was, there was a strong acrid odor of sweat, both fresh and stale, for on Wednesdays this is a cross-class church with many work clothes on the several hundred congregants. No visible blacks, but one Asian-looking family. Seven men on the dais in varicolored business suits, Criswell in his usual summer vanilla. One was merely a vocal soloist, although a female soloist, with exactly the same role, sat in the first row below (Criswell has strong negative feelings about women in the pulpit). Criswell didn't preach that evening and participated only in the Invitation, when those present are asked to convert and be committed. A dozen people walked up to the front and, after talking privately to Dr. Criswell, were assigned to the assistants. After one whis-

pered conference Criswell announced that "this appeal" was being turned over to the proper church agency, playing the classic role of Godfather or Tammany Hall chieftain. Prayers were asked for the basketball mission then visiting Poland and for a counterinsurgency team leaving for the Mormon heartland. The service was pleasant enough, full of nice detail, but without either a collection or congregational hymn-singing, it was truncated, unfulfilled.

Criswell, totally dedicated, totally unspontaneous, almost obsessive in his punctuality and regular habits, has preached the Bible *word by word* all the way through—the first cycle took seventeen years, the Word ritualized. He is one of the powers, if not the principal one, behind the current assertion of fundamentalist power (*l'Éminence crème?*). Directing the First Baptist Church from its geographically anomalous center—80 percent of the congregation drive 20 minutes or more to attend church there, and that Wednesday night they were profusely thanked for bothering to come downtown—Criswell inspires the whole SB fundamentalist movement from the archaic architecture amid the mirrored towers. (The only thing reflective about Dallas is the glass, cracked one reporter during the Republican Convention there.) This institution, internally class-segregated in the name of fellowship, flourished in the midst of one of the most striving and status-conscious cities of our time; it makes a profound statement about one of the potentials of religious institutions in this age.

This model, the Texas model with its new contradictions, is the winning one in the internal Southern Baptist struggle. Another aspect of its appeal is illustrated by another SB church, Houston Second, which serves a neighborhood of big houses on small lots, sociologically suburban but with a Houston postmark. "In a fast-paced city such as Houston," goes the booklet describing its new physical plant, "a person or family needs a subculture— a group of people and a place where they [*sic*] can build a lifestyle. For the Christian, this should be the church." Houston Second provides its parishioners with a total institution, for they scarcely have to leave it except to have a home (a base for their symbolically important family lives) and to go to work. The new sanctuary seats 6,000, with a 450-voice choir and a $2 million pipe organ. Also in the complex are a 900-pupil day school and a Family Life Center, including a 175-seat theater, eight lanes of bowling, four racquetball and two full-size basketball courts, a gymnasium with weight and exercise rooms and a track, crafts studios, and restaurants. The telephone is answered "Exciting Second," and the services there exhibit the skill in handling mass emotions so much a part of the television age.

The old sanctuary, "modified" Colonial, dominates a huge complex of matching buildings which shelters a gigantic parking lot full of the right sort of vehicles for the newly affluent. It holds about 3,000, and was packed: there was one black man in a three-piece gray flannel suit. The choir marched in to a fast-paced lilting hymn; they had memorized all the verses so they could briskly take their places on the steep array of seats. "UpBeat, UpBeat, we're going to have a positive experience," they seemed to sing.

"Ed" Young, in the bullpen for a future SBC presidency, led the service. Dignified, controlled, lithe energy in a dark suit. A sermon about family life—sentimental, freighted, sober, full of warnings of what may happen if we lose patience and don't pay attention to each other. Then, after a brief break, a stem-winder on the dangers of a Gay Rights proposal to be voted upon by the City Council that week: Would the congregation please make their views known to Council members by Tuesday? Political mobilization from the pulpit, an honorable tradition. (John Bisagno, at Houston First, was making the same plea to his congregation at the same time, but he pointed out that the Bible won't tolerate adulterers and fornicators either.) Scary stuff—Sodom and Gomorrah, auto-intoxication. Then the sky cleared, another upbeat, bouncy recessional hymn for the closing, and off to sign up for the annual Sunday School picnic, planned for a local country club. Young programmed his parishioners with a wide range of emotions and ended with triumph: they had gone through something, they had been moved out of themselves, they had prevailed, they felt good about him—and their worldly goods—and they were ready for another week. And it was very obvious how this all was achieved.

Though the parishioners may live from week to week, the denomination has a long and complex past. Southern Baptists' history of themselves tends to be inbred, drawing heavily on bureaucratic statistics and Th.D. dissertations at Southern Baptist seminaries, and thus usually serves to obscure their relationship to southern, American, and religious history in general and to deny the connections with material and social reality that an awareness of class factors implies. The following account tries instead to make exactly those connections and illuminate those relationships.

2 A Social History
of the Southern Baptists

It is bad to have your back and your blood taken, as blacks
have. But there is a sense in which it is worse to have your
head taken away . . . The job on the redneck was more extensive because . . . he still hasn't identified his enemy.
— The Rev. Will Campbell (1974: 112)

From the Beginnings to the New World

Southern Baptists are a part of Western civilization; they express the Judeo-Christian tradition and some of them take the Bible with
consistent seriousness. At the same time, they are Christians, believing that
Jesus was a unique historical figure, a Redeemer of all believers, and they
specifically see Christianity as, in some sense, an improvement over what
went before. The Old Testament theocratic model of the church and the
Roman Catholic authoritarian one are rejected, superseded by an ecclesiology of voluntary commitment by freely choosing adults who are assumed
to agree in their concept of church. That there are inherent contradictions
in these positions is the raw material for theology (the attempt to make
mythology consistent, as a smart observer of the process remarked) and
bothers most SBs not a bit.

Southern Baptists are Protestants; they grew out of a movement to release the hold on society of a monolithic institutional church. They adopted
an entire ideology of individual religious conscience in the process, em-
braced the Old Testament with all its tribal difficulties and tried repeti-
tively to breach the wall of separation between clergy and laity and keep
it down. Protestants were anti-Establishment in the beginning (until some

of them achieved their own Establishments) and each of their protests has contained the potential for further fission; they are congenital schismatics.

Although a direct link with continental Anabaptism has been disproved, there was plenty of a similar type of fervor and fierce individualism among Baptists in the English Reformation. Sixteenth-century English Protestantism was different from the continental kinds in being even more intensely political. Less philosophical at first, the Anglican Church first freed itself from Rome and then sought a theology to mark itself off. In England the Reformation in the sixteenth century was much closer in time to its seventeenth-century Revolution, the enormous transfer of power from a feudal to a capitalist form of organization that would not take place in France until the eighteenth century and in Germany for still another hundred years.

So Protestant theological and denominational developments in England were intertwined with this socio-economic Revolution. The poor and the dispossessed saw an Established Anglicanism as no improvement and increasingly demanded tolerance—for all non-Catholic Christians, anyway. Baptists' involvement in this effort was very deep and real, and many lost their lives for their efforts.

"Baptist" was a term first applied derisively by others to those who utilized the practice of complete immersion, undoubtedly Biblical, as a differentiating ritual. Folk beliefs about the danger of submersing the whole body have come and gone and come again, and possibly in some minds this added the sort of thrill that handling snakes or walking on live coals may give today. Some groups baptized children ("*Pedo*-baptists" as in *ped*agogy and *ped*iatrics), but the SBs come from a strain which insisted on believers', or adult, baptism only, with much vagueness about the age of adulthood.

At one with the Puritans in their basic Calvinism, an early group of Baptists actually traveled to Holland with those who took the *Mayflower* but then returned to England. There were theological nuances and divisions—and no unanimity—among those who came to the colonies, mostly to New England, with the first Baptist congregation in Rhode Island around 1640.

These early Dissenters in the colonies were poor or working-class farmers or petty artisans, but included a tiny minority more urban, more highly educated. Most of them saw their best future in cheap land, so their economic motivation pushed them continually toward the frontier, peopling it, composing it, expressing it, trying to discipline and tame it.

As economic marginals and doctrinal purists, they contained in the early period the potential for political disruption as well. "They were considered religious radicals of the most dangerous type and were frequently looked upon as enemies of all political and social order," William Warren Sweet says (1964: 3), and these qualities and characteristics made them particularly susceptible to the revival movement beginning in the 1730s which has been termed the "Great Awakening." Personified in the remarkable talents of Jonathan Edwards, this movement flowered in Northampton, Massachusetts, near where the Massachusetts frontier was at the time. And Edwards was a crypto-millenarian; as Paul Johnson puts it, "Much of his writing is capable of a political as well as a theological interpretation" (1977: 425).

The Awakening, with its emotionalism and self-consciousness, was accompanied by further splintering of denominations. "Religious competition," Johnson says (1977: 432), "produced an atmosphere of permanent revival," especially on the constantly moving frontier. The Baptists, with their passionate belief in local church autonomy and their do-it-yourself ministry, were ideally suited to take advantage of both tendencies. M. Darrol Bryant points out that lay preaching by blacks and women during the Awakening again raised the question of "the role of the clergy and challenged the fixedness of stations . . . the whole authority structure of pre-1740 society was shaken" (1974: 71).

Lay preaching had enormous advantages for expansion. Baptists need not wait for clergy to be trained, as the Presbyterians did, nor for the bishop to assign ministers to keep up with the shifting population, as did Anglicans and later their Methodist successors. Their own people, self-inspired and self-driven, were the medium, and a handful of families could form the nucleus of a congregation without waiting for anyone else's approval. Expand they did. Masters says there were 21,000 Baptists in the South by 1784, 15,000 of these in Virginia with the spillover going into Kentucky. A remarkable node had already been founded in North Carolina in 1775, whence a rapid spread westward to Tennessee. By 1790 the first Baptist church was established in the old Northwest territory, near Cincinnati.

Theological differences, now of only antiquarian interest, existed; there were the "Generals" and "Particulars" divided over the breadth of salvation, and then "Regulars" and "Separates" who varied as to their tolerance of emotional expressiveness. By 1800 or so these differences had faded away as bases for organization, but the kind of theological compromise that emerged, as after later controversies, was the result of organizational imperatives (to unite in order to compete) rather than any clear defeat of one position or another. Theological diversity and the potential for conflict continued below the surface. But as of this date there was broad agreement on five basic Baptist principles: the separation of church and state, conversion as a condition of church membership, individual responsibility to God, congregational church government, and immersion as the only scriptural form of baptism and symbol of commitment.

A case can be made for emphasizing the *continuity* of the emotional, evangelical, expansive strain in American religion from Edwards on through the camp meetings to Moody and Sankey to Aimee Semple McPherson and Billy Sunday, with a detour for the disreputable Fathers Divine and Coughlin, to Norman Vincent Peale, Billy Graham, and the current galaxy of television preachers. The Second Great Awakening can be seen as a continuation of the First; the American Revolution interrupted the stream and drew off, for a time, some of that enthusiasm and energy.

Post-Revolutionary Expansion and Pre-War Schism

Except for parts of the Carolinas, most Baptists were on the rebel (American) side in the Revolution amidst an Anglican, Tory South. "As a consequence of their political involvements they emerged from the war with enhanced respect and considerable support among the South's common folk," J. Wayne Flynt comments (1981: 35). It was in this period that Baptists left their lasting mark on the design of the American polity. Young James Madison saw an imprisoned Baptist minister preaching the Gospel through a jail window, and his horror of such persecution became part of the background of the First Amendment. Baptist John Leland, a Massachusetts man who spent fifteen years in Virginia during and after the Revolution, was a vigorous preacher of freedom of religion and reinforced Madison's views.

The Revolution was followed by a huge push of migration to the south and west from Georgia and the Carolinas, people often traveling first overland and then by river. Baptist members grew; by 1812, Masters says, there were 100,000 Baptists in the South, where two-thirds of their growth had taken place. Historian Walter B. Posey thinks that while one-quarter of the U.S. population was Baptist in 1800, it was by 1845 only one-sixth and by then concentrated in the South.

They spread primarily as family herdsmen and farmers, largely without resources, barely literate but independent and proud, and making virtues of all these necessities. In Alabama, for instance, according to the SB *Encyclopedia* (1: 17ff.), they "swarmed in" after the War of 1812. By 1825 there were about 5,000 Baptists in 128 churches. The preachers farmed, "lest someone should accuse them of preaching for money," and they tacked copies of Biblical passages to their plows as aides to memorization. "Their preaching was almost entirely exhorting . . . and they relied on physical exertion to compensate for mental deficiency." Sermons ran from two to three hours and were delivered in the holy or "ministerial whine" which "on a quiet night could be heard from one to two miles." Many of the churches were enlarged log cabins, whose only special feature might be a "candlestick" pulpit, a covered square or circular structure with a few steps and a door—a kind of lantern shape, in which the pastor became the flame.

In the lower Mississippi, Posey says, churches were often built near water to make immersion easier, but sometimes near the home of a wealthy family who had given the land. Other times they were "out on the edge of town by someone who wanted to raise property values," or "occasionally a donor had been persuaded to grant an obscure location by an old preacher who preferred that the better educated townspeople would not attend" (1957: 8).

Masters' maternal grandfather, the Rev. Bryant Burriss, a young man in 1815, was a substantial example of the period: "a Baptist preacher, a large farmer, a tanner, a brick mason, a cabinet maker, and trial justice and a community peace maker. He was a slave owner and worked more than any slave he had" (1915: 20). As he traveled about from one rural church to another he did not receive offerings sufficient to pay for the horseshoes he used up—one year all he earned was a pair of wool socks. Perhaps one out of fifty preachers was full-time. The people, Masters wrote, "favored free will gifts to the pastor . . . and then mostly forgot to give them" (1915: 41).

This was the era of the Great Revival and the development of the frontier camp meeting. One in Paris, Kentucky, in 1801 drew perhaps twenty thousand people. The night was lit with campfires, hundreds of candles, lamps, and torches. Popular reaction to marathon preaching was overwhelmingly emotional and featured wild physical abandon—rolling and jerking and near-convulsions—the model for the later frenzied worship style. Baptists, Presbyterians, and Methodists would celebrate communion (the Lord's Supper) together, making it necessary for the Baptists "either to stultify their principles or to seem unbrotherly" (Masters 1915: 30) and, of course, signaling their early wariness of interdenominational cooperation.

Frontier revivalism coincided with the heyday of "watch-care" or "church discipline" and was a result of some of the same circumstances – the paucity of social contacts and the tenuousness of the civil structure. The adults acted as a court, hearing witnesses and passing sentences for such transgressions as irregular church attendance, memberships in secret societies (especially the Masons), doctrinal disputation (if publicly expressed), excessive drinking (if it led to fighting), adultery, remarriage after divorce, lying, stealing, fraud, and gambling. Punishment was severe, and if the guilty ones objected they could only leave the community.

Masters concluded that in this period Baptists were "the great inconspicuous majority of Southern men [*sic*], the hardy pioneers who subdued the forests and caused the American wilderness to blossom with beauty and gladness" (1915: 19). And Southern religious historian Donald G. Mathews links their class membership with social cohesion and style:

> as a social, historical process, Evangelical Protestantism in the Old South enabled a rising lower-middle/middle class to achieve identity and solidarity, rewarding its most committed religious devotees with a sense of personal esteem and liberty . . . a volatile social movement providing a value system to raise converts in their own esteem, give them confidence in themselves and their comrades, and create the moral courage to reject as authoritative for themselves the life-style and values of traditional elites (1977: xx, xvii).

Although there can be no question that the vast majority of Baptists were of modest status, there was always a better educated, urban strain. They tended to get most of the publicity because they disproportionately became the leaders, the essayists and historians, and the spokesmen. Eugene Genovese's work (1974) suggests they were almost all in-migrants; almost half a million Yankees moved south between 1776 and 1860, many of them clergymen who then became assimilated to the southern viewpoint. Among them were Richard Furman and Thomas Meredith, whose names have been given to prominent Southern Baptist educational institutions. (The details that follow are from their biographies in the 1958 SB *Encyclopedia*, which here as elsewhere sometimes exhibits a bit of hyperbolic pride.)

Furman was born at Esopus, New York, in 1755 but moved south as an infant. With less than a year's formal schooling, by "persistent, personal study he learned Latin, Greek, Hebrew, French, German, metaphysics, logic, history and theology." Brown University and South Carolina College (now the University of South Carolina) both granted him honorary doctorates. Ordained at nineteen, he was for thirteen years pastor at High Hills, South Carolina, and became a Revolutionary patriot and anti-Tory propagandist. In 1787 he was called to the Charleston church, serving there until his death in 1825. The first national Baptist meeting in 1814 produced a missionary organization, of which he was the first president. He urged the upgrading of ministerial education, inspired the foundation of several institutions, and was active in Baptist politics. According to the SB *Encyclopedia*, he was "a Southern aristocrat," and when he died, twenty-seven of his slaves were put up for sale.

Meredith, a little later, was more formally educated and a more formal educator. Born in Pennsylvania in 1795, he earned a bachelor's degree in 1816 and a master's degree in 1819 from the University of Pennsylvania. He then moved to North Carolina, married, pastored around, and became professor of mathematics and moral philosophy at Wake Forest College and a trustee there for several years. A charter member of the North Carolina State Baptist Convention, he also founded the state newspaper, the *Biblical Recorder*, and was its first editor from 1835 to his death in 1850. In 1838 he advised education for women (very up-to-date, that, since higher education for women in the U.S. was just beginning) and in recognition of that urging, the Baptist University for Women in Raleigh was renamed in his honor in 1909. (Today it is known informally as the "Angel Farm.")

In between these two in time, and probably in class, was a native southerner, Jesse Mercer of Georgia. Born in 1769, he had a year of formal schooling at Salem Academy, founded by his father, and acquired "some knowledge of learned languages." He was ordained at age twenty and became principal of Salem Academy while pastoring up to four churches simultaneously, one for 39 years. Mercer was involved in missionary work to the Creek Indians, financed the first temperance publication in the South, and was active in Baptist state politics, serving as president of the state convention for nineteen years and writing its history. An "able advocate and liberal patron of education," after the death of his first wife he married a wealthy widow (the *Encyclopedia* is careful to say "Jewish"). She predeceased Mercer by a few months, and his inheritance made possible substantial bequests to religious causes, including Mercer University.

Church historian Martin Marty concludes: "By 1800 Baptists were strong in all the colonies. They seemed to embody the Great Awakening impulses and served as a means for people to 'get religion'. They were rural and urban, capable of dealing with the educated (Brown University) and uneducated; Baptists were locally autonomous, mobile" (1977: 168).

Continually, of course, there was contact and flow in both directions between the higher and lower status groups. Baptists needed both a radical egalitarian identity and an educated, articulate leadership, despite the tension between the two. For there was also competition, since to the extent that the continued excitement on the frontier took political form, it threatened settled society. But, through marriage alliances, the out-migration of the rebellious and restless, and the upward mobility of the best and the brightest, the kin networks could be extended and the perception of common interests continued.

After the cotton gin was invented in the early 1790s, slave-based production moved into the bottom lands of the Deep South and out into Missouri and Texas, and Baptists moved with it. Commercialization of agriculture has ever resulted in consolidation of landholdings, sharpening the distinction between wealthy and poor farmers, often to the point of landlessness for many. The South was no exception; in 1860 three to four thousand families received three-quarters of the total return from southern exports. The "federal" formula of counting slaves as three-fifths of whites for apportionment purposes gave large slaveowners massive political advantage as well.

While only a third to a half of southern whites owned any slaves (the median number was about five), those who held fewer, or none at all, could always hope to increase their number. Although there were many more Baptists among the small slaveholders, by the 1840s, Baptists held a total of 115,000 slaves (Putnam 1913). Comparatively, according to historian Dickson D. Bruce, Jr., "Methodism had overtaken Episcopalianism as the slaveowners' church, with the Baptists running a close second" (1974: 57).

The ideology of the slave-based society took a long time to develop. Wilbur Cash (1941) sees the plantation system in full swing by 1820, but notes that the rewriting of history, especially the mythology of a southern aristocracy, went back to the Revolution. The already wealthy, aided by their originally greater resources, family ties, and access to capital, moved into the best lands, pushing the poor whites (mostly kin to the wealthy, according to both groups) on to the poorer uplands. But with luck and hard work, there was sufficient mobility in the system to give everyone a stake in its perpetuation. A literary observer, William Gilmore Simms, comments that in 1832 slavery was rarely rationalized "except on the score of necessity." Twenty years later he found reference to the "perfect right" and "moral obligation" (quoted in Peterson 1978: 1).

The religious ideology, the sermons quoting Scripture, proliferated during the same period with a Biblical defense of slavery coming from South Carolina Baptists as early as 1822. The author of this famous document, titled "Exposition of the Views of the Baptists Relative to the Colored Population of the U.S. in a Communication to the Governor of South Carolina," termed by religious historian Milton Sernett "probably the most significant pro-slavery statement of the twenties" (1975: 39), was the abovementioned Richard Furman. His biography in the SB *Encyclopedia* does not refer to this accomplishment.

Not all the Baptists were on one side, of course. Cash (1941) states that four-fifths of the membership of abolitionist societies established before 1827 were in the South. The shift—the defensiveness, the myths of chivalry, gentility, and the unity of white interests—took place after that date. In fact, many Baptists who opposed slavery, or its expansion, left the South, or were made to resign their jobs: for example, Howard Malcolm as president of Georgetown College in Kentucky and James Pendleton as pastor at Bowling Green. Posey draws the connections: "Where slavery and cotton were not so vital as in the lower South, the Baptists either condemned or compromised issues. In the cotton areas the Baptists, owning more slaves than any other church group except the Methodists, found slaveholding profitable, defended the institution with great vigor, and fought its opponents with all the power that lay in the church system of the Baptists" (1957: 89).

Mainstream Baptists, north and south, had succeeded in joining together in a national organization for the first time in 1814. The stiff suspicion of any form of authority inherent in all of early Baptist history had made cooperation beyond the local congregation difficult and slow to come. The first "association," as district groupings are known by Baptists, was founded in Philadelphia in 1707, but it was half a century before there was another one.

Baptist reluctance to cooperate was overcome by extraordinary evangelical zeal; the purpose was missions. In the early American colonies there were missionaries to the Indians whose writings inspired William Carey, an English Baptist shoemaker, to found the first organization specifically devoted to missions when he went out to India in 1792. Carey's accomplishments ricocheted, inspiring U.S. Baptists to undertake their own foreign mission efforts—thus the beginnings in 1814 of what came to be known as the Triennial Convention. At the second Convention in 1817, domestic missions were added to the goals, but this distinction meant less in the U.S. because Americans had aboriginal populations within their own borders. Much domestic work was done, then as now, in cities: Masters states proudly that by 1845 the Mission Board had established a church in every southern state capital but one.

The new group was troubled from the beginning by the same agonizing questions of organization that continue to plague Southern Baptists today: how much centralization is desirable and how to balance democratic principles of management with plutocratic ones. Added to these political quandaries were various kinds of suspicion of the educated and effete East and North, and fear of loss of control to them. Some rural Baptists left the church at this point because they did not want to be the *objects* of condescending missionizing.

There were also theological problems. Some Baptists were actively antimission, believing, in SB historian Robert Baker's words, that "it was blasphemy for men to attempt to win people to salvation whom God had not elected . . . because these efforts amounted to taking the work of God out of God's hands" (1974: 151). There were "whiskey" Baptists, wary of the linkage of mission and temperance issues, and most of these groups were also against Sunday Schools. As a result, Baptists experienced the first major defections.

These disputes led to a drive for identity on doctrinal grounds. The three great southern denominations had shared more than they had quarreled about, since the lively frontier evangelism had separated the denominations principally on grounds of "taste," surely a reflection of education and class loyalty. Historian John B. Boles writes:

> The primary thrust of the theology of each denomination concerned experiential conversion; hence, most of the doctrinal ideas of the three groups were almost exactly the same. The differences were primarily ones of tone and organization. The Baptists were zealous in their support of believer baptism by immersion, the Presbyterians were often extremely rigid in their allegiance to the Westminster Creed, and the Methodists sometimes made a creed out of having none. But the shared beliefs outweighed the differences . . . The essential unity of a conversion-centered theology so shaped the course of religious development in the South that the popular denominations can be viewed as one large synthesis of evangelical pietism (1972: 129).

Out of this generalized southern Protestant evangelical background, teeming with personal rivalries and doctrinal quibbles, there emerged increasingly sharp denominational distinctiveness. On the surface it was theologically based, but in fact it was underlain by greater divergence in class interests developed in the context of the defensive sectionalism before, during, and after the Civil War.

The first major challenge to the big three was posed in the 1820s and 1830s by the Campbellites (later termed the Disciples of Christ). Thomas Campbell (1763–1854) was a Scotch-Irish Presbyterian minister in western

Pennsylvania who had gone back to a kind of elemental New Testament faith. His son, Alexander, "was bright, argumentative, aggressive and a good promoter," who combined "principles of rationalism with a return to scriptural literalism and primitive Christianity" (Boles 1976: 43). An appropriate element was total immersion, and the Campbells became nominal Baptists for fifteen years, joining the local association. Their basic view of baptism was different, however: "They rejected grace . . . celebrated communion on each Lord's Day . . . practically ignored the Old Testament in their total preoccupation with the New, and emphatically rejected all forms of ecclesiastical organization above the level of the local congregation. Mission societies . . . were abhorred as incompatible with the New Testament" (Boles 1976: 44).

Victor Masters points out that "if Mr. Campbell had organized his cult with the specific purpose of catching the backward Baptists of that day, he could scarcely have done it better" (1915: 122–23). In the Kentucky of 1820 there were 491 Baptist churches with 32,000 members. Between 1829 and 1832 about 10,000 of them became Campbellites. To lose a third of its membership is to challenge a denomination to change its definition; Presbyterians lost even more to Campbell, only to experience another schism with the Cumberland group and yet another with the followers of Barton Stone, who broke away to form the Churches of Christ. Hill says the Stoneites could prove that "theirs was the New Testament Church" (1980: 112). Shakers made inroads in them all.

These splinterings are talked about today as if grounded in theology, but actually, Flynt writes: "Class elements were more significant. In most cases, the dissenters were poor and mountain whites, those closer to the frontier experience who resented the increasing religious sophistication of their wealthier and more politically powerful lowland brothers" (1981: 25).

All this sorting out and shaking down was connected to southern evangelical Protestants' growing defensiveness because of the slavery issue. They turned inevitably to their religious denominations to provide an ideology, only to find reflections of their own divisions. When the Methodist Episcopal Church was founded in 1784, half of its members were Virginians, yet its charter contained an anti-slavery clause, almost immediately weakened. There was a tiny if outspoken anti-slavery society of Baptists called the Friends of Humanity organized in Kentucky in 1807. First the circumstances that led to its foundation (that cotton and slavery were strong only in one section of the state) and then the fact of its existence, helped to keep Kentucky in the Union. As late as 1835, when the national Anti-Slavery

Society was organized, two-thirds of the delegates were ministers and two-thirds of those were Baptists and Methodists.

Tensions among the nation's Baptists were public by April of 1840, when a New York "American Baptist Anti-Slavery Convention" wrote a warning "Address to the Southern Baptists." Before 1844 an anonymous member circularized his own region with a pamphlet entitled "A Calm Appeal to Southern Baptists in the Advocacy of Separation from the North in All the Works of Christian Benevolence." The South kept complaining of neglect, with justification, but northern missionaries were reluctant to work there unless they could educate the slaves.

The 1844 Triennial meeting adopted a resolution to cooperate in mission work; while "we disclaim all sanction . . . whether of slavery or anti-slavery, but as individuals, we are free to express and to promote, elsewhere, our views on these subjects, in a christian manner and spirit," founder William B. Johnson said (Baker 1966a: 119). But less than a year later a new qualification for missionaries was added, that they not be slaveholders. Objections were met with silence; the southerners were indignant at this "usurpation of ecclesiastical power" and what they perceived as an attempt to prevent them from "preaching to the Gentiles." Three of the southern states refused to send any more contributions north, and the southerners, as a test case, submitted the name of a Georgia slaveholder for missionary appointment, though it was predictably refused.

So they met in Augusta in May 1845 and, in what seems to have been a mood of quiet determination and enormous self-righteousness, the schism was approved. If, as Cash puts it, the coming war was seen as "Armageddon, with the South standing in the role of the defender of the ark, its people as the Chosen People" (1941: 83), the Southern Baptists felt themselves to be saving the faith from dictatorship and considerations irrelevant to the main task of saving souls.

Two boards were established, one for Domestic Missions at Marion, Alabama, and one for Foreign Missions at Richmond. A loose, central unfunded Convention was designed originally to meet every three years, but by 1866 gatherings were annual. Resources and target territories were divided with the North without too much difficulty; China was carved up, for example, and the "missionary cause . . . advanced by the separation . . . [On] the whole the separation served to provoke each section . . . to love and good works," according to missions historian Edmund F. Merriam (1900: 57–58).

The Methodists and Presbyterians also divided, and Hill emphasizes that all these splits not only reflected growing sectionalism, but helped to increase it; they brought "one more weight to the load that in the 1860s would break the bridge and create a second nation for a short time and an alienated regional society and culture for many decades" (1980: 63). Boles also underlines the interplay: "Regional spokesmen became aggressively defensive of the southern way of life. The passive traditional society became self-consciously conservative, and the conservatism evolved into a dynamic cause. Because southern life appeared particularly Christian to those churchmen whose theology allowed them to overlook the social evil of slavery, threats against the South were interpreted as threats against the last remaining stronghold of Christian civilization" (1976: 143–44).

For the new Southern Baptists, separation meant confidence and security in the southern context of the time. Once they no longer felt themselves social outcasts, their feelings of inferiority ("status anxiety" in sociological jargon) were no longer reinforced by what they perceived as northern condescension and their resentment of northern leadership, financial power, and control. The editor of the Georgia state Baptist newspaper, the *Christian Index*, wrote in 1850 that to join a Baptist church was no longer to "lose standing or influence in society" (quoted in Loveland 1980: 33). One had been redeemed for being Baptist, in other words, by becoming Southern.

Landmarkism

The Landmark movement, with its counterparts in other denominations, should be seen within the context of this drive for identity, specialness, and superiority as a response to the Campbellites and the north. The movement derives its name from Proverbs 22:28, "Remove not the ancient landmarks which thy fathers have set," and its chief proponent and propagandist was the Rev. James R. Graves. Born in New England in 1820, Graves was ordained a Baptist minister and became a skilled and enthusiastic debater as he fought the Campbellites. In 1848 he was named editor of the *Tennessee Baptist*, in Nashville, which was the center of both the Methodists (who had moved their publishing house there after the North-South split) and Campbellites, and Graves used his experience and his new platform to emphasize Baptist distinctiveness, albeit in his idiosyncratic and perhaps autocratic fashion. Part of this effort should be seen in the context of Graves' general exclusiveness and his interest in nativism; he editorially supported

Arena of the original Graves-Howell struggle: First Baptist Church, Nashville, Tennessee, 1837–1884 (now a Lutheran church). (Photograph courtesy of the E. C. Dargan Research Library, Sunday School Board, Southern Baptist Convention.)

the "Know-Nothings," a violently xenophobic, anti-Catholic political movement. In the *Tennessee Baptist* of 26 August 1854, he said, "The foreign element is increasing in fearful ratio. Nearly one million per annum of foreign Catholics and German infidels . . . are pouring in upon us, and the tide is increasing. These foreigners have already commenced their warfare upon the use of the Bible in our public schools – against our free school system – against our Sabbath – against our laws. They boldly threaten to overthrow our Constitution" (quoted in Overdyke 1950: 67).

Landmark tenets were a restricted version of such defensiveness. They are summarized by SB historian Baker thus: the local church was prime, with supra-church bodies only those based on local church authority. Communion was restricted to members (only to those subject to church discipline). Pulpits were limited to Baptist ministers, no other baptism was recognized, and cooperation with other denominations was discouraged. All this was very exclusivistic, and intended to be. Graves attracted thousands of followers; by 1855 the Landmarkers were able to force a lengthy debate at the SB annual meeting, and by 1859 they nearly caused the Convention to divide.

What was the source of the Landmark appeal? In large part, it met the needs for growing sectarian and sectionalist identity of an intensely defensive group of rural people. Some extremists claimed there were three types of Christians – Roman Catholics, Protestants, and Baptists – and the last were the truest. Another radical theory, now called "successionism," traced the Baptist lineage back from Anabaptists through Albigensians and Cathari to Novationists and Donatists – all the dissenters, in other words. For those with any knowledge of church history, this was going too far and threatened to invite ridicule. Graves' own ecclesial ideas were susceptible to development of an exclusive institution like the Roman Catholic Church. And his views, of course, threatened the interests of the supra-church organizations. As SB theologian Walter B. Shurden writes: "Landmarkism, with its emphasis on local church successionism and the exclusive validity of Baptist churches, Baptist ministers, and Baptist ordinances, gave to Southern Baptists a claim to fame as being the only ones God had . . . Many Southern Baptists . . . believed the non-historical assumption and felt much better about who they were" (1982: 9).

The influence of Landmark thinking has been very powerful. At the end of the century, a time of heresy trials in other Protestant groups as well, Landmarkers were able to remove from the presidencey of the Southern Baptist Theological Seminary a man (William H. Whitsitt) who, German-trained and with unclear motives, showed that Baptists were not always purists, that they had sprinkled before they became dedicated to dipping in 1641 (to use Roger Williams' nomenclature). Two groups of Landmark loyalists left the SBC at the same time and still flourish in the 1980s on the Southern fringe.

More important is the lasting undercurrent. By the end of the century, James E. Tull writes, "Landmarkism had ceased to be an alien infection in the Southern Baptist body . . . it had entered the bloodstream of the denomination as a chronic infection" (1960: 617). George McDaniel's popular work of 1925, *The People Called Baptists*, states proudly: "We originated, not at the Reformation, nor in the Dark Ages, nor in any century after the Apostles, but our marching orders are the Commission, and the first Baptist Church was the first church at Jerusalem. Our principles are as old as Christianity, and we acknowledge no founder but Christ" (quoted in Tull 1960: 631).

Even Albert McClellan's statement, "Our real life comes not from roots but being, not from history, but from God" (1978: 293), while unusually mystificatory, may be attributed to Landmark influences. More specifically, the Landmark legacy of ideas can be found in "a local-church-alone theory of the nature of the church, a denial of the validity of 'alien' immersions, an adherance [*sic*] to strict, local church communion, and a hostile response to the ecumenical movement" (Tull 1975: 18). (Tull continues with a caveat: "Some Baptists hold one or more of them but not on the basis of Landmark premises.") Exclusivism brings security and freedom from comparison. One is redeemed for being Baptist, then, by being unique.

That War and Its Aftermath

It is hard not to wax ironic and helpless about the next episode. There was a war, and the South lost. But, despite Emancipation, it would not relinquish its two-tier color system, and so invented new forms under the Black Codes. The North, not to be denied its victory, prolonged its military occupation. Southerners mythologized this period as a reason to develop a real hatred toward the North, unjustifiable, in the feudal code, on the grounds of military defeat alone. For more than usually shabby political reasons, the North withdrew its troops. The South redrew the two-tier society that, in part because more deliberate, lacking in large degree even the redemption of paternalism, was in many ways humanly uglier than the one before the War. "The system of race relations that emerged in the aftermath of emancipation was the closest functional approximation to the outlawed institution of slavery that white southerners could conceive, impose, and sustain," Black and Black conclude (1987: 75).

What part did Southern Baptists play in this charade of history? During the Civil War there were a few SB officers, but the vast majority were the foot soldiers and the sloggers who looked after the officers' personal needs and cared for their horses. The leadership was dominated by Episcopalians, and even Jefferson Davis, who had been a Baptist in Mississippi, was persuaded by his Episcopalian wife to convert to that denomination when they got to Richmond, "as much for social as for religious reasons" (Williams 1971: 34). So the Southern Baptists would have lost their men, in those insane battles, and suffered and grieved and mourned. At the same time, however, because of their place in the poorer segment of the rural masses of the South, they would have had less to lose financially, and an enforced retreat to subsistence-level living would have been felt as less of a deprivation.

The Confederate Army reluctantly recognized the need for chaplains and reluctantly paid them something, and the denominations supplemented this as they could. There were 400 Methodists, 100 each Presbyterians and Baptists (Williams [1971] remarks that this was low for Baptists, considering their numbers), 65 Episcopalians, and 35 Roman Catholics. The state conventions organized a great deal of the activity; Virginia Baptists alone printed and distributed fifty million pages of tract literature.

The 1863 *Annual Report* of the "Army Mission" section of the Domestic Mission Board to SBs, meeting again in Augusta, is poignant:

It is our privilege to cheer the painful monotony of the camp; to sustain its good order and discipline . . . Let a larger number of missionaries be appointed to converse with, and preach to men, to distribute tracts, testaments, and religious newspapers, and to hold meetings for prayer and exhortation. Let our best men be delegated to this work; it is one that no novice can effectually perform. We recommend also that the churches allow a furlough, at some convenient season of the year, to their Pastors so that they may visit the camps and hospitals at a distance . . . Our Lord commended his gospel by ministering to the necessities of disease and poverty; and the missionary who bears to the camp clothing for the naked, food for the hungry, and refreshing delicacies for the languid convalescent, finds the soldier's heart open with truth . . . Our soldiers have ample leisure to attend to the word; they are crowded together, already forming congregations that wait for the minister's appearance; they are easy of access; they are eager for books or tracts; they are in danger from exposure to temptation, and sudden death; they are dying now, many of them—the safeguard, the pride, the glory of the Confederacy . . . In some of our hospitals soldiers have died pleading for the benefit of prayer, and pleading in vain; in some of our fields they have been buried as brutes, and hidden out of sight without a word concerning Jesus and the resurrection being breathed over their cold remains. The spiritual wants of our troops are pressing. The field is white unto the harvest, but the laborers are few. Let Christian husbandmen arise and go forth into this inviting field and gather sheaves for the garners of their Lord.

In 1863, SBs also resolved to reiterate their support for the Confederate cause, "acknowledge the hand of God in the preservation of our government against the power and rage of our enemies . . . and confidently anticipate ultimate success," worry about the "privations of those reduced to poverty by the war, and especially the wants of the families of our soldiers," and show their concern for "the serious interruption of education, and the growing neglect of domestic discipline which the war has caused."

Some of the Confederate chaplains were quite active; Isaac Tichenor, later to become director of the SB Home Missions Board, personally killed six Union soldiers (although the SB *Encyclopedia* biography tells only of his "reputation as a sharpshooter"). The memory of the great revivals in the army camps tended to invest the entire war in retrospect with the aura of a religious peak experience, and thus the ministers, the former chaplains, became some of the main myth-makers. They "used the Lost Cause to warn Southerners of their decline from past virtue, to promote moral reform, to encourage conversion to Christianity, and to educate the young in Southern traditions," Charles Reagan Wilson concludes (1980: 11).

Victor Masters carried on the mythologizing tradition:

This unique awareness of itself and of its past is one of the richest treasures possessed by this section. Its consciousness of its own pains and sorrows, of the gallantry and chivalry of its sons . . . of its ability to build a civilization out of ashes, makes the present South worth far more both to the nation and to itself. Having had such experiences, it has become not merely a loyal part of the nation, but something more . . . the wisdom and the strength and a certain depth of soul which the South has acquired through the bitterness of trials which purged it of dross and have healed without hate (1918: 18).

This was written during the First World War; with every war the South has been able to draw upon the great epics to blunt lingering North-South rancor and particularly to reinforce the myth of cross-class solidarity. The Southern Baptists have been the largest identifiable group of victims of this myth, and Masters sometimes shows an awareness of this, as here:

In 1863 the Confederate Congress passed a law exempting from military service all planters who owned twenty or more slaves. This could not do otherwise than make a breach between classes. It is credited with having been responsible for many farmer-deserters from the army. Incidentally it suggests that the New South had better not get too close a view of the Old South life, if we wish to preserve intact the halo of romance with which we have enshrined that period" (1915: 61).

The economic impact of the Civil War – and losing it – upon Southern Baptists can only be estimated. In 1860, 45 percent of the assessed value of all the property (including the value of slaves) in the United States was in the South, and the per capita wealth of southern whites was almost twice that of whites in the northeast and mid-Atlantic regions, according to the New South booster Richard Edmonds (1912). The total value of the slaves was estimated at $700 million; the greatest loss the South sustained was the value of these people as property. Precisely because Southern Baptists owned fewer slaves on the average, their losses would have been proportionately less – which is not to say that some individual SBs did not suffer enormously on this account. There was also the loss of life, of male labor (free and slave), and of productive capacity due both to battle and the scorched-earth policies of the victorious army. But again, since SBs were poorer and more rural, their property was more likely to have been overlooked.

The severity of the losses in the seaboard states, richer to start with, meant a savage diminution of Baptists' resources. It led to the move of the earliest theological seminary, which had invested its entire endowment in Confederate bonds, from South Carolina to Kentucky. Two and a half million whites fled the South between 1865 and 1900, one million of them to Texas and the Southwest, spreading SB churches and other aspects of southern culture to new territories.

A vast and fateful change took place when the blacks left SB (and other southern Protestant) churches and established their own. Slaves had been encouraged to join Baptist churches before the war, and much active evangelizing had gone on; Masters says about 125,000 of the 350,000 Baptists in the South in 1845 were black. Usually they attended the same churches as the whites but almost always sat in segregated sections – in the balcony, for example – and worshiped under white pastors and white supervision. (They were, of course, usually prevented before the war from having their own social organizations of any kind.)

Arthur F. Raper tells of Bethesda Baptist Church in Greene County, Georgia, which had a "balcony on three sides for Negroes," numbering seven members in 1846, seventy-three in 1866, and none (officially) in 1886, except for "'old Uncle dad' [who] continued to sit in the remaining gallery – the two side galleries having been removed – and retained his membership in the church until his death" in the late 1920s (1936: 355–56). The

SB *Encyclopedia*, in its account of the South Carolina Convention, says that "segregation was begun in the churches 'where the colored members became restiff [*sic*] from the continuance of such relations'—that is, when the Negroes became to feel that segregation was better for them" (2: 1225).

Bailey on the other hand states that the blacks, in most cases, were pushed out. He cites as "the most reliable regionwide indication" (1977: 468) the 1869 Southern Baptist Convention, during which, in a day-and-a-half of spirited debate, even the most modest proposals for cooperation were denied on the grounds that they might lead to social equality. Kenneth K. Bailey also points out that neither Rufus Spain nor John Eighmy ever mentions this debate, though their social histories purport to focus on SB "racial" attitudes. Foy Valentine, for twenty-five years head of the SB social action agency, wrote in his doctoral dissertation on the same subject: "The whites, for the most part, favored such a separation because many of the freedmen had become so drunk on their new liberty that compatibility was almost impossible" (1949: 18). This expulsion was very much a part of preparation for the legal segregation that was to come.

All of the mythmaking is heavily involved with the fact that Northern Baptists had moved in to work with southern blacks even during the war. A federal order had authorized the Home Mission Society (the Northern agency) to take over church buildings abandoned by SBs as the war advanced. By 1869 one-third of all Northern Baptist missionaries were working in the South, and the North had vastly greater resources. Northerners desired to humble the South, to pressure it into renouncing former opinions and to allow the North to lead. "It was inevitable," Walter Lynwood Fleming writes, "that ecclesiastical reconstruction should give rise to bitter feelings" (1919: 196). SB historian Joe Wright Burton notes that the SBC "insisted that workers in the South should be Southerners selected and approved by Southern Baptists" (1977a: 25–26), and its missionary agency moved from Marion, Alabama, to Atlanta, the better to raise funds and to be in a position to compete. The underlying drive was not merely to meet the competition but came from a desire to retain control of black education and aspirations of all kinds.

The First "New" South

The South seems to have risen again and again and now yet again, but the phrase "New South" was first used shortly after northern troops departed.

In this period Southern Baptists developed new mechanisms to overcome their defensiveness and help them flourish as an organization.

The Civil War, Reconstruction, and Progress enormously complicated the white class structure and the delicately crafted myth of cross-class solidarity. As many writers have observed, whites before the war were linked across class lines: by kin ties – real or fictive or exaggerated in their closeness – and by real social mobility reflective of the open frontier, with its cheap and initially fertile land, that offered the constant possibility of bettering status, in part by becoming slaveholders. According to James L. Roark (1977), on the eve of the Civil War, class-consciousness was growing and the chances of mobility were increasingly being seen as limited. During the war, combat and the harsh conditions at home had a leveling effect which was resented by the planter class. On the other hand, the slogan "rich man's war, poor man's fight" was coined as a result of the slaveowners' exemption, which led to widespread desertion. And some planters continued to grow cotton with slave labor while poor white women and children struggled for subsistence food in the next field.

After the war many other factors worked to fracture white solidarity. Planters had lost their principal source of wealth, in human beings, and many found it next to impossible to raise enough cash to bring in a crop. Land prices fell and led to many forced sales. Who the buyers were is not completely clear; there seems to have been little circulation of the rural elite, and only limited land redistribution; by 1910 plantations were larger than ever. The rapid economic expansion of Reconstruction introduced a new commercial class, not all of whom were carpetbaggers: "construction contractors, business speculators, and railroad promoters, or their agents," as Kenneth M. Stampp (1969: 180) describes them. As always, those with the greatest resources, especially in non-agricultural investments, were in the best position to ride out the storm. Their ability to survive tended to split even the planter class and raise doubts about loyalty to the Cause, in which so many had invested and lost everything they had. Economic differentiation exposed the potential for class conflict and led to fears of a collapse of white solidarity.

The initial solution was sharecropping, with both black and white tenants. In order to raise owner incomes, cotton production was extended and intensified, leading, before the end of the century, to a glut in cotton with a resultant drop in prices. As this was happening, there was still enough development taking place to keep the myths alive, and much was done to ameliorate the situation of poor whites, as in South Africa. But still there

was the constant specter and occasional reality of poor whites "being reduced to working side by side, and on the same place, with the black man,"
as W. J. Cash characterized it (1941: 172).

Out of this awkward balancing act came the Populist and Progressive
movements, with the possibility of an alliance of poor whites and blacks.
Success would have meant splitting the Democratic party, the mechanism
of Bourbon control. Flynt (1979: 53) describes the reaction to Populism:

> Among Methodists and Baptists denominational leadership came from larger,
> better-educated, and more affluent churches, the First Church elite . . . The offi-
> cial stance of this leadership was typically hostile to Populism . . . Beneath this
> religious elite existed a subchurch dominated by poor whites. Their uneducated
> preachers frequently earned a livelihood on the land or in mill villages in the
> same occupations as their parishioners. During the early 1890s the *Alabama Bap-
> tist*, state journal of the denomination, was filled with mission reports chiding
> churches for the decline in offerings due to political divisions among Baptists
> over the issue of Populism.

Poor whites had to be persuaded that they were part of the structure
of power. "To keep the Negro in subserviency, it was necessary to consolidate poor and middle class whites and these groups found themselves en-
dowed with new political importance," historian Harold Faulkner comments (1931: 10). Class solidarity had to be frustrated and color solidarity
reaffirmed.

The political and legal technique which made this possible was the gigantic structure of segregation: Jim Crow legislation, denial of black voting
rights and the evolution of a dual-track and immensely disparate educational system. The economic means was the textile industry. The rhetorical
terms in which the mills were described make the effort sound like some
latter-day Crusade: "'The establishment of a cotton mill would be the most
Christian act his hearers could perform' . . . 'this was not a business, but
a social enterprise . . . people were urged to take stock in the mills for the
town's sake, for the poor people's sake, for the South's sake, literally, for
God's sake'" (Cash 1941: 181–82, citing several sources). This effort ostensibly worked; the mills, lily-white or job-segregated for generations, saved the
poor white from black economic competition. "Progress had snatched his
supreme value, his racial status, back from the brink of peril and made it
secure once more," Cash maintains (219), but the South as a whole lagged
evermore behind the North, the rural environment continued to deteri-
orate, and conditions in the mills led to the unions they had been designed
to prevent. The devices used to keep blacks off the voting rolls often disen-

franchised poor whites as well. And male powerlessness may have led to strengthened claims of male prerogatives, challenged just at this time by social movements for women's suffrage, more equitable divorce, and the spread of contraceptive technology. After all, maintaining white solidarity was men's work.

The ideological responses to these threats shaped the special features of Southern Baptist development. To the principal contemporaneous developments in American religion as a whole, SB reactions are predictable in light of this history. German "higher criticism," the application of scientific philology to biblical texts, was roundly rejected in a renewed commitment to millennialism-fundamentalism. The "Social Gospel" reformist movement, associated with the American-German Baptist Walter Rauschenbusch, was defined as applying only to the North because of its urbanization and industrialization, even as SBs were vaunting these developments in their own territory. By evading the Social Gospel approach, churches could avoid the tensions between segregation and Christian concepts of social justice.

They would work on social problems in their own way. The pervasiveness of ministerial power led to southern legislative successes in prohibiting or controlling liquor sales, prostitution and gambling, and enforcing strict Sunday observance. Here the dilemma—still troubling to SB intelligence and logical consistency today—of acting practically like a political party on some issues while backing off completely from others shows clearly for the first time. But there was a divergence in SB class membership which was the basis for that selectivity. Matters of "private" morality on which general agreement (if not general behavioral conformity) could be attained would be defined as ones for religious involvement. Those which included shifts in socioeconomic power and thus threatened middle-class interests would be rejected as divisive and interpreted as fit only for politicians.

During the same period the churches tried to lead in the development of southern culture, what historian George Tindall calls its "peculiar 'Americanization' . . . The idea that the South embodied the purest American (with overtones of nativism and fundamentalism) grew into an established article of regional faith" (1976: 2). William Vines, pastor of the First Baptist Church in St. Joseph, Missouri, wrote in Masters' 1912 volume of essays (150–52):

> The suffering and poverty of the South became a means of emphasizing not wealth but goodness, truth and righteousness as the highest aim toward which the young manhood and womanhood of the South might aspire . . . The young

people of the South were taught that they had not time to become rich but rather to be good and useful . . . As the South has stood most conspicuously for Christian idealism and as commercialism is now invading the South as never before, the conflict is on and the result is not yet announced . . . Verily, America holds the key to the future. And if our contention concerning the place of the South in the religious life of the nation is correct, then in the final analysis an opportunity which becomes a responsibility too great for words to express rests upon the Christians and especially upon the Baptists of the South.

Churches were reflecting social and economic changes, and at the same time helping people with ways to think about them. An ethic of purity that did not condemn personal wealth was ideal, for it formed another means of buffering potential conflict. It was all-encompassing: "Mass solidarity was required for the legitimization of an entire society . . . the elite was broadened to include every (white) person," Hill concludes (1972: 40). One could be redeemed for being Baptist, now, by being white, and pure.

Between the World Wars

After the First World War, in which presumably the world had been made safe for democracy, Southern Baptists claimed that both the death of tyranny and the success of their own promotionalism were harbingers of the coming of the Baptist era. SB historian Tull cites the pronouncement of SB leader James B. Gambrell: "'The time for which Baptists have suffered and waited through the long, bloody centuries has come. The world is open to the Gospel and we may preach unafraid . . . The old aristocracies have collapsed and are passing. The star of democracy is in the ascendant. The Baptist day has come'" (1960: 662–63).

In the First World War, SBs once again had been the footsoldiers, and their evangelists had rejoiced at the great concentrations of men ready to listen to their messages. The victory of the national Prohibition amendment was a tremendous source of encouragement, although its enforcement problems led SBs to new levels of concern for the law. And yet, according to the assessment by historian J. J. Thompson (1974: 351):

The events of the Twenties deeply troubled America's conservative Protestants . . . moral standards seemed to . . . be crumbling . . . Darwinists roamed the land corrupting America's youth . . . Biblical critics mocked the Holy Scriptures . . . Social Gospelers appeared ready to discard the message of eternal salvation. Roman Catholics, drunkards, immigrants and city folk stood united behind Alfred

E. Smith, determined to wrest the presidency of the United States away from the godly. Everything conservative Protestants cherished seemed about to be swept away.

What went wrong? The nature of the economic development in the South inevitably increased further the internal divisions among the Southern Baptists and paralyzed to a greater extent their ability to do anything about them. Demagogues, Cash writes, had issued an open invitation to the Northeast to "come South and take advantage of the 'cheap and contented, 99 per cent pure, Anglo-Saxon labor,'" and offered "inducements . . . of free sites and tax exemptions," with resultant export of profits and loss of control (1941: 266). Absentee ownership grew in manufacturing, and the better-off farmers moved into the newly enlarged small towns, with their automobile dealerships and moving picture theaters. The war boom had served to raise the floor of living standards for mill workers, and this further increased the gap between the towns and the countryside.

"Calculation," or the spread of the business mentality, was particularly damaging to the religious ethos and its concern for the always-with-us poor. Social policy changes, like the strongly resisted and weakly enforced child labor laws, were for the growing middle class only those "relatively minor ones as would plainly serve to further their chances of making money . . . they were in fact growing distinctively more conservative, if that were possible, precisely because of the gathering knowledge within themselves that the Southern *status quo* presented a nearly perfect stage for the working out of their personal ambitions" (Cash 1941: 228).

This process of economic development is so familiar. What looks like the boat-lifting rising tide turns out to be a change in the productive system that serves to enrich a few, raises the level of more than a few, and leaves the vast mass bought off by meager improvement but transformed in the process. The problem that seemed most insurmountable was the rural churches and the underclass they purported to serve.

The mythmaking machine continued to operate. But what an enormous distance from the Thanksgiving Prayer of SB college president William Louis Poteat which "induced visions of 'clean sweet air,' 'mellow and fragrant soil,' and a land with 'its crops so heavy, its hay so high, its apples so red, its grapes so blue, and its honey so sweet, that it is truly a marvel to everyone who beholds it'" (Thompson 1974: 356) to Harry Ashmore's dismal summary of these same 1920s when "one-horse farmers still tried to eke out subsistence on the few leached acres that represented the family inheritance from six generations of hard labor" (1982: 5). This was the literal *Barren*

ethlehem Baptist Church, Clarksville, Georgia; economic misery, cultural poverty, rural
urity. (Photograph courtesy of the E. C. Dargan Research Library, Sunday School Board,
outhern Baptist Convention.)

Ground of Ellen Glasgow's novel, and William Faulkner, Eudora Welty,
and James Agee would all support the gloomier view.

Southern Baptists tried to mount a program of urban evangelism, to pursue the numbers and the greater resources, but they despaired of its success. What they yearned for, of course, was the kind of control a church
as a total institution can exercise in an old-fashioned rural community;
what they feared was precisely the diversity and cultural competition that
urbanity implies. To attempt to slow the migration from the rural landscape would involve facing up to their role in the social structure of the
South—the high birthrate, the eroded soil, the low investment in public
sector activities like schools and libraries, not to mention roads and sewer
systems and clean water supply, the epidemic diseases and malnutrition—
and underlying these symptoms the system of segregation which, aside
from morality, equity, justice, and mercy, made no economic sense.

The migration continued, away from the economic misery, away from
the cultural poverty. A country church would continue to lose resources,
to be underserved by an uneducated pastor, as James J. Thompson, Jr.,
notes, "who cared nothing for such programs as the Sunday school and the
Baptist Young People's Union, choosing instead to devote his time to emo-

tional sermons recounting the glories of personal redemption" (1974: 359). This lack of interest in the denominational agencies and their resources would also increase the qualitative gaps between urban and rural churches, yet the ideological value of rural purity and a shared rural past remained very great. John Jent (rural church expert for the SB Sunday School Board as Masters was for the Home Mission Board) could write in 1924, "To neglect our country churches and let them die is to commit *denominational suicide*" (Thompson 1974: 360). A few SB leaders preached that keeping blacks down also made victims of their own poor whites, but others could only repeat exhortations against divisiveness.

The tidal wave of fundamentalist reaction washed over the SBs, leaving them terribly shaken but largely intact. Despite deep internal disagreement, as the battle was fought out in the different southern states and nationally, there was no formal schism. The denomination stood against evolution, conveniently betraying its stand on church-state separation, and was forced for the first time to adopt a creed-like statement. Another loser was the long-professed primacy of the individual conscience.

The election of 1928 came as a relief and a unifying experience for Southern Baptists as their pastors led them in a holy war against urban (and northern) diversity, Catholic infiltration, and the repellent realism of Repeal. Their victory had unfortunate side effects: a loss of ministerial authority as Hoover's election was blamed for the Depression, and an exhibition of Southern Democratic disunity which left local leaders defensive and apologetic.

Then came the great Depression, worsened perhaps for SBs since it followed a previous decade of agricultural depression, and certainly because the denomination had just centralized its fundraising system, embarked on a major capital campaign and then spent according to the pledges without waiting for the receipts. Also in the late 1920s there were embezzlements at Baylor, Furman, and the Foreign Mission Board, as well as a very large one at the Home Mission Board, and SBs lost 58 of their 140 seminaries, colleges, and schools between 1922 and 1931 due to heavy debt. It took until mid–World War II to get clear. But the South as a whole – the nation's number one economic problem – and poorer SBs with it, probably gained from the New Deal response. Trickles of minimum wages, Social Security payments, agricultural extension programs, Farm Home mortgages, public works building, and rural electrification actually got through to the people they were designed to help and gave them a touch of security and hope that had been missing before, even as these programs antagonized the better-off. Federal investment and installations, particularly in military bases, gave some solid diversification to the economy, although a net migration away from obsolete agricultural enterprises continued for both blacks and whites.

A rebirth of romantic regionalism, southern style, took place with the birth of scholarly treatments such as Howard Odum's sociological studies at North Carolina and the *Journal of Southern History*, and in 1930 with the publication of the Agrarian Manifesto, *I'll Take My Stand*. All this self-consciousness fostered a healthy measuring of how people actually lived and how they felt, and even included, in William T. Couch's *Culture in the South* (1935), an essay by SB Edwin McNeill Poteat, "Why the South was so reluctant to submit religion to analytical treatment." Another type of reponse was the *Koinonia* Community in rural Georgia founded by SB pastor Clarence Jordan. This pioneering social experiment went on to spawn Habitat for Humanity, which helps poor people (with aid from friends like Jimmy Carter) to build their own housing. Then the Second World War arrived, relieving the United States, the South, and the Southern Baptists of the urge toward further introspection or social engineering. Once again, the sloggers and a few officers went off. The South swarmed with ships and soldiers and production, and SBs worried about liquor in army camps and marital breakdown.

Boom, Quake, and Aftershock

Peter Schrag gives this wonderful picture of a cultural occasion at the University of Mississippi in 1971, when the orchestra played only Glenn Miller songs from the late war: "What they were trying to preserve was that one short moment . . . when the South, having been part of that war and having been part of what seemed to be a kind of reunified country, seemed to be part of America, was beginning to rise in some way and at the same time, had not yet needed to confront the reality of that reunification, and particularly the Brown decision" (1972: 54).

Southerners had come back from this war and had gone to college on the GI Bill in unprecedented numbers (the first generation to do so) and had participated in and enormously profited from the kind of economic growth characteristic of the go-go years of the fifties and sixties, with their consumer-oriented construction and services. Southern Baptists, deeply involved in the power structure of state and local government in the South,

Hendricks Avenue Baptist Church, Jacksonville, Florida; post-war modernity in the heartland. (Photograph courtesy of the E. C. Dargan Research Library, Sunday School Board, Southern Baptist Convention.)

were by now in position to shape that development and benefit from it. And they rejoiced in the denominational increase which seemed to validate their own success even if other denominations were growing just as rapidly.

They supported Joe McCarthy and the Cold War and served in Korea. And in 1954 the rigid, fragile Southern world was shaken and left reeling by the Supreme Court. There were SB preachers in the marches and demonstrations, and some of them lost their pulpits for it. There were many more SB laymen professionally handling the fire hoses and the attack dogs, as in earlier generations they had privately ridden beneath the sheets. They thundered and shrieked and howled and fantasized; they sought, in one way or another, new definitions of meaning; they fled out of the "cities."

Urbanization and suburbanization in the South are beginning to get the full-scale study they deserve, and the results underline southern distinctiveness as an economic region. Because of the late urbanization (the other side of agrarianism and rural virtue) when cities finally came, they were able to grow to remarkable degree by annexation since there were no established political entities to resist. The increase of metropolitan central-city population resulting from annexation was 21 percent for the decade of 1950

(First Baptist Church, Quincy, California; post-war reality on the Southern Baptist frontier. Photograph courtesy of the E. C. Dargan Research Library, Sunday School Board, Southern Baptist Convention.)

to 1960, and 13 percent for 1960 to 1970 in the South, while during the same periods the growth rates in the Northeast were zero (Berry and Kasarda 1977: 185). It is this fact that makes the rural-urban distinction, with its cutoff point at 2,500 population used by the federal census, so difficult to interpret for the South. Suburbanization, in the sense of the development of class-homogeneous, primarily residential communities, can and does take place *within* the ever-expanding city boundaries. And "rural" areas, by the census definition, can become suburban in the same cultural sense as the cities expand toward them. The fact that these transforming processes were occurring in the South at a time when dependence on private automobiles was nearly complete has given the landscape new dimensions of sprawl.

Some "white flight" had preceded the Brown decision, of course. But much more followed it, and the impact on settlement patterns—and thus on the churches—was profound. Some congregations packed up and moved to the outskirts, to new neighborhoods maintained white by low density or other zoning devices. Some suffered and sputtered and died, the remaining members dispersed. And a few stayed and struggled to form new urban ministries. But "suburbanization" (as a loose term describing the complex shift in the mixture of rural-urban relationships as it took place in the South) enabled SBs to escape the old version of class conflict precisely because it was that very suburbanization, the particular economic sectors involved, that moved the center of denominational power into the middle class. Southern Baptists participated in these changes both in their residential-congregational and their vocational-professional lives, and adjustment to desegregation would have been far more difficult if economic and geographic expansion had not occurred simultaneously.

When the period of general growth was largely over, the Sunbelt advantage — differential Southern prosperity — continued to soften the transition for Southern Baptists and create new New South mythologies. But the recent migrants and transferred employees, including some upper-middle-class blacks, have transformed the southern cultural landscape (some of the largest Unitarian churches in the United States now are in southern metropolises). Politics is also kaleidoscopic, fluid, unpredictable. The tertiary urban centers (like Atlanta) are islands of glitter and boom, but middle-sized cities struggle for survival as well as for identity. Most blacks are still a marginal labor force, the educational system is color-separated in new ways and vastly disparate in old ones, and rural areas are once again depressed. One SB mission expert acknowledges the problem: "our people are being hurt . . . the rural and smalltown South more than fifty miles from a major city seems to be caught in the backwash of a major change in the economy" (Farley 1987: 4).

Southern Baptists in the late 1980s have reacted to these multiple changes by putting on their own version of the Civil War. But meanwhile they have built an enormous institutional organization, which both expresses and attempts to resolve some of the contradictions inherent in their attempt to maintain solidarity — and sometimes creates further contradictions in the process.

3 The Southern Baptist Polity: Denominational Structure and Financing

> The necessitie of Politie, and Regiment in all churches may bee held, without holding any one certayne form to bee necessary in them all. Nor is it possible that any form of politie, much less politie ecclesiastical should be good, unlesse God himself bee authour of it.
>
> — Richard Hooker, *The Laws of Ecclesiastical Politie*, 1594

Obsession with Bureaucracy

All religious groups in democratic societies have these awkward dilemmas: how to remain authentic to the original reason for existence while serving diversity and meeting challenges of change; how to raise and manage resources in order to ensure economic survival; how to make decisions and settle disputes in ways that will further the cause of the institution while keeping an appearance of fairness; how to cooperate with other religious groups without too much compromise; how to perform these institutional tasks within the legal and constitutional strictures of the country.

Such dilemmas can be faced honestly and openly and the necessary compromises arrived at. Southern Baptists, however, face them with excruciating self-consciousness to the point of obsession — they are constantly explaining who they are and where they came from and what they stand for in terms of how they work. It distorts their view of the past and makes them sound as if they were constantly selling themselves to their own membership.

The six videocassettes produced with much fanfare by the Historical

Commission contain one-quarter history and three-quarters bureaucratic establishment and increase. The most detailed history of the denomination, Robert Baker's 1974 book, *The Southern Baptist Convention and Its People, 1607–1972*, while invaluable for reference, is loaded with detailed descriptions of committees meeting through the night to reject long-dead proposals.

The premier *theological* journal, *The Review and Expositor*, devoted a special issue (Spring 1980) to the district association as a level of organization. (It's as if the *American Historical Review* did a whole number on the siting and administration of, say, the local offices of the Internal Revenue Service.) The same journal later devoted an issue to Southern Baptist – Roman Catholic dialogue (Spring 1982). In the pair of essays on "scripture," the RC writes of ideas, documents, and liturgy; the SB of publishing houses and Sunday School curriculum. In the pair on "spirituality," the RC mentions history, theology, and forms of prayer; the SB talks about conferences and seminary programs of field education and supervised learning. In a discussion of "evangelism," the RC emphasizes concepts, a cooperative spirit, and ecumenism; the SB recapitulates the entire SBC organization chart. Only in "eschatology" did a programmatic approach fail the Southern Baptists.

James L. Sullivan's *Baptist Polity as I See It* contains this prideful bit (1983: 69): "It is my studied belief that the Southern Baptist approach in developing its polity has more strength and fewer weaknesses than any other denominational system available." Why the defensiveness, the chauvinism, the obsessive detail?

First of all, emphasizing organizational distinctiveness in the 1845 split appears to shrink the slavery issue in proportion. In all the SB histories there is no shred of evidence for this. Founder W. B. Johnson said "the Constitution we adopt (in 1845) is precisely that of the original union (of 1814)" (Sullivan 1983: 237).

But vaunting a "convention" (centralized) form involves a contradiction with cherished Baptist principles of freedom of conscience and individual church autonomy. Paul Harrison, in one of the few political science treatments of American church structure (1959), points out that the extreme emphasis on the individual is the product not of seventeenth-century Baptist beginnings but of the eighteenth- and nineteenth-century secular spirit of individualism, reinforced by the American frontier tradition. "What authority does this Convention have over either individuals or churches?" the SB *Encyclopedia* (2: 1262) asks. "The answer is, absolutely none." Yet people in the local churches and the several seminaries and the state agencies have

complained chronically of "dictation from Nashville," even before fundamentalist pressures began to be felt.

The insistence on absolute freedom can become an escape, a retreat from
responsibility. One tiny but telling example: the Raleigh *News and Observer*
(11 July 1982: 1) surveyed churches in the tobacco-growing eastern region
of North Carolina as to their moral pronouncements on smoking. The
newspaper quoted Rev. Foy Valentine, then head of the Southern Baptist
Convention's Christian Life Commission: "We happen to be on the right
side of a moral issue. We give thanks that others are now recognizing it
and see the moral dimensions of it." But the Rev. Ray Hodge, minister of
the First Baptist Church in Kinston, North Carolina, denied that the lack
among North Carolina churches of a stance on smoking had anything to
do with the state's tobacco industry: "Baptists have no organizational structure to speak on these issues."

And an SB expert critic charges: "Southern Baptists have come to the
strange pass of having developed one of the most authoritarian religious
structures in America, while deceiving themselves by their own ecclesiastical pronouncements into being almost completely uncritical regarding
these very structures" (Moore 1977: 29).

In general, SBs are reluctant to face issues of power. How can there be
a basic democracy of 14.7 million people? is a question they don't want to
ask. Do they want a plutocracy or a democracy? On the other hand, do they
want to grant authority to people who are not paying their way? How do
they enjoy the advantages of size, including greater resources and a greater
opportunity for public influence, yet accurately reflect their varied constituency? Rather than facing the inherent incompatibility of some of their
goals, and the necessity for compromise—a prospect that SBs find intoler-
able—they react by denying contradiction and paradox.

One of the signs of this malaise is megalomania, an obsession with doing
big things. The modern period has been marked with a succession of gran-
diose goals for growth: the $75,000,000 Campaign, a Million More in
'54, the Thirty Thousand Movement (churches), 8.5 (millions in Sunday
Schools) by '85. A current effort, to witness to every person who has never
heard the gospel by the year 2000, is named "Bold Mission Thrust." [The
unconscious phallicism of this term was noted in *The Christian Century*
(1980: 692) by Jean Lyles, who called it "vaguely suggestive."] A previous
version of the same program bore the label, "Operation Penetration" (SBC
Annual Report 1965: 88).

Many of the efforts have fallen short in the scheduled time. Sometimes even the annual agency budget targets are not met, and the Lottie Moon offering for foreign missions has set unrealistic goals. In 1983, notwithstanding, when a mere $3.1 billion was given by all SB churches, a plan was announced to increase this total to $20 billion annually by the end of the century.

Despite all this, it works. They are successful—by the standards of growth in numbers and resources against which modern churches, even folk churches, are judged. There is inevitable friction among the various levels of the structure, and the different interest groups, but considering its vast size and geographical dispersion it seems responsive to its members. The Reformation coincided with, indeed was part of, a gigantic movement to redesign polities, civil as well as ecclesiastical, which made all the denominations self-conscious about their structure. Many of their common names—Episcopal, Presbyterian, Congregational—reveal a concern for the locus of authority. Baptists lack such an inherent commitment, and may still be fighting the Campbellites and the Landmarkers over the validity of any supralocal organization. But the tone is different—more intense, less balanced by other involvements—and getting more so. The result is a structure that works, but only at the cost of hypocrisy, evasion, and constant improvisation. Criticisms are met with shibboleths, and the reluctance to face problems and make rules leaves much room for opportunism. "The Southern Baptist Convention . . . can do whatever it wishes and produce an ecclesiastical reason for its action," said the loyal critic LeRoy Moore (1977: 22).

The Corporate Structure

The most striking feature is the way a tight organization is achieved without geographical concentration (the groupings here are by function and are not the ones used by SBs). The SBC is like the United Nations, with its secretariat and corporate headquarters in one place and the specialized agencies scattered about in others; the FAO in Rome, WHO in Geneva, UNESCO in Paris, and so forth. In the case of the UN, the purpose was to prevent domination by one country—and to spread around the prestige and the patronage opportunities. The same motives are undoubtedly at work in the SBC, although nothing openly indicates such awareness. W. B. Johnson said in his long speech in 1845 that the Boards should be in different places, but there is no explanation of what was in his mind. The agencies started that way, with offices in Richmond and Marion, Alabama, and have continued to sprinkle themselves throughout southern urban centers as the agencies grew. There seems to be no functional reason for the placement (and the many moves), except for a lobbying presence in the nation's capital.

Only slightly less striking is that there was no central coordinating organ until 1917, and it had no secure funding until 1925. To continue the UN simile, it would be as if the specialized agencies went about their business all over the world without the New York secretariat, and minus budgets. The corporate headquarters wound up in Nashville because the Sunday School Board was there. And the Sunday School Board, the largest publisher of religious materials in the world, is unique since it is not only self-sustaining but contributes (almost $3 million in 1987–88) to the central and the various state organizations.

When the missions emphasis became paramount, fund-raising efforts had a clearer appeal—but were no less difficult for all that. Luther Rice, employed by the old Triennial Convention to raise the funds for missionaries in India, wrote in 1817:

> I have travelled 6,600 miles—in populous and in dreary portions of country—through wilderness and over rivers—across mountains and valleys—in heat and cold—by day and by night—in weariness, and painfulness, and fastings, and loneliness; but not a moment has been lost for want of health; no painful calamity has fallen to my lot; no peril has closed upon me; nor has fear been permitted to prey on my spirits; nor even inquietude to disturb my peace. Indeed, constantly has the favourable countenance of society towards the great objects of the mission animated my hopes . . . and . . . I have, besides many other aids and liberalities, received for the missionary object, in cash and subscription, more than $4,000 . . . The Lord hath great things for us (McClellan 1975: 50).

Causes proliferated throughout the nineteenth century—educational institutions, homes for the elderly, orphanages. (The magnetic appeal of the children was always resented. "Why," one pastor said, "they'd just parade the orphans around to all the churches and they'd get all the money there was!") Masters gave this version of the situation at the end of the century:

> A number of preachers . . . [were] . . . employed by the Boards to itinerate in order to stir up the pure consciences of the brethren . . . The State bodies in general seemed to get pretty tired of the agents, and there came a time when these had to cease their activities. The severe straits of the General Boards after the War once more turned thoughts longingly toward field agents as an aid in

the efforts to finance the work, but the poverty-stricken States and the urgent cries of the intra-State needs that must be supplied, made the agent for the General Board have an unpleasant time of it (1915: 181).

So the solution to all this insecurity and competitiveness was found in the "Cooperative Program" (CP), a central fund that would furnish the absolutely essential fiscal underpinnings of the growing denomination while using the missions, the modern magnet, as the come-on.

Under the CP, money is collected from the local churches and forwarded to the state conventions. They take off the top a proportion for state-wide activities and send the rest to Nashville, where the Executive Committee distributes it to the various agencies according to the budget it has prepared for ratification by the annual meeting for the SBC as a whole. The CP is an ingenious plan, a commonsensical, realistic, logical answer to an obvious problem, yet the SBs feel a necessity for continually selling it to the membership. As ex–SBC president Duke McCall comments, "The Cooperative Program is much more than a way of collecting money and dividing it among the state and Southern Baptist agencies . . . It has molded the structure of the denomination by being the main channel through which Southern Baptists have expressed their sense of mission under God" (1978: 16). A former SBC president says he believes that the Cooperative Program was "revealed to Southern Baptists by God," and another one adds, "It's almost easier to be against the Virgin Birth than the program."

The agencies have relinquished their right to do independent fund-raising for operating expenses except for the two principal missions campaigns. At the same time, substantial proportions of CP funds also go to the two Missions Boards. McCall explains: "One major effect of the Cooperative Program has been a slight revision of the meaning of 'missions' to Southern Baptists. With such slogans as 'The Cooperative Program is Missions,' church members have learned to think of every denominational enterprise as interlocked into the mission outreach of the church" (1978: 17). The figures and the percentages vary from year to year; the numbers in the various Annual Reports never add up. It is obvious that the missions' mission is being used to bring funds into the central organization and that the fund-raising bureaucrats are shy about asking for money for copying paper, cleaning services, and coffee machines in Nashville and elsewhere, and middle-class salaries and modest fringes for themselves. While all non-profit organizations have this problem, the SBC has the missions appeal with which to overcome it and an overwhelming reluctance to be honest about it.

Another chronic source of contention is the division of CP funds between the central SBC and the states. Originally, in the mid-1920s planning, a fifty-fifty split was foreseen. The annual percentages are worked out in, no doubt, agonizing negotiations; on the average about 62 percent goes to the state and 38 percent to the central organization. With the understanding that the newer state groups may need to retain more resources for their own consolidation, fresh efforts are intermittently forecast to reach the fifty-fifty goal.

SBs as givers, compared to other religious donors, are in the middle; their enormous total resources result from their being so numerous. According to the 1987 *Yearbook of American and Canadian Churches*, annual per capita giving (rounded off to whole dollars) amounts to $268 for SBs, $297 for the Lutheran Church of America, $280 for the United Church of Christ, $554 for the Episcopal Church, $769 for the Seventh Day Adventists (*Quarterly Review*, Third Quarter 1987: 76). In order to evaluate these figures as results of zeal rather than affluence it would be necessary to relate them to income.

Tithing (giving a tenth of one's income, with arguments as to whether it should be figured before or after taxes) is encouraged, but practiced by somewhat less than a tenth. A seminary student was outraged that her aunt sent money to Jerry Falwell. Asked whether the aunt tithed, she replied, "Oh no, she wouldn't go that far."

Most of this $4 billion (all such figures, unless otherwise noted, from the SBC 1987 *Book of Reports*), every year over 90 percent, stays within local church control, to build and maintain buildings and run programs ranging from child psychiatry to bowling leagues, some of which are construed as missions. Part of the balance goes to feed the state coordinating bodies which provide important services to local churches and support state-wide institutions, the rest to the relatively tiny central SBC superstructure, where it underpins the evangelistic efforts at home or abroad.

The central headquarters, housing the secretariat and a few other agencies, is located in Nashville on land donated by the Sunday School Board. The actual Executive Committee consists of the SBC president and recording secretary and the Woman's Missionary Union president, and fifty to one hundred members, elected by the annual meeting from a proposed slate, with a wide geographical distribution. All states have at least one member, the larger ones more, but none more than five. Neither pastorate nor laity may have more than two-thirds of the membership, and terms of office are staggered over four years. The Executive Committee meets at least twice in Nashville, in between the annual meetings, but there are numerous subcommittees to consider special problems *ad hoc*. The members are not paid, but they get expenses, and their tasks are to supervise the complex budget and to consider by-law revisions for presentation at the annual meeting and any number of ideas—some worthy, some bizarre, some too hot to handle in public—thrown them by the Convention for study. Some of these involve real issues of power, theology, and attempts to redress grievances resulting from structures that have turned out to be unfair, while some are pious cries for attention. The committee ducks a lot of issues: one that size has to behave more like a legislature than an executive committee. But it works, and the messengers at the Annual Convention have trusted it, most of the time.

There are three other central financial bodies (the distinctions between boards, commissions, and committees are meaningless to the SB membership). The *Annuity Board* in Dallas handles annuities, pensions, and life and health insurance for pastors and their dependents and some church employees. "Southern Baptists were later than many denominations in providing some economic security for their aged ministers," Baker writes (1974: 432). With the gradual professionalism of the ministry, increased longevity, and, some would add, a breakdown in the American family system, pensions had to come to supplement Social Security benefits. In every discernible respect the Annuity Board is like a small insurance company; in 1986 it held assets of almost $2 billion. The average monthly pension check, however, is still under $250. At some annual meetings the board gave *video* presentations of its activities which had all the high drama and visual excitement of the typical meeting of the mortgage committee at a small town bank.

The *Southern Baptist Foundation* in Nashville is like an investment trust company. Besides holding funds for individuals, investing them and transferring the income to the Convention, it also invests idle or endowment funds for SBC agencies. Market value of assets managed in 1986 totalled $51 million.

Also in Nashville is the *Stewardship Commission*, which operates like an in-house fund-raising firm, providing services to churches and other groups which plan money-raising campaigns, selling others. It runs its own sales promotion service, with filmstrips, kits for local committees, books and pamphlets, and other items (like paper napkins with the printed message "Give Boldly: Declaring My Growing Commitment"). It competes, of course, with private fund-raising consultants, which advertise in the various SB publications. The Stewardship Commission has raised over a quarter of a billion dollars since 1969. The report that the head of a new "Planned Growth in Giving" promotional program received over $80,000 in yearly salary and benefits brought reactions of mixed envy and outrage.

There is also a Standing Committee on the Denominational Calendar, which works five years or so ahead. It has to, if only because of the logistics of the annual meeting. Lacking any but the most minimal liturgical year, Southern Baptists find the seasonal round marked with Outreach and Make-Your-Will Months, Jewish Fellowship Week, and Start-a-Church-Commitment, Christian Literature, and On-to-College Days, among a long list of such celebrations. (The committee, ostensibly impossible to politicize, had just that done to it by the fundamentalists' insistence on designating a Sanctity-of-Human-Life Sunday synchronized with the national Right-to-Life movement's January observance.)

A central denominational press is curiously lacking. The only publication the SBC itself has is the *Baptist Program*, which is given away free to 65,000-odd pastors and other full-time church workers as a promotional piece for the Cooperative Program. Most of the contents of the *Baptist Program* deal with selling the CP to the laity and encouraging generosity. Otherwise, the vast task of informing the multitudes is carried by the state papers, thirty-eight of them, wire-serviced by Baptist Press. Besides its small staff in Nashville and several representatives in Washington, Baptist Press uses stringers from the state papers to carry regional news of general interest. Baptist Press reporters, especially those in the Washington office, seem quite independent, sometimes commenting quite acidly on the temper and tone of the annual meetings. Several autonomous, lay-edited periodicals with well-defined viewpoints have been started since the rise of "theological" controversy, and they also serve as carriers of news and opinion across state lines.

The Annual Meeting and the Presidency

What historical theologian and former SB Samuel Hill wrote in 1967 is still true:

> The annual meeting of the Southern Baptist Convention . . . is a magnificent sociological experience. For here are gathered under one roof (few buildings in the South are sufficiently cavernous enough to contain this assembly) thousands of individuals normally isolated from the power structures of any organization but very much a part of an immense, destiny-conscious, muscle-flexing in-

Display area, Southern Baptist Convention annual meeting, 1950. (Opposite, above): Coffee break, Southern Baptist Convention annual meeting, 1948. (Below): Prayer time, Southern Baptist Convention annual meeting, 1986. (Photographs courtesy of the Southern Baptist Historical Library and Archives.)

stitution in which the accents and concerns of its leaders, because similar to their own, are intelligible. Complex issues which transcend their grasp and concern, when raised at all, do not stay on the floor very long . . . It is remarkable how these annual meetings have so effectively brought together institutional grandiosity and the psychology of an agrarian, inferiority-ridden people (167–68).

Ostensibly the annual meeting (how can there be a convention of a convention? although that is what both are called) is a business meeting, embodying the only legal power, charged with election of officers, the care and feeding of by-laws and procedures, the adoption of the budget and other legal matters, the self-promoting reports of the denominational agencies, and resolutions on public policy issues. These have absolutely no binding effect on either churches, seminaries, or individuals, but are, besides the election of the top officers, what the national media will cover, and of tremendous symbolic importance. Recently, however, some of them have

been used as if they were dogma, to justify policy or to discipline denominational employees.

The annual meeting also has, of course, many latent functions. Many pastors (and perhaps 70 percent of those attending are pastors and wives) use the occasion as the family vacation. For many it is combined with an alumni/alumnae reunion (60-odd percent of SB pastors with seminary and college degrees have attended SB institutions). It has many features in common with the business convention or trade show, at which the latest products/techniques/sermon anecdotes are exhibited. The plenary sessions serve as showcases for ambitious pastors, laymen, and bureaucrats in one role or another, and obversely, the review and assessment of such by the multitude. Beyond these functions, the sessions are full of inspiration—preaching, music and prayer; they are educational, not only regarding denominational affairs but national and international issues; and they are a gigantic spectacle, a form of entertainment, in which passive viewing and listening, shrewd analysis, and gossip have roughly equal parts during "one furious, flaring week of life each year" (Frady 1967: 39).

What goes on? The current format is Tuesday-through-Thursday in mid-June, sessions of three-plus hours morning and afternoon and three hours in the evenings. The auxiliary women's organization and several specialized groups hold conventions the preceding weekend, and in the main arena on Monday happens the "Pastors' Conference," a preaching and evangelical marathon, the leaders of which are often subsequently elected to high office in the SBC itself. In 1984 a simultaneous and to some extent competitive affair, the Forum, was organized to serve as a focus for "moderate" sentiment. Wednesday afternoons are off for seminary alumni luncheons, shopping, sightseeing, and some of the "ladies" have their hair done—again.

The sessions start with music and prayer. There are two formal sermons by the president and a selected superstar preacher, and frequent congregational hymns that serve exactly the purpose of the seventh-inning stretch. Baptists usually stand to pray, which also helps the circulation and is the only way to achieve quiet; they will not talk during a prayer, although they may continue to ambulate, tiptoeing with bowed heads and slitted eyes. The scheduling is careful and thoughtful, deliberately sequencing business sessions and set pieces with physical and aural relief to maintain interest and minimize wear on the body.

The audience/congregation are called "messengers"; the term "delegate" is eschewed since they don't represent anyone, and speak and vote only for themselves. The basis for selection has changed many times; currently both size of church and financial contribution are criteria. Since each church may send one messenger, but no church more than ten, the group is potentially overwhelmingly weighted in favor of the small churches. And since there are 37,000 churches, the present system of selection has been preserved only by the post–World War II erection of sports temples. There are many of these, but a lot of them are in places where there are not also the thousands of nearby hotel rooms that the Convention requires.

Despite the thoughtful scheduling and the afternoons off, people – including those on the platform – get tired and testy. Sometimes the atmosphere is exciting, and more than a bit ugly; sometimes it's at its best when most tedious because this enormous effort at basic democracy has seemed so genuine. Group emotions are expressed, of course, not only through the ballot but in American style – with applause, boos, catcalls, and even an occasional rebel yell or whistle. The sports arena atmosphere encourages such open displays and relieves the tensions. One year the women's organization provided a huge net of balloons – interesting colors of sky, grape juice, and dried blood – which were released late in the evening of the contested presidential election and popped with cathartic abandon.

The congregational singing, involving not just the lungs but the whole body, is also marvelous therapy. Despite the deplorable influence of Delius, Glazunov, and Hollywood on most of the music, the overdone, hoked-up arrangements, and the mixed quality of the performances, at some meetings the conductor of the congregational singing has in the middle of one of those touching nineteenth-century hymns cut the accompaniment so that fifteen or thirty thousand voices floated on *a cappella*, authentic and very moving. Just for one short verse – it could not be sustained.

The circumstances and the format have changed many times since the beginning. In 1845 "delegates" celebrated the Lord's Supper, "something that would be unheard of today, on the grounds that the Convention is not a church," LeRoy Moore has judged (1977: 17). A charming account is given in Burton's history (1977B) of the Sunday School Board of the special train put together to travel to Fort Worth in 1890. It cost $150 to hire a whole twenty-four-berth sleeping car from Louisville; the roundtrip fare per person was pegged at $26.35. To think of those days of travel with the cinders and the dust in the clothing of the period is to start to sweat, itch, and ache. It was in May that year, but still scarcely temperate weather in the South. There were no women messengers; in 1885 the qualifier "brethren" was added but was changed back to "messengers" in 1918.

Now the thousands come by plane, sometimes chartered to save pennies, by car and antique yellow school bus or sleek heavy expensive van—an "AGAPE-6" Texas tag decorated the Superdome parking lot in 1982. And the leaders are still tinkering with the machinery. The starting times were later in Pittsburgh in 1983; the non-Baptist exhibitors were sharply segregated and sent over to another building. The eighth session was restored in Kansas City in 1984. The huge crowds have meant awkward adjustment for many microphones in several rooms, and the pseudo-intimacy of "image mag" screens. The order of events is clearly manipulated to coincide with peaks and valleys in attendance. Packets of cardboard ballots are utilized in random order; a messenger in Pittsburgh asked why, was told "to prevent their being marked in advance and to make sure you all listen carefully to the instructions," and riposted with a snarl about trust—a major problem for both leaders and followers (there have been charges of ballot fraud back to the early 1960s, increasing as the controversy grew).

There are many rituals not necessary to the program, and the details have varied with the personnel over the years. The families of the new and outgoing Presidents are introduced to the crowd. Bailey Smith, retiring, asked for thanks for his wife— "I've been away so much she's had to raise *my* children for two years" (emphasis added). Many in the audience sat on their hands. The children of the president are pressed to read the Bible or give a prayer; Smith's teenage son did the former abominably (SBs seem uncomfortable reading out loud) but Jimmy Draper's offspring and, later, his wife prayed adequately. Joyce Rogers, who had written a song, sang it (she was introduced as "my precious wife"). Prayers may be interjected by floor motion: one arched over a sick man in a Missouri hospital, the Convention workers, and pastors' wives, "all those who are usually overlooked."

There is a clutch of printed materials: the reports for the previous year, a pamphlet which among other things contains the words to the hymns (which the SBs rarely need), and a really remarkable daily *Convention Bulletin* produced in a press run of many thousands between midnight and eight in the morning. Transferred to the incoming president is a collection of gavels made from trees growing on the banks of the River Jordan and the timbers in the prison where John Bunyan languished ("Works fine," said Draper, swiftly obliterating the symbolism). The home-church musical ensembles of the president and the Convention sermon-giver are featured—a nice, if sometimes expensive touch. There is child care, a day camp for the independent types and a nursery for the little ones. There's a prayer room supposedly staffed by the state groups about eighteen hours

a day; sometimes there is no one there. The unspeakable problems of sup-
plying food to thousands who have less than two hours for lunch in the
middle of what passes for urban renewal are seemingly insoluble.

Where does the power reside in this circus? Legally, with the messengers, the ad hoc multitude. There is a commitment to basic democracy,
and to Robert's *Rules of Order* as modified by the president's inexperience
and the ignorance of everybody else. The opportunities for manipulation
are many and have been increasingly exploited. Professional parliamentarians are now used but have added only a facade of impartiality.

One of the most basic and intractable difficulties lies in the age of the
messengers. Ten-year-olds finger packets of cardboard ballots as they ask,
"Daddy, how shall I vote now?" (Women may ask the same question, for
some call their husbands "Daddy.") Every effort to establish a minimum
age of, say, thirteen has been ignored by the current leadership. The possibilities for undue influence are obvious, but to change the situation would
collide with some cherished principles – local church autonomy and individual freedom. Obviously, there are financial considerations, and the pressure to continue is inevitable.

Another and not unrelated problem is the relation between the site of
the Convention in a given year and the availability of expense money from
sources other than local church budgets. Most SBs believe that events are
greatly affected by location and thus the political/theological coloration of
the messengers most likely to attend. By-law changes must be approved in
two successive meetings, smoothing out some of the differences, but the
proximity factor remains.

The president has a few powers and a great deal of influence. On paper
he has the right "in conference with the vice-presidents" – a stricture most
recently honored in the breach – to appoint the Committee on Committees,
which will select the slate for the Nominating Committee that works out
the proposed officers and the various boards of trustees for the seminaries
and agencies. The president's predilections can obviously influence selection, but it is checked by a system of staggered terms. (The junta of inerrantist leaders announced that its takeover would be a ten-year operation,
now completed.) The president also appoints the Resolutions Committee,
which shapes and selects those which will be voted upon by the SBC as
a whole. Although these resolutions are nonbinding, they have high public
visibility and do a great deal to form the SB image.

The president presides over the annual meeting, sits on the Executive
Committee and ex officio on many others, and serves as the principal spokes-

man for the denomination during his term of office (since the 1950s limited to two consecutive one-year terms). His church pays many of his traveling expenses and tolerates his absences as long as he is back home for the "preaching service" most Sundays. Both Draper and Rogers published two books while in office and traveled thousands of miles to press encounters, college commencements, state conventions, conferences abroad, making umpteen speeches as well as attending the requisite committee meetings. Although some of these may have overlapped with their almost weekly preaching, their stamina was impressive.

Most presidents in the past have been pastors, or at least ordained, with an odd governor or two. The father of Brooks Hays, U.S. Congressman from Arkansas in the '50s, was asked whether he'd rather have his son elected a president of the United States or of the Southern Baptist Convention. "Guess it'd have to be the country, 'cause he ain't smart enough to be head of the Baptists," he is supposed to have replied. In this century, a seminary professorship and some bureaucratic experience, as well as pastoring large churches, have been good paths. More recently, the evidence of evangelical success has become the test: "You're judged in this business by the number of baptisms," said one young pastor.

There is a fairly sharp break between the latest five presidents and their predecessors; not a whole generation, but more like fifteen years, and a totality in orientation and culture. The same change can be seen in U.S. senators, a trend toward prettiness and slickness. The difference is due, beyond doubt, to television. The fundamentalists organized in advance of the 1979 SBC meeting in Houston and elected, unprecedently on the first ballot in the absence of the usual list of favorite sons, Adrian Rogers of Memphis. There were widespread criticisms of irregularities in messenger registration which led to tightened procedures in subsequent meetings. Rogers joined North Carolina Senator Jesse Helms in asking to restore voluntary prayer in the schools, and he made some very conservative appointments to the key committees. Unexpectedly, and very late, Rogers announced that he would not run for a second term, supposedly for reasons of health.

His successor was Bailey Smith, then pastor of another over–10,000-member church, elected in St. Louis in 1980 and reelected on the first ballot again in the 1981 Los Angeles meeting. Smith had a reputation as a "soul-winner"; his church had led the denomination in baptisms for several years. Smith will endure in American religious history for his remark that God doesn't hear the prayer of the Jew; he may live in SB history for his committee appointments and his hard-line, almost incoherent president's sermon.

Elected in 1982 on the second ballot by a 57–43 percent vote against a "moderate" candidate, Jimmy Draper came from another of the mega-churches, in Euless, Texas, and started his term determined to be less controversial, more conciliatory, more moderate in tone. His first sermon— long, delivered at breakneck speed, studded with quotations from Baptist and other theologians and embellished with a couple of foreign terms, one even German—amounted to a restatement of the fundamentalist platform of seventy years ago except for his omission of all reference to the Virgin Birth and was greeted with enthusiasm. His second and valedictory effort contained some very specific criticisms of SB operation and was received with total silence.

Charles Stanley of Atlanta, the fourth of the current inerrantists, was elected in Kansas City in 1984 in a deeply divided Convention and re-elected in Dallas in 1985 to near hysteria, followed by lawsuits challenging his use of parliamentary procedure. In Atlanta in 1986, Adrian Rogers came back for a second term, an event carefully engineered from the beginning in the minds of many on both sides, and he repeated his victory in St. Louis in 1987. Jacksonville's Jerry Vines won in 1988.

The resolutions process can be bewilderingly arbitrary. Some seem not germane, some repetitive, some contradictory, some predictable, some trivial. Most of them are just titled and their full texts never released. The committee then takes the drafts off and disposes of them. Some are dismissed as "inappropriate" (and some of them indeed are, or seem to be, but there's no explanation made as to why), some combined, reworded, or reshaped.

All of these decisions are dependent on the composition of the committee, which depends on the president. There is no recourse except an attempt at further action from the floor, in which case the frustrated protester may be shouted down by the angry, tired (or hungry) crowd, ruled out of order by the chair, or defeated by lack of time, a technique which has also been manipulated, particularly in 1987 and 1988. One messenger wanted to pursue an obviously unpopular subject and was referred to the parliamentarians. A young pastor commented, "Well, we'll never see him again."

There are vice-presidents, too. In 1982 the first vice-president was a woman, the second a Korean-American pastor. When the ritual time came for a surrogate to preside, it was the Korean male who took the gavel. An Arkansas pastor remarked that this showed "spiritual insight," for even the possibility that a woman might speak to them is still taboo to some. Since then all have been white males, until 1987 when a Choctaw became second vice-president. Over this period, the number of blacks among the messengers has shrunk by a factor of at least fifty; the number of women in formal roles has also been decimated, as white male authority was reestablished.

Central Mission Organizations

The mission impulse in Southern Baptist history is scripturally grounded in "The Great Commission" in Matthew 28:19–20: "Go then, to all peoples everywhere and make them my disciples; baptize them in the name of the Father, the Son, and the Holy Spirit, and teach them to obey everything I have commanded you" (*Good News Bible*). The 1845 Constitution spoke of eliciting, combining, and directing "the energies of the whole denomination in one sacred effort for the propagation of the gospel." However, most denominational leaders assume a unanimity about the purpose, function, and value of missionary effort which seems not borne out by facts. In the past few years of controversy and confrontation, many of the pleas for unity bewail the danger of losing missionary strength through dissension and division. Missions are used as the come-on for much fundraising, and the meaning of missions has been made ever more ambiguous.

The first formal missionary society was founded by the Baptist William Carey, who went out from England in 1792. The Anglicans followed in 1799, the Congregationalists in 1810, and the U.S. Baptists in 1814. In the post-Revolutionary effort to sharpen denominational distinctiveness, Baptists in the South had to walk a tightrope. On the one hand, there was much opposition within the fold, as largely illiterate folks who hadn't accepted the idea of cooperative missions effort at home were asked to support it in India. The Campbellite competition, legitimating only local church activity, and the Landmark movement, which even more actively opposed supra-church organization, made the effort even more difficult. The missions impulse, then, brought elements of SB theology and polity into reciprocal tension.

The present *Foreign Mission Board* (FMB) is a creature of the 1845 split, one of the two original agencies specified by founding father W. B. Johnson. Its siting in Richmond is clearly due to the influence of early SBC officers who were Richmond residents, and the support of the Virginia state paper, one of the most powerful at the time. Its original functions were recruitment, training, and screening of missionary personnel, supporting them abroad, providing a clearinghouse of the necessary legal, financial, and medical arrangements, and promoting the whole. For the rest of the century the story is one of gradual growth and consolidation.

Work was concentrated in China, "opened up" just at the right time, and to Yoruba country in present-day western Nigeria, one of the early African centers of commerce, including the slave trade. At first, efforts were confined to evangelism; only gradually were added the benevolent activities of hospitals, schools, and orphanages, the training of indigenous personnel, and publications in the necessary languages. Japan was "opened" at another convenient moment; Italy became more hospitable after 1870. Activities were slowly expanded to the Pacific and South America and eventually to more than a hundred countries.

There is a built-in dilemma in missionary activity, since it is hard to emphasize common humanity and common problems while simultaneously proclaiming the superiority of one religious system and associated behavior over another. Critics of missions, Sydney E. Ahlstrom thinks, saw the movement as an "escape and an evasion . . . It began to appear that the foreign missions revival may well have arisen as a half-subconscious effort to divert Protestants from intellectual problems and internal dissensions by engaging them in great moral and spiritual tasks – only to have deeper problems and dissension appear" (1972: 866–67).

The treatment of women as missionaries is still full of ambiguities. One married woman M.D. had to be listed as a "homemaker" when she signed up to go overseas. The position of black missionaries is also fraught with tensions; there are only a handful, and they tend to work in countries where skins are dark. And there are more suspect statuses: "[E]xisting sentiment against divorce in Baptist conventions overseas precludes the appointment of persons who have been divorced," states the FMB information request form.

Southern Baptists are aware of the missionary field as an outlet for "overproduced clergy." The seminaries graduate about 2,500 potential ministers a year; the turnover is about 1,500 a year, and in fiscal year 1985–86 there was an increase of only 137 churches. Yet, for example, recruiting for the Baptist colleges has been stepped up on the grounds that they will produce mission vocations, part of what Langdon Gilkey called "the operation of expanding itself" (1963: 64n.). "Our Task is evangelism that results in churches. But it is a continuing emphasis. The evangelism that results in churches results in evangelism that results in churches," said the head of the Foreign Mission Board (Kruschwitz 1984: 71).

The official position is overwhelmingly positive, however. Most missionaries focus in urban areas, aiming for human concentrations in the Third World. (American-type amenities are available in cities, if anywhere, and this makes recruitment easier.) About 3,750 professionals work in 108 countries, with a budget of $173 million in 1988 for them and the headquarters staff and services in Richmond. The results for 1986 were 186,000 overseas baptisms and a dazzling list of schools, theological students, medical projects, skills training, disaster relief, twenty million copies of tracts, books and periodicals. There's a lot of anecdotal material about benevolence and baptisms, but it seems thin on the social consequences of conversion, and "national" leaders do not control their own budgets.

Foreign Mission Board goals, beyond expansion, have to do with missionary job security, provision for pensions, life and health insurance, MK (missionary kid) education (a source of real anguish), and furlough travel—reasonable aspirations of middle-class Americans. They use the phrase "career missionary," and every effort seems to be made to professionalize the job, make it less the domain of the "overcommitted." Yet the little touch of glamor remains. At the finale of one annual presentation, furloughed missionaries, many in something like native costume (including an authentic nineteenth-century Japanese court prostitute's outfit) and some in dinner dresses, paraded out of the arena, swirling in spotlights and carrying flags of the countries where they work. Both totalitarian and authoritarian regimes, Fascist dictatorships, Bantustans, African socialisms, many bourgeois democracies, and one each illegally occupied trusteeship, Islamic monarchy, and Jewish theocracy—the politics were irrelevant. Unanimity is assumed in the one place where all is serene, all are united.

Asked if there were any transfers between the foreign and domestic mission fields, an FMB staffer replied patiently that they were run by different boards. What if someone were overseas and a relative got sick—could that person arrange to work within the United States? She glared—well, it could happen, but not very often. It was a stupid question, like asking a United States Marine if he'd ever thought of transferring to the Air Force. There is no evidence of direct competition, tugs of war, but there are grey areas and enormous problems of boundary maintenance. Some American territories are overseas—the Home Mission Board covers American Samoa—and some foreign countries are next door.

Home Mission Board (HMB) efforts are *here* and involve more SBs because of their propinquity, their visibility, and more opportunities for temporary volunteers. There was also early antipathy. According to historian

Bertram Wyatt-Brown, the "Antimissionists . . . [were] . . . primarily a rural, economically insecure people . . . The controversy exhibited deep-seated class antagonism within the South itself" (1970: 511). For whatever mix of reasons, Baptists lost 45 percent of their membership—entire churches and district associations—to anti-mission movements between 1810 and 1845.

Those who remained Baptists, and who supported the new SBC, clearly saw value in mission work and used its goals as a rallying point. The HMB was duly begun with headquarters in Marion, Alabama, where the presence of two Baptist colleges and a substantial church assured its support. But the life sounds even harder than it had been for Luther Rice thirty years earlier. One agent described it thus: "The domestic missionary must not expect to enjoy many of the luxuries of life, otherwise he will be sadly disappointed. In the performance of my labors, many times a little bread and milk was a sumptuous fare. Often I have made dinner and supper of a little cold fat bacon, cold cornbread, a little coffee without sugar or cream. I have slept on beds (so called) not bigger than my hand, a bunch of rags for my pillow" (Stephenson 1982: 33).

Fund-raising and missionary activity of any kind were largely pushed aside by the Civil War, but resumed thereafter even with limited resources. The worst problem was competition from Northern Baptists. The continuation of mission fund-raising was considered essential to the survival of the Convention itself; cooperative effort would dissolve if there were no concrete reason for it.

The Moody-Sankey team of revivalists had burst on the American scene between 1873 and 1875. "Using methods and money of big business, Moody reconciled the city and the old-time religion to each other," Ahlstrom claims (1972: 745). This was part of the consideration to move the board, under the guidance of a successful SB pastor-businessman, to bustling Atlanta in 1882, where it has mostly flourished ever since.

Securely based to meet northern competition, the HMB found new forms of rivalry in state, district, and local church mission efforts. A good deal of imagination and ingenuity have gone into finding the niches, the interstices, where real service could be given and souls won, without treading on the territory of other agencies. This has meant moving in where the local churches and district associations were unwilling to go. By the end of the nineteenth century the HMB was running missions in the Appalachian Mountains, a study course on fundamental doctrines for "Negro" pastors, language missions to German, French, and Italian immigrants in the East and to Chinese in California. The military chaplaincy during the

Home Mission Board camp counselor Mike Haywood holds blind child, Camp Piankatank, Virginia, 1983. (Photograph by Everett Hullum, courtesy of the Home Mission Board, Southern Baptist Convention.)

Foreign Mission Board volunteer nurse Mary Saunders hugs healthy child, relief camp, Rabel, Ethiopia, 1986. (Photograph courtesy of the Southern Baptist Historical Library and Archives.

First World War again offered concentrated target populations; later came city missions, a rural church program, student summer missions, correspondence Bible work, a ministry to migrants, juvenile rehabilitation, literacy missions, hospital chaplaincies, work in U.S. territories overseas.

"Baptists will live or die, win or lose, by their ability to reach the cities," said one pastor at a missions conference. This imperative leads them into areas of ambivalence. Orrin Morris, Home Mission Board research division director, predicted another period of white flight in the mid-1980s and probably a second in the 1990s. "Baptists will totally lose the cities if we don't become sensitive to social and racial trends revealed in the 1980 census data," he wrote. "There is little hope for Baptist church growth in Southern cities apart from aggressively starting new churches among blacks, Hispanics and other ethnics" (Newton 1982: 42). And church planters will have to be paid more than $600 a month, the executive director acknowledged in 1987.

Another huge area of potential expansion is "language missions," or work with non-English-speaking minority groups. Already the SB experts are forecasting problems: About 90 percent of those in SBC non-English-speaking churches are immigrants who have reached or are moving toward citizenship status. It is the second generation ethnic, born in the United States but retaining the native language and cultural ties with the parents' homeland, who is "the greatest challenge facing Southern Baptist language missions," says Oscar Romo of the HMB, admitting that of the U.S.-born ethnic groups, "we're only making progress among the American Indians and the deaf groups" (quoted in Newton 1982: 42).

It sounds as if part of the success with the first generation is based on the friendly interest and the provision of really critical material services which may not be appreciated to the same degree by the second. And if the goals might include true assimilation of the members of these missions into the structure of power, the current SB leadership may not be able to satisfy their needs.

Who hasn't been mentioned? The blind. Prisons. Internationals, temporary visitors like seamen and diplomats. The elderly, and many more. The HMB is working with some groups who are helped in concrete ways just by being paid attention to. The efforts to involve more SBs on temporary bases and short-term mission assignments can remove some of the limitations of a provincial education and provide the HMB with some volunteer help. (Jimmy Carter did a stint of crusading after the political defeat that led to his own spiritual revival.) The HMB employs about 3,600 missions personnel and planned for 1987–88 a total budget of $75 million.

The Sunday School Board

The Southern Baptist Sunday School Board (SSB) is the largest publisher of religious materials in the world. Operating income for 1987–88 totaled over $170 million. Because of its independent financial base it holds secure power (and pays its top executives better than most pastors; one president retired with annual life income of almost $60,000 plus elaborate gifts). Besides its publishing houses, it works like a gigantic advertising agency for its product, the Gospel, and also like a large retailer, with 63 stores and a huge mail-order business, marketing other manufacturers' products — from choir robes to electric chimes to directional signs (over 6,000 items in the catalog). It wasn't always that way. Church historian Posey writes: "The Baptists, under the influence of the antimissionary movement and the general opposition to organizations in churches, were quite reluctant to form or encourage Sunday schools of any type" (1957: 109). As the denomination fought for distinctiveness, frontier antieducational biases prevailed. Ann Douglas (1977) points out that the women, early involved, and the ministers were in competition. The Sunday School movement gave organizational experience to women but left ministers with a dilemma — to get support from women but retain power over a vital aspect of their churches. Control of the curriculum was an important part of the solution.

Again a precipitating factor was competition and growing acceptance of printed materials prepared by Northern Baptist organizations. Southern Baptist churches were buying their materials and Southern Baptist pastors were moonlighting for them. As the early Southern Baptist head Thomas C. Teasdale argued: "If we can command the general patronage of our own Southern people, we will give them a Sunday School paper, at once most excellent and attractive, which shall be alike free from offensive sectionalism and unsound theology, and which shall be in every respect adapted to the peculiar civilization of the South, and the scriptural piety of our people" (Baker 1974: 245). Although Isaac T. Tichenor of the Home Missions Board called the refoundation of the Sunday School Board "the heaviest denominational conflict of the century" (Baker 1974: 270), it seems inevitable in light of SB exclusivism and expansiveness.

It was approved at the annual meeting in 1891 and established in Nashville, then the center of Southern Baptist density, and full of printers and printing houses partly because the Methodists had moved their publishing operations there after their own North/South split in 1844. In addition, Tennessee had been a center of religious controversies that implied an active market for such literature.

The Sunday School Board from the beginning has reached out for the most up-to-date technology and promotional and organizational techniques. According to SB historian Shurden: "No institution has done more to denominationalize and synthesize Southern Baptists. It lassoed every inter-denominational movement that came down the churchly pike in the latter nineteenth and early twentieth century and promptly 'Southern Baptistized' it" (1982: 10).

The process of extending a church-related activity to a special group—market segmentation—was always carefully placed within the church context. So with the concern with individual psychological problems, carried forward into enormously elaborated pastoral counseling, the recreational ministry, which results in such imaginative combinations as Bible Ski Weekends held at one of the two "Christian resorts and conference centers" which the SBC owns and the SSB runs, and the tremendous concern for conventional family life which is realized through an entire department of Family Ministry within the SSB, with its own married couples' retreats. College students, and not only at Baptist colleges, have their Baptist Student Union, and singles and seniors have their own programs and publications.

In 1986, in the service of these aims, the SSB shipped 156 million pieces of literature. There are vast quantities of audio-visual materials, slides, filmstrips, films, and cassette tapes. The SSB was quick to use radio in its early days, then TV, and now the system of closed-circuit television with its own leased transponder and "Nashville-based uplink satellite facility." The programs offered are mainly for training church workers and teachers—local church people must be supplemented, not supplanted.

There are substantial supporting programs and publications in the fields of church music, administration, and libraries; architectural advice and stock building plans with all the problems solved in advance; entire recreational programs. There are two publishing houses: Holman, an established Bible printer, and Broadman, a trade house whose name is an acronym of two early SSB leaders. (Broadman, appropriately, published Jimmy Carter's campaign autobiography, *Why Not the Best?*)

Some of the church supply items involve a field largely unpublicized, the technology and logistics of total immersion baptism indoors in a formal setting. T. Lee Anderton's denominational building guidebook states:

> The baptistry should be located so as to be a major focal point in the auditorium. Traditional arrangements place it above and to the rear of the choir. The water level should be a minimum of five feet above the last choir row floor . . . It should be elevated sufficiently to be seen by everyone in the audience . . . A glass panel should be used to improve sight lines . . . Prefabricated fiberglass tanks are recommended . . . Walls above baptistry should be spot resistant, and should harmonize in color with the auditorium (Painted scenes detract and are not recommended). . . . Lighting should be concealed on sides so as to accent the pastor and candidate (Use separate circuit with dimmer control for creating appropriate atmosphere) (1980: 92–93).

Broadman markets one-piece fiberglass baptistries with such features as built-in water heaters and molded seats for maximum visibility. Special clothing is also sold. The pastor may wear "Baptismal boots/trousers" (like waders), with a "large inside chest pocket," a pouch presumably for his Bible. The baptismal robes, all sizes and for both sexes, are designed with gathered bands across the chest so as not to reveal the body contours of the soaking wet candidates. Garments are weighted in the hem so they won't fly up when the candidate enters the water.

The stunning scope of SSB activities is only possible, of course, because SBs are so numerous and the market is so large. Only a denomination this size could afford to be diverse, to pioneer with new technologies, and to make bold, if not risky, investments. There is evidence, however, that in terms of content, experimentation is avoided. Baker quotes in his history SSB instructions to its contributors that its "work . . . should be constructive and for the promotion of the generally established views of our denomination," and that "our writers shall avoid the discussion of questions at any time which are unsettled, and the occasion of sharp issues among our people" (1966B: 123).

The SSB is aware of the danger of conflict. Some of the doctrinal battles of this century have been started by its publications. It pays the salaries of liaison professors in each of the six seminaries and contributes to salaries of state convention employees who work on curriculum. These subventions have other functions but keep the SSB in touch with producers and consumers as well and assure an interested constituency in some of the potential sources of dissension. As the fundamentalists consolidate their control, the SSB is feeling their pressure in both direct and subtle ways and can be expected to respond like any market-sensitive organization.

The Seminaries

Forget Bernard Shaw's crack that a Catholic university is a contradiction in terms. A theological seminary is not a university, although many observers think it would be better off if it were a part of one.

Here again the bulk is staggering. About one-fifth of all American theological students are in SB seminaries – more than thirteen thousand people. Four of the five largest seminaries in the world are Southern Baptist. Their position is so anomalous, the ambivalence so massive, the contradictions so pervasive, that the whole exercise is another gigantic balancing act. How can they have open admissions and high academic standards? How can they pride themselves on the non–SB doctorates their faculty hold and still require them to sign fuzzy and conflicting statements of doctrinal purity? How can they grant research degrees for dissertations written with almost complete fidelity to the latest style manual and almost no idea of what questions to ask?

These present circumstances result from all the compromises made since the beginnings of Baptist identity in the South. A paid ministry was associated with the Established Church, and Roger Williams – Baptist or maybe not – wrote a piece, *A Hireling Ministry None of Christ's*. In Tennessee in 1848 only two Baptist pastors were full-time. "For this shrewd and successful group, the job of being a Baptist minister was more of an avocation . . . the role gave a prestige that was highly courted," Posey writes (1957: 19). But Richard Hofstadter adds that compared to Methodists, Baptists were "still more uncompromising, still more disposed to insist on a ministry without educational qualifications" (1974: 104). "The Baptist laymen were divided between their desire for respectability and their desire for a congenial and inexpensive ministry" (1974: 106). The ambivalence as to the value of an education had theological roots as well, Posey comments: "Support of theological institutions implied the inadequacy of the Divine Being and his power to call and equip ministers . . . An education could actually be a serious handicap and impair rather than add to the ability of a Baptist preacher" (1957: 21).

But even as the other denominations founded undergraduate colleges which no longer were exclusively for training ministers, they found it necessary to add specialized theological institutions with their increasingly professionalized task: Newton and Rochester in 1825, Crozer in 1868. Baptists on the frontier established the Western Baptist Theological Institute at Covington, Kentucky, in 1845, but it foundered in state rivalries in the context of the approaching Civil War. The first lasting institution grew in 1859 out of the Religion Department at Furman University in Greenville, South Carolina. Work was almost immediately interrupted, and it had great difficulty picking up again after the War, since all its endowment had been invested in Confederate bonds. One of the Baptist heroes of the time, John Broadus, remarked, "Suppose we quietly agree that the Seminary may die, but we'll die first" (SB *Encyclopedia* 1: 184).

James Boyce, the principal energy behind the institution, gave it much of his diminished fortune and sought a better home for it in another part of the South. After much trial, such a place was found in Louisville, and the seminary held its first session there in 1877. Boyce's concept of theological education included three principles: an open admissions policy serving the needs of all regardless of educational background; advanced training for the highly gifted, "for Baptists need their own thinkers and writers," and a requirement that "each professor should subscribe a doctrinal statement, or 'abstract of principles,' agreeing to teach nothing contradictory to the statement, thereby insuring doctrinal soundness" (SB *Encyclopedia* 1: 184). So many of the problems of logic and consistency were with Southern Baptist seminaries from the beginning. Boyce's principles are still followed, however, not just for tradition but because they continue to serve current purposes.

The Louisville seminary, The Southern Baptist Theological Seminary (or "Southern"), is the premier one and, according to some evaluations, superior in quality. As the center of Baptist density moved to the West, Southwestern was founded in 1908 in Ft. Worth, as an outgrowth of the Religion Department of Baylor. Then New Orleans in 1917, Golden Gate (San Francisco environs) in 1944, Southeastern at Wake Forest, North Carolina (occupying the former campus of the university which the Reynolds tobacco money persuaded to move to Winston-Salem in 1951), and Midwestern in Kansas City in 1958. All of these except Southeastern grew out of institutions previously supported by state conventions but then taken over by the central SBC. Southwestern is by far the largest, with 5,070 students in 1985–86; Midwestern is the smallest with 688. About nine-tenths of the students in each institution are enrolled in degree programs, with the balance, usually those without bachelors' degrees, working for various certificates and diplomas. Of the degree candidates, about half are in theological or ministerial training, and the rest in religious education and church music.

Student fees are almost unbelievably low; the Southeastern 1986–87 bulletin, for example, cites a per-semester matriculation fee of $350 for Southern Baptist students (there is no tuition) – half that for an attending spouse – and offers three-bedroom apartments for students at $200 per month. This is made possible by support from the Cooperative Program, amounting to nearly $29 million for the six seminaries in the 1987–88 fiscal year. Such a high degree of financial support – among the highest of any denomination – is a great part of the source of control over the seminaries, and it helps to assure pastoral support for the Cooperative Program. One seminary shows on its student billing statements the dollar amount provided to each individual in "scholarship" from the CP. At the New Orleans meeting, a pastor heatedly suggested that anyone who wanted to criticize the activities financed by the CP should first repay the full cost of his eduation.

There are at least four doctrinal statements used by the Southern Baptists – not creeds, they say, but confessional statements. One is the "Abstract of Principles," or Articles of Faith, developed in the context of Boyce's imperatives at the time of the Southern foundation. Two more are the Faith and Message Statements of 1925 and 1963 (about which, more below) which themselves were drawn up in an atmosphere of bitter theological controversy involving professorial orthodoxy. New Orleans has its own Articles of Religious Belief. The statements do not say the same thing – if they did, it wouldn't be necessary to have four of them. The obvious difficulties were handled with careful equivocation by Herschel Hobbs, a former SBC president: "Of course, Southern Baptist Theological Seminary continues to require all faculty members to sign the Articles of Faith adopted by the seminary in 1859. This statement is in harmony with the basic theological elements of 'The Baptist Faith and Message.'" Southeastern does the same, but adds, "We refer to 'The Baptist Faith and Message' statement as the most recent and definitive for Baptists." Midwestern, Southwestern, and Golden Gate faculty are required to sign the "Faith and Message" statement.

"In each instance where an agency has adopted 'The Baptist Faith and Message,'" Hobbs goes on, "it has been done voluntarily by the institution. The Southern Baptist Convention . . . has in no case *required* this action." In a footnote, he adds, regarding Southern, "Though the writer taught there for only one month in 1973, he was required to sign these Articles of Faith" (1978: 40). These statements are not creeds, Hobbs says, because Southern Baptists are not creedal people. The SBC itself does not require their use, but the constituent agencies may. Anyway, it is voluntary; nobody refuses to do it. He subtitled his article, oxymoronically, "Anchored but Free." The internal pressures on the presidents and faculty members at these institutions as a result of these external ones have been until recently carefully concealed. The fundamentalists are now requiring adherence to specific tenets of inerrancy, or biblical literalism, as well as loyalty to themselves.

The presidents are usually not scholars but bureaucrats, and they're on the way elsewhere, not primarily concerned with "development," faculty parking, and football tickets, but with growth, academic freedom as they are permitted to interpret it, and staying out of trouble that might jeopardize the support on which they depend. Such imperatives may lead to arbitrariness and misuse of authority, but these are characteristic of other kinds of educational institutions as well. The seminary faculty have had considerable freedom within the classroom but sharp limitations on what they might try to publish. If they are people of erudition and experience, as some of them are, these qualities may largely go unused.

Three of the seminaries—Southern, Southwestern and New Orleans—grant doctoral degrees, and the Ph.D. is supplanting the Doctor of Theology because the former means access to more job opportunities in college and university teaching. The seminary faculty are overwhelmingly trained in other SB seminaries, leading to an incestuous educational system. Southern's 1985–87 catalogs showed that of a total of forty-six full-time permanent faculty members in the schools of theology, thirty-two were their own doctorates and one was from Southwestern. Southeastern, not one of the doctorate-granting institutions, listed thirteen faculty, of thirty-four total, with doctorates from Southern plus two from Southwestern and one from New Orleans.

Southern encourages faculty breadth through extra study at another kind of institution, and at Southeastern, tenure is not usually granted until after the professor's first sabbatical, which he is strongly urged to take at a large university or abroad. Although salaries are very low ($29,000 average for a full professor at Southeastern in 1987–88 compared to, say, $62,200 at Duke, according to the AAUP), he will get full pay for his sabbatical; otherwise he couldn't afford to go. There are few women; almost all of them are in religious education, social work, and music. The first black joined the Southern faculty in 1986 to teach courses in the black church and black family.

The titles of Southern Baptist Ph.D. and Th.D. dissertations are inward-looking: "Practice of ministerial ordination among Southern Baptists: a theological analysis," "Southern Baptist churches which disband: implications for theology and terminal ministry," "Pastoral care of ministers in the Southern Baptist Convention," "Study of changing concepts of ministry at the First Baptist Church of Houston from 1917 to 1976." They seem more like exercises in management and bureaucratic history than research into theology or philosophy. The seminaries also give doctorates in education. Two Ed.D. topics from the same period were "Course of religious education at the Southern Baptist Theological Seminary 1902–1953: A historical study" and "Image of Southern Baptists: A content analysis of *Time* and *Newsweek* 1967–1977." The most recent ones seem to ask bigger questions and range more widely – over the theology of Gutierrez and Mary Daly, for example, and sociopolitical topics like hunger.

For comparison, the titles of dissertations done at Catholic seminaries show as much interest in what might be called denominational history, but the Roman Catholic Church is redeemed by its catholicity, by the breadth of place and depth of time. Catholic seminaries today also go out of their way to broaden their students' exposure. According to a 1982 survey, 40 percent of them had Protestants, Anglicans, or Orthodox among their full-time faculty, 7 percent had full-time Jewish faculty, and 58 percent had entered in formal consortia with Protestant schools of theology (Beifuss 1982: 26). For once, Southern Baptists cannot point to their rural environment; all of their seminaries are in large metropolitan areas, although they do seem to have found, or created, sylvan oases within them. In contrast, many Catholic seminaries are noted, if not notorious, for their rural isolation.

Because of their commitment to open admissions, the SB seminaries face formidable problems of complexity, level, and meeting everyone's needs. As the registrar of Southeastern put it, "[we] have given good theological training to some very raw material." This, he said, was in contrast to, say, the Methodists, who have higher academic standards. (Methodist theological students at Southeastern have additional requirements of thousands of pages of reading.) In 1983, 43.2 percent of SB pastors held post-college degrees. Those with only college degrees rose to 13.5 percent. But these figures mean that 43.3 percent had no degree at all.

The curricular requirements vary from seminary to seminary and cannot easily be compared with those of other theological schools in the United States. A very large proportion of the courses in church history seem narrowly concerned with Baptist denominational affairs, a focus which no doubt contributes to the mole-like limitations of much SB historical writing. In its Ph.D. program Southern gives a substantial number of credits (24 of the 66 required) for seminars in "Graduate Research," "Teaching Principles," and "Higher Education," and for "Dissertation Form and Content" and "Dissertation Defense." In general, the seminaries appear to give a great deal of credit, even toward the Ph.D., for applied work, various forms of supervised fieldwork experience or practicums. The language requirements are as unrealistic as they are in most American graduate programs of any type, although the huge volume of printed aids available for those who will only want to translate bits of one book from time to time for the rest of their lives changes the nature of the problem.

Southwestern seems to have more of a pronounced regional flavor, partly because of its size. CBS-TV did one of its Sunday dawn religious programs on the Ft. Worth seminary (17 October 1982). It ducked theological questions entirely and tried to be "visual," but what it did with the rest was very Southern Baptist. "When you think of the Kingdom of God, think 'Christ,' and when you think Christ, think 'missions,'" one professor was filmed saying, writing the words "Christ" and "missions" on the blackboard in appropriate pauses. Students were "involved in recreational ministries – the total man – mind, spirit, body." But, pronounced one student critique, "We think he spends too much time with books and literature and not enough time with people." Student preaching exercises were videotaped, and the body language evaluated rather than the content.

Southwestern is famous for its preaching teaching; some churches elsewhere, it is rumored, even seek pastors who had trained in Texas because of the more dramatic style of oratory. (A Chair of Evangelism, founded at the beginning of the seminary in 1908, was popularly referred to as the "Chair of Fire.") There is much ambivalence about this style because of the associations with old-fashioned revivalism and black southern religious expression. The perfect balance between substance and dignity, on the one hand, and emotive power, on the other, is still being sought.

One study of graduate education in religion found the libraries in the doctorate-granting SB institutions inadequate. Nonetheless, the one at Southeastern was ideal for some purposes because of the strength of its holdings in not only SB history and denominational organization but also American Protestant history and theology. The superb and expensive periodicals go largely unused; there are theological journals in at least six foreign languages, some with uncut pages. A few of the book titles – *CB for Christians, How to Operate a Cassette Tape Ministry, Phone Power* – emphasize again the eager adoption of modern technology and vocabulary in this religious milieu. The library also, however, subscribes to *World Marxist Review* and the *Secular Humanist Bulletin*. There are at least two SB theological journals. The one from Southern, the *Review and Expositor*, seems generally meaty and well-produced. But a whole issue on "The Baptist Association" (Spring 1980) means that denominational organization is creeping in at that level, a kind of theology of bureaucracy, or that associations are on the defensive, or both. The *Southwestern Journal of Theology* did its entire Spring 1982 issue on "Home Mission Board Resources for City Churches," which implies that there's trouble there as well.

Southeastern students talk a lot – loudly, in the middle of the stacks, of course – about the strategy of their education, how they are "playing" such a professor, what they are choosing to concentrate on and what to neglect in studying for an exam, how short a paper can be to get by, just as students do at every institution of higher education. (One pair nattered about the difficulties of securing ordination and loving God, in that order.) Most students are men, of various shapes and sizes, 75 percent married with lots of children who liven up the campus. The availability of on-campus jobs for "spouses" is advertised in the various catalogs; some are professionals like nursery school teachers or librarians and some not. Many of the students, male and female, must hold outside jobs to stay in school even at subsidized rates.

Students at Southeastern are asked for their marital status on the "Request for an Application" form bound into the catalog. Divorced applicants would have a special interview, not to screen them out but to inform them in advance of the prejudice they face in the churches when they get ready to seek a pastorate. One administrator reported that a student's *spouse*'s previous divorce might be an obstacle in some places; this is a curious echo of the prohibition of *digamy* practiced in the first few hundred years of the Christian church, when priests were expected to marry only virgins. When interviewed, many students and administrators thought this focus on divorce unfair and outmoded; after all, other clouds in their past were not held against them. An administrator, asked if that included alcoholism or a prison record, replied politely and evasively, "We get all kinds."

Women and blacks have as vexing – if changing – roles in the seminaries as they do in the denomination as a whole. There are lots of women in the religious education and music programs, many fewer in theology. Like most other Protestant groups (no matter what they say), SBs are challenged with professional placement problems just as the historic monopoly of white males is itself being questioned. Southern Baptists, who only recently admitted women at all, are a long way from experiencing the kind of change that has taken place in some of the liberal denominations, where over half the seminary students may be female. To link women and blacks, however, according to one administrator, was troublesome to the blacks, since there were perhaps only 20 of them to 120 women. But blacks (all males) had their own forum, while the women didn't even have a "support group." At Kansas City in 1984 in answer to a challenge from the floor, the Southeastern president had to affirm that there was *no* feminist group on his campus. In 1986 there was one female faculty member, in theology, and seven visiting instructors. There is increasing fundamentalist pressure to unsettle, if not unseat, any women in positions of authority.

Even if a woman survives the difficulties of obtaining a theological education, she may have trouble getting ordained by one of the local churches, which have that responsibility. There are rumored to be 450 women of a total of 50,000 ordained Southern Baptists. And if they clear that hurdle (and home churches cannot always be relied on), they may be unable to find pastoral employment. The military, however, welcomes women and black chaplains, and women are filling hospital posts to the point where some observers fear a kind of ghettoization. (One female SB hospital chaplain said her definition of stress was more than six or seven deaths in one shift.)

As for homosexuality in the seminaries, it exists no doubt in at least the same proportion as in the general population, but unacknowledged. "We're all holding our breath," said one Southeastern faculty member privately.

The American Baptist Theological Seminary, Nashville, has the status of a full commission of the SBC but in fact represents a valiant but somewhat pathetic attempt to aid black pastoral education. Wrote John Lewis, a black Baptist pastor and now congressman, "It's primarily the financial burden of the Southern Baptists, a missionary school in a sense, from the whites to the blacks. It was started in 1924 primarily to keep black Baptists from going to the white seminary in Louisville" (1981: 194). The real estate and administrative history of the relationship are checkered, to put it generously. In 1985–86 the SBC provided scholarship funds of $1,100 each for 142 students and $110,000 toward operating expenses. It might be better not to include an aerial photo in the SB *Encyclopedia* than so to expose the pathetic discrepancy between its facilities and those of the SB's own seminaries. At one meeting the rationale for helping at all was given in the following way: "To be sure that the gospel is properly interpreted and that regardless of the color . . . " Then this anecdote was told: "When you pass Bible class, you know you're at a seminary but not at a predominantly black seminary. When you pass the theology class, you know you are at a seminary but not at a predominantly black seminary. But when you pass the preaching class you know you're in a predominantly black seminary—they *know* how to preach!"

Even though the Bible schools are run by the states, it seems appropriate to mention them here. Their number changes as their status may be changed—maybe four, five, six. They have mixed histories and today can be characterized as a combination of high schools for people who otherwise couldn't go and adult education. One in San Antonio has become an Hispanic branch of Southwestern Seminary. Together the seminaries also operate an active and growing program of pastoral extension courses in line with the national trend toward continuing education.

There are also three schools attended by many SB theological students that are not so far supported by the Cooperative Program nor controlled by the Southern Baptist Convention: the Mid-American Baptist Theological Seminary in Memphis, Luther Rice Seminary in Jacksonville, and the Criswell Center for Biblical Studies in Dallas. These are more conservative in theology than the official six and several of the new leaders have close ties to them. As the fundamentalists consolidate their hold on the Convention, pressure will be felt to extend SBC funding to these institutions. "Even in their seminaries," Charles Hudson pointed out, "Southern Protestants have a rather shallow sense of history and a somewhat undeveloped tradition of theological scholarship" (1972: 122). The current crisis will simply increase those tendencies among Southern Baptists.

The Lay Organizations

Although the two agencies serving adult men and women have very different statuses in terms of the SB bureaucratic structure, their respective foundations are intimately connected and their similarity in goals should be stressed. The timing and the form (and in a sense the failure) of the men's organization are in response to the particular attributes of the women's activities and they should be seen as complementary and related.

Here, as elsewhere, the nineteenth-century documents come from the upper and upper-middle class, and Baptists were not well represented in either until late in the century. They were, of course, influenced by many of the same ideas. Feminist historian Barbara Welter summarizes the mid-century view: "Young men looking for a mate were cautioned to search first for piety, for if that were there, all else would follow" (1966: 225).

The problem for Southern Baptist women was that the concrete expression of pious impulses was so fraught with danger. Most of the causes that engaged nineteenth-century women elsewhere were taboo to them. Women's suffrage, dubious enough in itself, was allied with abolition. The temperance movement led to concern with prison reform and health education.

The modest dress reform involving the wearing of bloomers was linked to socialism and agrarian radicalism.

There had been women messengers at the annual meeting since 1845, and they played similar roles in several state conventions. But in 1885, on the defensive, the men challenged their presence, and the constitution was changed to qualify only "brethren." As SB historian Leon McBeth says, "Baptists were seriously concerned not to appear to endorse any part of the women's movement of the time . . . For almost twenty years the women who attended Southern Baptist Convention sessions at all sat in balconies" (1977: 14).

Out of passion for missions, the one safe issue around which women could organize, and out of their exclusion from any other role then, the Woman's Missionary Union (WMU), Auxiliary to the SBC, was born in 1888. The WMU found it prudent to channel its funds through the existing agencies rather than sending missionaries independently. On at least one famous occasion the two Boards were invited to compete for WMU funding; more than once WMU fund-raising ability rescued the Convention as a whole from financial distress, and in the early 1930s from bankruptcy.

From the beginning the WMU had a forthright bureaucratic structure, adopted deliberately to promote efficient fund-raising. One of its founders, Annie Armstrong, knew that the average gift per SB woman overall was 2.25 cents, while in Maryland, the Methodists, who had a more formal structure, averaged 37 cents. This reflected more than disparity in resources, and the early WMU adopted this successful model.

But, Anne Scott tells, what happened to the Southern Methodist women was this: they had built Foreign and Home Mission Societies. In 1906 the men in the General Conference, without consultation with the women, "decided to combine . . . [them] and put them under the control of a male-dominated Board of Missions." In 1910 one Methodist woman wrote of feeling like "a helpless minority in a body opposed to independence of thought in women" (1972: 110). A similar fate met the early Mormon and Southern Presbyterian women's groups.

This could not happen to Southern Baptist women: although they had a central organization, the Convention itself lacked one until 1925. Their very exclusion from full participation, which forced them into an "auxiliary" but autonomous position, rescued them from domination or co-optation. Thus their independence, their vital control of financial contributions, and election of their own board, have combined to create a remarkable situation.

Boundary maintenance problems have existed here as elsewhere, but

Leaders of the Woman's Missionary Union, 1950. (Photograph courtesy of the Southern Baptist Historical Library and Archives.)

there is every indication that the women have handled them with knowing tact. Victor Masters wrote of the way women worked "with a quiet and modesty which has measurably kept the more loud-speaking brethren from understanding the bigness and blessedness of their work" (1915: 152–53). WMU promotion is careful and well thought out, and they take pains to promote their value to pastors and church staff. When, after suffrage became a settled issue, women were accepted once again as Convention messengers, the WMU nonetheless allowed men to give their annual reports as late as 1928.

From the beginning the WMU took on the job of "missions education," that is, education about missions to children and young people. The programs have changed in function, combining recreation with witnessing and cooperative work projects; the girls' programs are still in their hands but the boys and young men have gone to male direction. The WMU was responsible for the initial training of female missionaries at a special school in Louisville, now incorporated into the seminary there, and founded a home for missionary children and later a scholarship fund for their college education. Currently it produces eleven magazines, lots of promotional material and curricular literature, and separate programs for women, young women, teens and younger girls, and very small children of both sexes (even the pre-schoolers are divided into three grades). Over $66 million was raised in the Christmas 1985 Lottie Moon offering for foreign missions, organized and promoted by the WMU, and over $27 million for the Easter 1986 Annie Armstrong offering for domestic missions, although neither campaign met its goal. The WMU, presently headquartered in Birmingham, in 1986 operated on a budget of over $10 million.

The historic fund-raising capacity is even more astounding when the poverty of most of the women and the lack of control over their own funds is remembered. Sharecroppers' wives were largely outside of the cash economy, and mill workers made pitifully small wages. A seminary professor writes:

> I suspect, though I cannot prove, that the enthusiasm for missions was in part an escape from their rather hum-drum lives. But I would not be so reductionist as to think that was all. I have seen too many people—including my own grandmother—who worked and gave quite sacrificially because they had a deep concern for the eternal welfare of unfortunate souls around the world . . . and because they had a dream, perhaps unrealistic, that they would have a part in making world conversion come true. The whole world could be changed if they only worked hard enough (Hewitt 1983).

The Southern Baptist *Brotherhood Commission,* functionally if not legally equivalent and complementary to the WMU, was founded in 1908. It emerged in part *in reaction to* the organization of women. This was a period which saw the foundation of the graduate schools of business, the beginning of the service clubs, and the addition of Father's Day to the American ritual calendar (1910). An alliance between women and the clergy had created a new ethos of sentimentality. Ann Douglas comments, "In the midst of the transformation of the American economy into the most powerfully aggressive capitalist system in the world, American culture seemed bent on establishing a perpetual Mother's Day" (1977: 5). And besides the still-controversial suffrage question, other issues had become widely discussed—homosexuality, contraception and divorce—that added to male insecurities.

There were two routes taken. One, a formalization of the Social Gospel, was a direction unthinkable for most Southern Baptists, since it raised questions of social power which they had, by and large, recently agreed not to ask. The other route was the formation of the Federal Council of Churches in 1908, but that was ecumenism, and Southern Baptists were, and still are, wary. The version finally found suitable was the Laymen's Missionary Movement, begun as an interdenominational organization in 1906 and "Southern Baptistized" in 1908.

"It never really worked," said an SB bureaucrat in Nashville. "The men will take leadership roles, not group roles." Many others have made the point that men didn't need this avenue for their organizational talents and energies since they were running the churches and the denomination as a whole. Establishment of men's organizations was slow: in North Carolina not until 1924, Tennessee 1925, South Carolina 1941, Mississippi 1944. The additional fund-raising potential among laymen, beyond what they pledged as family heads to the local churches, was not there in the way it had been with women, with their scrounged pittances and ability, through extra effort, to earn small sums on the side. Sometimes, however, the men's group was used as an organizing focus for fund-raising as a whole, for example in every-member canvasses.

The principal current role of men's organizations is in the leadership of boys for mission education, although they also do some direct evangelical work, participate in many scouting-type activities, and engage in some useful work projects and disaster relief, all of which make for feelings of drama and critical importance. Some of the most successful men's work is the construction of small churches. Individuals with good skills spend their vacations putting up a new building for a group, in a rural area or in pioneer territory. Sometimes they take their families.

In 1954 the teenagers were moved from WMU to Brotherhood auspices; in 1971 the 6- to 8-year-olds were added. During this period the widespread public feeling, misguided or not, that boys needed male leadership in order to grow up heterosexual was surely a factor in these transfers.

In 1985 and 1986, Brotherhood enrollment was about 569,000 (half that of the women's group), a decline from the previous year. Headquartered in Memphis, the organization had a projected 1987–88 budget of over $3.3 million. Its current programs stress intricately age-graded work with older boys and young men (in the "drop-out period," 18–34) and vocationally based Fellowships of Baptist Men in Agriculture, . . . in Transportation, . . . in Construction, . . . in Medicine, in an acknowledgment of the importance of class.

The Social Concerns Agencies

What another denomination might call "social concerns agencies" (or even "social justice" or "social action") are the most often criticized and the most vulnerable of the SB agencies, since the stuff of their concerns is political. In the SBC there is one, with offices in the headquarters in Nashville, called the Christian Life Commission, whose agenda is "family life, race relations, Christian citizenship, daily work, and . . . special moral concerns." It has a small staff of professionals and a budget for fiscal year 1987–88 of $1,490,200, with which it does research, public speaking, conferences, and publications—"applied Christianity support materials" for use by groups in the local churches.

Its history goes back to the previously mentioned heyday of the Social Gospel. A Social Service Commission was established in 1913, in addition to a Temperance Committee in operation since 1908, seeming to imply a broadening of focus. They were shortly thereafter merged under a "Social Service and Temperance" rubric, but the director was the temperance addict A. J. Barton, who during part of his long tenure until his death in 1942 was employed by the Texas Anti-Saloon League. In some years only two-thirds of his annual report was devoted to alcohol and prohibition and its enforcement.

In retrospect it is understandable that he was allowed to focus the commission so narrowly for so long. There were rumblings of dissatisfaction, but the situation must have served the purposes of the majority, and of the Reverend Mr. Barton himself. One unsuccessful attempt to establish a program with a wider agenda, Eighmy points out, "exposed more clearly than ever the deep ideological division in the minds of the Southern Baptists between the evangelical and social-gospel traditions" (1972: 123).

In 1946 significant reorganization led to the present name, Christian Life Commission, and the employment of a professional staff. Also that year a new and major emphasis was proposed: "race." The former director, Foy Valentine, had written his dissertation at Southwestern on "A historical study of Southern Baptists and race relations, 1917–1947," which helped prepare him for the stormy years to follow. Although liquor and gambling have continued as concerns, in recent years more emphasis has been placed on world hunger and peace and disarmament issues. Adding these new directions to the kinds of "social" issues that are of more interest to the fundamentalists has led to ingenious combinations like a conference on "Moral

Concerns" which included the director of the NAACP and an expert on child pornography who specialized in graphic and lurid descriptions.

The commission's journal, *Light*, is light years away from the center of current SB thought, as shown by its circulation, a mere 19,000. Although the commission does patient work with the local churches in an effort to buttress awareness with information, its accomplishments seem often overridden by the emotionality of the resolutions process at the annual meetings. A 1987 proposal for a Washington office clearly is designed to strengthen the SBC influence on abortion and other New Right issues.

The other social concerns agency is the *Baptist Joint Committee on Public Affairs*, which some call the "Baptist lobby." This is a cooperative effort with eight (black and white) Baptist groups and grew out of a common interest in the problems of the military chaplaincy during World War II. Its current program involves public relations, research, reporting, and denominational service. The greatest problems of the tiny Washington staff lie in explaining themselves to their constituency, at least the Southern Baptist half of it.

There are a surprising number of points at which religious groups have to pay special attention to government directives, and the Joint Committee spends much of its time explaining one side to the other. The "double deduction" for a housing allowance for ministers, stemming from the time when parsonages were considered exempt from income, is threatened. (A pastor at one annual meeting remarked, "If we had any integrity, we wouldn't take it anyway.") The best way to include pastors under the Social Security system, whether a theological seminary must file Equal Employment Opportunity reports for nonteaching personnel, and whether the government has the power to determine who falls into that category—these are not exactly the substance of martyrdom but are very much part of the constant dialog that has to go on in a pluralistic system.

The Joint Committee has consistently stood against government-mandated "prayer in the public school" despite the SBC 1982 resolution of support, the only such disagreement in 50 years. As fundamentalist power waxed, pressure grew to establish an independent Southern Baptist voice in Washington. But in 1987 a compromise instead increased SB representation on the Joint Committee, and created a new role for an SB Public Affairs Committee. This latter group tried to divert the SB subvention to the Joint Committee for its own use, and then took several public positions contrary to Joint Committee sentiment. Meanwhile the director of the Christian Life Commission was eased out after a brief and shaky tenure. With both internal agencies firmly under fundamentalist control, social policy activities can be expected to follow the New Right line, and the SB relationship with the pan-Baptist Joint Committee is increasingly tenuous.

Miscellaneous Denominational Agencies

Most religious broadcasting goes on the air as part of public service programming, and the SBC is the world's largest producer of this material. It began to explore the potential with a radio committee in the 1930s which became the *Radio and Television Commission* in 1953, with offices now in Ft. Worth and a 1987–88 operating budget of over $8.1 million. The current slogan is "a wholesome viewing alternative on the channel you can trust." Even though studies show that members of conservative churches watch "morally unacceptable" TV series in the same proportions as the American population as a whole, network programming has been inveighed against at many annual meetings, and there is much resentment of television evangelists and the competition they offer to local churches.

The commission has tried to build a backlog of programming for release, set up a network of local low-power stations using Baptist educational institutions as bases and cable affiliate channels, and train local church people in the technological aspects and necessary skills for whatever additional local programming they might wish to do. The "Southern Baptistization" of these technologies has proved to be much more expensive than anticipated, and anxious efforts are being made to retain control of programming even if the network must be sold. The Commission hopes to benefit from the difficulties of some of the best-known televangelists and pick up both audiences and outlets.

The *Education Commission* is not well known even by dedicated SB-watchers and has the reputation of being defensive about its mission, since it has been involved in many activities subsequently assigned to other agencies. It grew out of the chronic need to promote high-quality education. Since the institutions are to a certain extent competitive themselves and receive financial help only at the state level, and there is a working Association of Southern Baptist Colleges, the function of a central denominational agency has sometimes been unclear. It organizes a faculty placement service (free to Baptists), various research tasks, and, importantly in this demographic era, recruitment of students. The commission has a staff of half a dozen or so headquartered in Nashville and a 1987–88 budget of $548,000.

The colleges are under pressure from the fundamentalists to become more exclusively Baptist in faculty hiring and to some extent in curriculum.

The *Historical Commission* was chartered in the 1950s; in a way, history is something one has to be able to afford. The commission occupies greatly expanded space in the recently built corporate headquarters in Nashville, where it accumulates archives of institutions and individuals and helps both groups with specific inquiries and general techniques for doing history, on a 1987–88 budget of $537,400.

The Historical Commission has produced a monumental SB *Encyclopedia* and publishes a quarterly, *Baptist History and Heritage*. The men who run the Commission and edit *BH&H* are not trained historians. In fact, they all have Th.D. degrees from SB seminaries, with such dissertation topics as "A history of the Home Mission Board of the Southern Baptist Convention, 1845–1882," "The origins, development and use of church covenants in Baptist history," and "Claybrook Cottingham [a Louisiana SB educator and Rotarian], a study of his life and work."

Similar difficulties plague the *Encyclopedia*, which nevertheless can be used with profit and read with pleasure. Volumes 1 and 2 came out in 1958, Volume 3 in 1970, and Volume 4 in 1982. There are no obvious errors of fact, nor even typographical ones—remarkable in more than 2,500 pages. It contains a lot of material on defunct institutions, which indeed should be remembered and kept in the record, and it is very frank about some elements of controversy (the Landmark polemic, for instance). It is in biography that it is most lacking; individuals are defined and described almost completely by the offices they have held, and they emerge as cardboard figures moving in an ahistorical field.

One example is the treatment of Josiah ("Holy Joe") Bailey, editor of the North Carolina state paper, the *Biblical Recorder*, for a decade and later U.S. senator. Not only his role in North Carolina progressive era politics but the way he utilized the newspaper and its Baptist constituency go unmentioned. Vann Woodward said the *Recorder* became a "defender of trusts" (1951: 177). None of this gets through into the *Encyclopedia*. In fact, any connection between SB accomplishments and history in the larger sense is ignored, if not denied.

One Samuel Palmer Brooks was largely responsible for making Baylor a full-scale university. When asked to sign the strong anti-evolution statement the SBC adopted in 1926 (as all leaders of SB denominational institutions were), Brooks replied, "I would die and rot in my grave before I would sign the Houston resolution" (Shipley 1927: 180). Yet he survived at Baylor until the year of his death. Neither the incident, nor the questions it raises, are mentioned in his *Encyclopedia* biography.

Thomas Dixon, a Southern Baptist preacher and friend of President Wilson, whose novel *The Clansman* was the basis for the famous D. W. Griffith film, *The Birth of a Nation,* doesn't make it into the *Encyclopedia* at all. Nor does M. Ashby Jones of Atlanta, an SB pastor and member of the Interracial Commission formed to combat lynching and ameliorate social conditions, who published widely in scholarly journals about the commission's work. If there is a political bias operating, it is not a consistent one; it's more of a looking inward, a shriveling away from the outside. Pope Leo XIII, on opening the Vatican archives, said with pride that the Church has no fear of history. The Southern Baptists are as yet not that secure.

The last central affiliation of the SBC is with the *Baptist World Alliance* (BWA). With an office in a Washington, D.C. suburb and a subvention of $368,500 from the Executive Committee's budget in 1987–88, the BWA is the binding organization of world Baptists, totalling 34 million in 143 countries. They communicate and visit and confer on many shared problems – a kind of tiptoe ecumenism. The Southern Baptists over the years have intermittently expressed worry about "liberal" tendencies in the BWA, and occasional letters in state papers express surprise at the proportion of the SB contribution to the whole BWA budget – although SBs make up over 40 percent of the membership. The cooperation is cautious, therefore, but real – especially when a Baptist missionary program is threatened by one of the increasing number of unfriendly host governments.

The State Level of Organization

There are thirty-seven state conventions and additional fellowships on the frontier. The stated purpose of the earliest, South Carolina's in 1821, was to create a "bond of union, a center of intelligence, and a means of vigorous, united exertion in the cause of God, for the promotion of truth and righteousness" (SB *Encyclopedia* 2: 1223). As the Southern Baptists have grown and spread the patent advantages of regional organization have been persuasive, not least that of legislative lobbying at the state level.

Most basic of state functions are the thirty-eight newspapers, twenty-two of them weekly, with a total circulation of 1.7 million. It is a wonder that in nineteenth-century America, a person could found, write, edit and publish a newspaper, sell subscriptions and sometimes advertising, and occasionally, with luck, make a living at it. Many of the papers started this way; others began thus and perished. In the 1920s most of them passed to the ownership and control of state conventions, which continue to subsidize them since they have suffered greatly from the huge increases in second class postage costs.

They contain a few ads for such miscellany as church furnishings, pre-owned school buses, and charter tours to the Holy Land, and are full of people doings: personnel changes, retirements, deaths, missionary appointments, and college and seminary commencements. And real estate, building designs, cornerstone layings, dedications, and mortgage-burnings. And meetings – of associations (districts), Woman's Missionary Union, youth groups, pastoral conferences, and the annual state conventions which are miniature versions of the SBC itself, with much the same format. There are lots of letters, a rich source of social historical data as well as public opinion about strictly Baptist matters.

One summary analysis of Southern Baptist state papers concludes that after takeover by the state conventions they added more comment on social issues (Sumerlin 1968). They were, however, James D. Bernard stated in the twenties (1926: 146), "unanimously silent on the question of the Ku Klux Klan," and wound up as weak journals because of their minister-editors. How much leeway do these men have? Each issue, presumably, they write an editorial on a subject and with a tone of their own choosing. Some of them are very bland, glowing reports of Baptist bonhomie, but the editors can be very frank.

The second area in which many of the largest state conventions play an important role is the colleges – forty-seven senior institutions, five junior ones, and a clutch of miscellaneous academies and institutes (even two military academies in Virginia left over from some previous era). Almost all of them are in the Old South; the five best ones, with national reputations, are generally agreed to be the University of Richmond, Wake Forest University and Furman in North and South Carolina respectively, Mercer University in Macon, Georgia, and Baylor in Waco, Texas. All were founded in the great age of denominational colleges, 1825–1845, some with a manual labor approach, all in intense competition with those of their rival denominations. Evaluation of their quality can be left to the accrediting agencies, which count earned doctorates and publications among the faculty, percentage of the graduates who go on to graduate schools, and number of volumes in the library.

After the anti-intellectualism and distrust of those who might have learned

aptist Student Union booth at Louisiana Tech, Rustum, Louisiana, 1939. (Photograph
urtesy of the E. C. Dargan Research Library, Sunday School Board, Southern Baptist
onvention.)

religion from books without a real born-again experience, even to the attitude of one of Flannery O'Connor's characters who "learned to read and
write but that it was wiser not to" (1949: 17), it is perhaps miraculous that
over half the pastors now have gone to the Baptist senior colleges. One
Wake Forest graduate and former Southern Baptist, however, said that especially for women, "it wasn't that they didn't teach you to think, they tried
to teach you not to think."

The colleges' underlying problem is the same as the seminaries' —
the built-in conflict between academic freedom and denominational spon-
sorship. "Surely," Masters wrote, "may we have too much education in
America, if it turns its back on God, and confines its efforts to the intellect
rather than the will and the emotions" (1918: 171). This dilemma leads to

oxymoronic statements such as a recent administrator's commitment to "biblically based intellectual inquiry," or to that of Associate Pastor Fred Powell, First Baptist Church, Atlanta: "I don't think Mercer is concerned about the Cooperative Program money they get . . . they would rather have academic freedom" (Hefley 1987: 141). Some of them have begun to cut the cord.

The third general area shared by many of the state conventions – those old enough to have an historical consciousness – is support for SB historical societies. Perhaps out of traditional female interests in "family" and genealogy, there are more women represented in this area than any other outside of the WMU. Most of the older states have set up repositories for archives, documents, and personal papers at a Baptist institution (Wake Forest in North Carolina, Furman in South Carolina, for instance). Many have state histories, of uneven quality, and some are microfilming and indexing the state newspapers, rich lodes of social history. J. Wayne Flynt, a Southern Baptist who is a professional historian and has been head of the history department at Auburn University in Alabama, has shown what can be done with them.

In the larger, older states the form of the organization is likely to be an adaptation of the national bureaucracy (although sometimes the ideas have gone the other way). North Carolina, for example, has departments of Sunday School, Church Training, Church Building and Planning, Music, WMU, a Foundation (some people want to leave their estates to the states), and Evangelism and Missions (Fort Bragg and other military installations, hospitals, and prisons; the many congregations of new wave immigrants in the cities; some work with Indians, the deaf and "the silent"; and youth and campus ministries). The state convention also manages four or five camps and conference centers for various age groups. A coordinating council works with the seven institutions in the state, and a social service group oversees several children's homes, half a dozen homes for the elderly, and one very large hospital in Winston-Salem. There is also a social concerns agency which prides itself on its unusually large staff and lay trusteeship, a separate structure for the *Recorder*, and the necessary logistic and administrative underpinning and fund-raising and public relations support for all this.

Different states have different problems: migrants from Pacific pindots with languages nobody in the U.S. knows how to speak; intense involvement with "internationals" (temporary aliens like seamen and diplomats); a different competitive situation in, say, Mormon territory; larger groups of young people; or accidents like a wealthy donor with a particular interest in an uncommon disease who pushes the convention in that direction. Texas has twenty-six camps for various conferences, an All-State Baptist Youth Choir and Band which holds annual noisy bashes, and many programs of cooperation with the enormous Spanish-speaking population. The newer, smaller states are understandably more concerned with church planting and getting organized.

District Associations

The association was the earliest (the first one was formed in Philadelphia in 1707) and remains the smallest unit of supra-church affiliation. The local church is paramount, certainly, but the advantages of cooperation have been apparent from the beginning. They started with just a small number of churches, perhaps only three. Now they tend to be much larger. North Carolina has exactly 100 counties and 3,489 SB churches, and about 80 SB associations, an average of 44 churches each. But the internal boundaries are ever shifting, with urbanization and other population changes and various sorts of petty politics. Since the local church takes the initiative to join the association, it may move just as easily over policy differences or even personalities, or population mix. Most associations stay within state lines, but an occasional church may stray, and "suburbanization" may divide the churches in one town, some staying with the rural association, others feeling closer to the city.

The functions of associational membership have changed, too. Early on, in frontier conditions, they were largely social: "Not missions," Masters wrote, but "union and fellowship" (1915: 102). Cooperative missions were first run by the Charleston Association in 1755. There was opposition in the beginning to the associational form, and as the states developed their own conventions, to the associations joining those. Finally they became acceptable, and even a little routine.

There are faint calls for a more hierarchical structure. One, from Oklahoma, would require that a church belong to an association before it be affiliated with a state convention. Some associations are already serving as agents of discipline, denying fellowship to churches which have ordained women, for example. The SBC as a whole is bound by its own By-laws to stand off. Article IV states that "the Convention does not claim and will never attempt to exercise any authority over any other Baptist body, whether church, auxiliary organization, associations, or conventions."

The opportunities for metropolitan, county, or district cooperation seem clear. The pastors enjoy the chance to talk shop, compare notes, share ideas, and make reputations. Plans are made for district scheduling, vacation Bible schools, revivals, church music festivals. Some associations manage special facilities themselves, like children's camps. In the Washington, D.C., area the entire association is "dually aligned" with the SBC and the American (Northern) Baptists, although generally this gesture, symbolic of divided loyalty and suspected liberalism, is undertaken by the local church.

One of the reasons for the revival of interest is the increasing ethnic diversity of the denomination as a whole. If local churches are becoming increasingly homogeneous, the association then becomes the organizational level within which social intercourse takes place. Home Mission Board publications support this. There is "pride over emerging pluralism of SBC churches and associations, reflected in integrated and racial/ethnic congregations that fellowship on an association level . . . the district association will emerge as the most crucial unit in the denomination. The local congregation will always be central in SBC polity, but apart from it, the association will best understand the context of Christian outreach and ministry" (*Missions/USA*, Winter 1982: 3). And the local congregation will then be free to develop into something else.

4 Congregations, Pastors, and Families

I learned about democracy in a Baptist church. I learned about the freedom of the individual in a Baptist church, I learned about the inviolability of the conscience in a Baptist church, I learned how to scheme in a Baptist church, . . . I learned how to listen in a Baptist church, I learned how to speak in a Baptist church, I learned about caring in a Baptist church.

— Bill Moyers (Hastey 1982A: 10)

The Church as a Total Institution

Typical (200–299 total members) Southern Baptist churches reported the following statistics in 1987 (*Quarterly Review*, Aug.-Sept. 1988: 27):

246	members
179	resident members (exclusive of college attendance, military service, unknown whereabouts)
15	baptisms and other additions
120	Sunday School
55	Church Training (graded membership instruction)
29	Woman's Missionary Union
24	Brotherhood
$51,754	gifts
$ 7,920	mission expenditures
$ 3,968	Cooperative Program
$47,089	church debt

Of the total 37,000 churches, 60 percent have fewer than 300 members; 8 percent have more than 1,000, the largest being the First Baptist Church in Dallas, with more than 25,000, which calls itself the largest country church in the world. Of the 5,800 churches in metropolitan areas (with a population greater than 50,000) about 40 percent have experienced significant social or "racial" change.

The functions of the local church were distilled by one pastor to "Bible study, minister, and worship." Bible study is an enormous enterprise. Southern Baptists are exhorted to study the Bible constantly, and many certainly read part of it every day. They may also work on it formally through the Sunday School, which in SB life includes everyone from toddler to senior in graded classes. Although the adult classes were for many years segregated by sex, now the trend is to meet as couples with singles separated (some age divisions imposed as well), on Sunday mornings before "the preaching service." The Bible is read and preached from then as well as at the Training Union meetings, which again include almost everyone in instruction that directly promotes denominational participation and leadership. Training Union meetings come before the Sunday evening service, which are also biblically based, as are the Wednesday evening meetings. Until very recently even in middle-sized southern cities teachers gave no homework on Wednesday evenings (Methodists and Presbyterians often have meetings then, too), and such activities as Little League baseball are still scheduled around church demands, or criticized when they aren't. Not every devout Baptist will attend all these meetings, but some will, and at the very least Sunday observance is well ritualized.

The irreducible minimum of local church organization is a pastor. As Samuel Hill wrote:

> The exalted status enjoyed by the clergy throughout much of southern history — in some respects, they have been like an untouchable caste — was partly deserved, owing to the quantity and quality of their services to the people. In many a community, the minister was one of a very few persons, perhaps the only person, from whom any sort of stable leadership could be expected . . . the figure of the local preacher incarnated what was ultimate for an uncritical society. Small wonder that such a society should vest him with an authoritative role (1967: 168).

Twenty years ago even the density of clergymen in the South was higher than anywhere else in the country: 135.6 per 100,000 of population compared to 121.2 for the U.S. as a whole. Hill also wrote that "[in] the tendency of ministers to overrate their own authority and in the acquiescence of the laymen . . . the pastoral office has been one of the most direct paths to fame and power in southern society" (1967: 169).

Yet in the mega-churches, the very ones that produce the old-new breed of super-evangelists, it is growing into almost an imperial pastorate. The legendary W. A. Criswell of Dallas said, "A laity-led, layman-led, deacon-led church will be a weak church anywhere on God's earth. The pastor is the ruler of the church. There is no other thing than that in the Bible." And another (anonymous) pastor said to an SB bureaucrat, "You need to tell those deacons to support their pastors more. After all, God has given the pastor to the church to tell it what to do. The deacons shouldn't argue; they should just do what the pastor says." Recent fundamentalist insistence on clerical authoritarianism, as in a controversial 1988 resolution, formalizes these power hungers and plays into the very American tendencies to create cults of personality and publicity. As the laity yearn for leadership, they also have much more practice in their business lives with board-staff relationships, and as Baptists with a commitment to basic democracy and freedom of the individual conscience.

Church structure is even more complicated because about one-quarter of SB pastors are still "bivocational" (in anthropological jargon they would be called "shamans," or part-time religious practitioners who make their living in the same range of ways as others of their age and sex in a given society). About a quarter of these are professionals, doctors and lawyers among them. In 1790 the average tenure of New Hampshire pastors was 30 years; the average tenure for Southern Baptist pastors now is thirty months, and only eighteen months in some big states. Since the relationship between pastor and congregation is said to be God's will, there is much (deeply ambivalent) laughter about God changing his mind so often. But there is much awareness of other factors: the low level of pastoral support in which SBs have historically been at the bottom of the large denominations ($19,070 average total compensation in a National Council 1984 survey), and the increasing complexity of the relationship, the ambiguity of the expectations, the inability to control the contradictions that are responsible for the tensions. Tharp's study (1985) found 1600 Southern Baptist pastors forced out within the previous eighteen months, 40 percent of them without warning. This was a repeated event for many churches, yet pastors were not aware of the pattern. Eighty percent of the terminated had found employment, but only two-thirds with SB churches.

Some churches, thus, don't even have a full-time pastor to themselves. A few have professional staffs of thirty, an "Executive Minister" plus "support staff"—secretaries, bookkeepers, a sexton or six, and many full-time kitchen staffs for all the necessary catering.

Then there are the deacons, a vexing term with changing definitions.

In the smaller churches the Board of Deacons functions like a board of trustees, with legal responsibility for raising and disbursing funds and handling property, hiring the pastor, deciding what color to paint the church, and other issues that are the stuff of congregational life. Early in southern history Baptists had presbyteries (Boards of Elders); Articles of Faith adopted by Southern Seminary in 1859 speak of "Bishops or Elders, and Deacons." "Deacon" and "minister" are both words for "servant," the former being a Greek term and the other a much later Latin one.

All of these distinctions are or have been fraught with theological or denominational significance and now, of course, Baptists would eschew the Methodist or Episcopalian connotations of "bishop," and "elder" for its Presbyterian sound. In the mid-nineteenth century deacons were responsible for works of charity or social service, and some of them were women. Toward the end of the century there was a shift to a business model of church management. In this shift (and perhaps, to an extent, behind the shift itself), women were barred from the diaconate in many areas except where their eligibility was part of the written theology, and the WMU took over much of the service work.

Class has been a vexing issue. Catholic parish (geographical) churches could manage to separate class-based groups by timing the services so that, informally, there would be a servants' Mass. Or as sociologist Kenneth Underwood (1957) described, Catholic parish boundaries could even be drawn to accommodate class divisions so that rich and poor would not have to worship together. The pressure to do this has increased as social and recreational functions have become more important, with churches moving toward total institutions in the American context.

Baptist churches have had different solutions to these problems. "Many urban Baptist churches at the beginning of the twentieth century contained a representative cross section of classes," wrote historian Flynt (1969: 533). Now, however, in the cities and large suburbs, the "gathering" church principle of traditional SB practice provides the means for class separation to take place. "Baptists are not a 'parish' church people," said a Home Mission Board official. A pastor reflected:

> Church swapping is definitely on the increase in American religious life. When I was a child, we always went to the nearest Baptist church and never even considered any other option. But today many people 'shop' for churches on the 'open market' . . . Here . . . there are six other Baptist churches less than five minutes away from ours . . . [In six and a half years] . . . we have gained 322

church-swappers from other local churches and have lost 320 church-swappers to nearby sister congregations which is about the way I like it (Hull 1982: 4).

He went on to give lists of good and bad reasons for a swap. It is "unwise . . . when one is interested primarily in furthering business or social contacts rather than in loving all Christians regardless of status," but all right "when one who cannot grow spiritually in one setting finds powerful incentive to grow in another setting." How, though, does one know the difference?

The emphasis on fellowship within each congregation serves, of course, to mask class differences. As Carol J. Greenhouse says, these differences "are not undesirable or unacceptable in themselves, but they have no relevance in the church community" (1986: 109). The result is a tendency toward homogeneous congregations which are regionally stratified.

Local church structure—and the class, demographic, and philosophical factors underlying it—are expressed even in the form of the worship service. Herewith one local service in a Deep South state capital:

Sunday Morning
Congregation moved out here to new part of town to avoid blacks downtown, according to local observers. Off straight wide boulevard, much construction, desolate. Destined to be solid strip in ten years, in another ten there will be some shade. Big complex—moderne, undoubtedly architect-designed—brick inside and outside the color of bottled Russian dressing.

Nice sparkling stained glass on exterior side of sanctuary, theme or objects shown, if any, unclear. Color-coordinated fresh flowers. Five hundred people in congregation, maybe three times as many women as men. Age-graded hair, bouffant or tight curls, Farrah Whatshername, Princess of Wales—no punk. Well-dressed, clean and shiny. Men in suits (air-conditioned building, of course). Some young families sitting together, but many older people. No blacks.

Organ prelude, but people chatting steadily in normal volume. Ministers (three) and four deacons arrive on dais in non-matching business suits, choir in two-tone gowns, ranked behind them. Number Two minister requests prayer for the coming annual meeting, says resolutions will be important and controversial.

Announces 531 in Bible School, over 400 in Vacation Bible School, with six professions of faith. Hymns led by Minister of Music, who conducts from the pulpit. Lively, spirited anthem with a lilt, a little like "Wearin' of the Green."

"Brother Charles," the senior pastor, announces the opening of the nominat-

ing process for the coming year. Seven hundred family units in the church: 1200 adults, 400 "leadership positions." Then prays, extempore, standing at side of pulpit, eyes closed—hands on hips, hands behind, hands in front.

Offertory solo, a young woman wavering in tone and sharp in pitch. Melody and accompaniment right out of an unsuccessful Broadway musical. A few murmured Amens. *Lights in chancel out.*

The program says Children's Sermon, Solo, Message; *but the solo has already happened and the pastor runs the two messages into each other awkwardly without making a transition. Children's sermon starts with baseball metaphor (Little League game the day before): what would baseball be like without any rules, any foul lines? Even God when he built this world included some foul lines, "not to prevent us from having a good life but so we may have the best life." Occasional grammatical mistake, mispronunciation—"everyone has their life," "preé-miss," "mis-cheé-vus-ness." Goes on with same theme to adults, not many of whom are active parents: "Parents stand in relationship to their children as God does to us—and God intended it that way." Quotes from "famous preacher of our denomination," then from Horace Bushnell's* Christian Nurture *about how important discipline is in the home. Brings in the Prodigal Son, doesn't connect it up. Then the etymology for the day—the Hebrew word for* discipline *means* train up, create desire. *Discipline has two sides, firmness and love. Powerful rationalization for authority.*

Then the Invitation, replied to by an assorted group, mostly children with proud parents. One boy is with his mother only: "Of course, his father is Catholic, or Presbyterian—oh yes, Catholic—and we're especially glad that he's made his decision for Christ." Another hymn, the benediction, and the congregation breaks up, talking avidly, bustling off.

Some SBs are well aware of their limitations. The Oakhurst Church in Decatur, Georgia, has become a focus for moderate leadership. It went through a traumatic period of transition and chose to remain in what became a nearly all-black neighborhood. The pastor, while praising its accomplishments, excoriates its background:

> Oakhurst faced this struggle with all of the liabilities which plague our churches and incapacitate them for mission; a basic biblical illiteracy in terms of knowing the great themes of God's Word, a weak and partial theology of church, a commitment to secular standards of institutional success, a culturally homogenous [*sic*] white, middle class congregation, an ethicless gospel manufactured over the years to perpetuate the status quo, a preoccupation with the cultivation of personal piety, a strong concern for the soul of man and corresponding lack of

commitment to the kingdom of God, rigid church structure, a bias against intellectualism which long ago declared a moratorium on new ideas, the absence of the cross in the call to discipleship; in short, the almost complete accommodation of our witness to the standards of our culture (Nichol 1969: 24).

Yet some of the whites remained, and some more have moved back to "be present in Christ's name on one of the frontiers of alienation in our land." The pastor says the church is "unique among the churches I have pastored for the warmth of its fellowship and the pastoral concern of its membership." In its mixed congregation it is indeed rare, for most SB churches anxiously seek diversity in ways other than including blacks.

Columbia Baptist Church in Falls Church, Virginia, a heavily urbanized Washington, D.C. suburb, is at the large end of the distribution with a professional staff of nine, and numbers among its members Chuck Colson, Senator Strom Thurmond, and other transplanted southerners. Its pastor described its activities in the context of "strengthening families" at the Christian Life Commission seminar of that title (Jones 1982: passim).

When he arrived at his new pastorate several months before his family, he could spend most weeknights meeting in the church parlor with small groups of families. His church has over one hundred deacons, including women, and their function has been redefined back to the earlier model, "from a broad concept to a servant mentality" and "fellowship before business." Inclusive of two women, the staff are not all ordained; the leadership style is like a family in "affirmation, correction and improvement."

There is an attempt to reach out: a quarter of the children enrolled in the day-care center are non-SBs. The staff, including a volunteer child psychiatrist, are available to work on individual and family problems. All this grows in summer to include a day camp staffed by college interns from his congregation. "This participation by returning college students," he commented, "is an aid to maintaining church family ties." Although Falls Church is not a community of young parents, the child-centered ministries help to keep the congregation young.

There is a counseling ministry with a full-time professional, a rural "Retreat Center" in the West Virginia hills, "eating meetings" on weekdays and after all three Sunday services, and luncheons for new members. Worship (number eight in his list) features two formal morning services, an "exciting" Sunday evening informality with a "variety of choirs," and the Wednesday evening prayer meeting. The pastor explained: "We feature prayer around the dinner table and children learn to pray with their parents. Many sick folk receive cards from little children who prayed for them on Wednesday evenings." There is less emphasis on large WMU meetings, more focus on using the women as "catalysts" to foster mission activity.

A full-time missions minister organizes the program; "carpenters, woodcutters, clowns, basketball teams, musical groups, bicyclists, and beachcombers have gone to places such as Canada, England, Ocean City, Vermont, Maine, a highrise for elderly people in Pennsylvania, and the Appalachian Mountains." The church gave $200,000 "through our Cooperative Program . . . to mission work." The large local population of internationals is subject to special attention; three families have been sponsored, English lessons serve 66 people who are brought in on the church's own buses, and there is an international Sunday School class and worship services in Korean and Spanish.

> We seek to make these a part of the larger family as opposed to groups using our facilities. We are not against separate congregations, but it is our desire to be a family. We have Spanish deacons. We seek to enlist internationals in the integrated activities. This is difficult but rewarding . . .
> A black cultural attache attended one Sunday with his delegation. The following night he awoke to the spectre of a cross burning in his yard. Our members have befriended hm. He has eaten in our homes and some of our folk have eaten in his. Remarkable things are happening.

There is also a family mediation service set up by a lawyer member, a ministry for families of prisoners, an AA group and "course to understand alcoholics," and a singles ministry making an effort to "integrate singles into the larger family."

Every theme encouraged by the denominational leaders and professionals is brought out here. There is a marketing philosophy behind it: find out who the congregation really is, not what you think it is or would like it to be, and set about meeting its needs. The result is the expansion of the local church in the lives of its members. For those at its heart it begins to approach Erving Goffman's "total institution" through which all potentials in the human personality claim to be expressed, and membership within which marks off its participants from the outside world. The church at McKinney, Texas (near Dallas), is a "life center planned to include education space, a theater, bowling alleys, handball courts, gym, craft room, weight room, sauna and a jogging track." Why ever leave it? Especially when the social world outside is shifting, probably dangerous, certainly diversified.

Josiah Strong, at the end of the last century, recognized that the expanded services throughout the week in American Protestant churches extended certain family functions when the family system didn't work. The model, interestingly, was the black churches, which operated as community centers highly valued since they were the only institutions blacks were allowed to control. Now the white SB churches have become symbols of attempted ownership of the cultural core, and centers of subcultural social life.

The local church can give individuals the security of the family situation without the potential for manipulation. The enormous psychological power of the central evangelical Christian message—that, as SB pastor Will Campbell says it, "Jesus love [*sic*] you no matter what you done [*sic*]"—can create a sense of security and self-worth that may never have existed before. Television ministries can make the delivery of this message both widespread and seemingly intimate; in the local church it has to be delivered face-to-face by complex living, human, beings. This can only be done by persons of real sympathy who can accept diversity and attract those from outside the traditional SB in order to meet the imperative to grow. There is, in the Falls Church example given, no mention of American blacks.

A New Rationale for Church Segregation

Christianity has a mixed record of dealing with social heterogeneity. Some of Paul's letters imply that masters and slaves attended the same meetings, but other passages indicate that missions were custom-made for different groups as defined at the time. The issue is entwined with that of the validity of group conversion; does a leader, as in the early Middle Ages, really bring his whole tribe along with him? The Scandinavian kings brought entire countries into the Lutheran camp; were their subjects truly Lutherans?

Fueled by the Baby Boom and "suburban" expansion, post-war growth trends continued up in all the large Protestant churches until about 1965. Then the "mainline" or "Main Street" denominations, the more "liberal" ones, just about the list of National Council of Churches members, stopped growing while the evangelicals—including the SBC, which is not formally part of that movement—continued to expand. Why? What was the magic secret?

One of the principal answers to those related questions has been institutionalized into the Church Growth Movement (CGM). The CGM is based on anthropological understanding and founded in the experience of one Donald McGavran, formerly a Disciples of Christ missionary in Kerala

Senior Baptist Young People's Union in an "ethnic" congregation; Spanish-American Baptist Church, East Las Vegas, New Mexico, 1920s. (Photograph courtesy of the E. C. Dargan Research Library, Sunday School Board, Southern Baptist Convention.)

on India's southwest coast. According to tradition, St. Thomas the Apostle brought the Syrian Christian Church to Kerala, and there are Jewish immigrants from the same period. Islam arrived in the eighth century, but all of these diverse groups have been affected by Hindu caste consciousness.

McGavran became convinced that sensitivity to the endogamous (inmarrying) restrictions of the Indian caste system, as practiced by all religious groups in Kerala, was the key to successful proselytizing. If an individual became a Christian in that situation he outcasted himself and could find no marriage partner. Thus it was necessary to attempt to convert entire groups — extended families, tribelets, occupationally based subcastes, in order not to cut off new Christians from their social environment.

McGavran started publishing his theories in the 1930s, but only after he retired to the United States did they start to find wide acceptance. In 1965 he settled his Institute of Church Growth at Fuller Theological Seminary in Pasadena, California. Its services have been used by many denominations, but with consistent success by the Southern Baptists.

Why is this message so appealing? Religious endogamy in American society has been maintained only within the three great traditions (Will Herberg's "triple melting pot") of Protestant, Catholic, and Jew; the time is long gone when marriage between Roman Catholics of, say, Irish and Italian backgrounds is considered a breach of endogamic restrictions. Except – of course – black-white endogamy in the South. It is to maintain this endogamy that some Southern Baptists are using the CGM and its "homogeneous unit principle" (HUP) to shape the changing nature of the local church, particularly those in urban and large "suburban" communities in the south. One approach they use is to blur, carefully or carelessly, the distinctions between "language", "race", and "ethnicity."

Examples of such blurrings are easy to come by. From *Baptist Adults* is the statement, "The question is not whether you can accept God's love for people who are different from you. It is whether you personally will love, relate to, minister to, witness to a person who differs from you in looks, culture, race, language, status or in any of the other ways that separate us into groups" (3rd Quarter 1982: 24). A Home Mission Board executive comments, "America is becoming retribalized. The melting pot theory is not working. Racial identity is the 'in' thing. New ethnic and language arrivals hurry to be with familiar people" (Driggers 1981: 4). Another HMB bureaucrat gives his definition of pluralism: "A state of society in which members of diverse ethnic, racial, religious, or social groups maintain an autonomous participation in and development of their traditional culture or special interest within the confines of a common civilization" (Tilton 1976: 93).

Another HMB statement says proudly: "We're in the business of changing lives . . . regardless of ethnic background. There are more than 200 different ethnic-culture groups living on American soil . . . More than 1200 language missionaries serve these groups that compose nearly one half of the American population" (1982: n.p.). (But most of these groups have been English-speaking for three generations or more.) And an associational missions director uses the code words like this: "When race is mentioned we will not automatically think of the blacks as the only ethnic group" (Rose 1980: 11). A former WMU president refers to *Fiddler on the Roof*, where, she says with a naiveté that borders on the insulting, the village milkman "sees the whole family in society collapsing around him, culminating finally in the decision of his youngest daughter to marry someone from another ethnic group" (Sample 1982: 72). (The daughter in question married a Russian, a Christian; for Jews in the diaspora this was equivalent to death.)

Rejecting the melting pot, many Southern Baptists like the *stew pot* simile, confusing themselves since *pot à feu*, that classic French delight in which the beef and the chicken and the vegetables are cooked separately to preserve their individuality before being combined, has been translated that way, and most southerners are more familiar with Dinty Moore. They have happily borrowed the misnomer *mosaic* from Canadian sociology, since it implies that color separation is part of the design. Both of these metaphors duck questions of power and pretend that all the groups are equivalent—black and brown and red and yellow—and that there is no history of one-way domination, exploitation, and repression.

Quite carried away, a study guide from the Sunday School Board proclaims, "At the present time, we are the most integrated denomination in the United States. We worship and study the Bible in more than eighty-seven languages and dialects" (1986: 6). Former Southern Baptist Ralph Elliott makes the obvious comparison of the homogeneous unit principle with South African apartheid, and asks, "Can it be that the church simply cannot minister and succeed in a community of diversity?" (1982: 56). "Of course not" must be the answer, if the church is perceived as a total institution/community center for a particular band of the caste continuum, terrified of mixing with one other particular band.

This approach explains part of the Southern Baptist attitudes toward Israel. The relationship between conservative Protestantism and Israel has many other elements, but the separatist/"ethnic" church/homogeneous unit approach is also applied. The existence of Israel enables those Southern Baptists who are inclined to be anti-Semitic simultaneously to be pro-Zionist and forge coalitions with some American Jewish groups in defending support for Israel: it gives Jews their own place, *over there*.

One of the Southern Baptists' interesting lines of thought is their insistence, when pressed, that blacks are in a different category because of their liturgy, their style of worship. Here is how it's done by C. Peter Wagner, McGavran's disciple and faculty member at Fuller Theological Seminary:

I give an example . . . Temple Church in Pershing Square in Los Angeles. It's a Baptist church right in a mosaic of inner city ethnic groups. In one church they have an Anglo congregation, a Spanish congregation, a Chinese congregation, and a Korean congregation . . .

They have to worship in four different languages. But the first Sunday of every quarter they all get together in the "Sounds of Heaven" celebration. No sermon, since they couldn't understand it. But they minister to each other in music, in testimony, in baptisms . . . Each congregation maintains cultural integrity. Yet there's a sense of interdependence and love among all the four congregations. . . .

I live in an integrated neighborhood. Our children go to integrated schools. Blacks need Christ. Whites need Christ. But there's no way one church can meet the needs of both of those communities. If we began having a service with soul music that ran two-and-a-half hours with the kind of black preaching that appeals to our black community, we would be considered ridiculous by everybody. We would stop winning people to Christ. But why should we do this, when New Revelation Baptist Church is winning numbers of unbelievers who are black, and we're winning numbers of unbelievers who are white? Neither one is racist (Stafford 1979: 12).

There it is: interdependence and love – respect for "cultural" differences – but not with blacks because of the disparity in liturgical style, and the identity of language which obviates that argument. Leo Hawkins quoted the generalized feeling of white congregations in 1964: "I have been pushed by law, economics, and society all the way back into my church. Now you can't push me any further (1964: 57). In the 1970s a Florida woman protested, "Our kids have to go to school with them and eat with them and go the picture shows with them. We ought to keep the church apart, where the kids can go and get away from them" (Baker 1973: 700).

Despite widespread SB enthusiasm and participation, there are many Southern Baptists who are explicitly and vehemently against the CGM approach on Biblical and other grounds. They spurn the emphasis on numbers, and the gimmicks, and the homogeneous unit principle. Then there is the question of true integration at the centers of power. A hint of this development has already taken place in California, as CGM leader C. Peter Wagner suggests:

the Southern Baptist open society attitude was recently tested by an event similar to secession. The Southern Baptist principle has been to form homogeneous unit ethnic congregations of local churches, but to unite these congregations in heterogeneous associations and conventions on a geographical basis. In the California Baptist Convention, churches have been started among thirty-seven different ethnic groups. But leaders of the twenty-two Hispanic churches and missions in the Los Angeles area felt that in order better to evangelize the vast Southern California Hispanic community, it would be better to have an entirely Hispanic Association. So, in March 1979, the Hispanics "seceded" from the mixed Los Angeles Association and started the *Asociacion Bautista*, much to the consternation of the Anglo leadership of the State Convention (1981: 80).

There have been black association and state leaders, and even in the early 1970s a black second vice-president of the whole Convention. But mixing in the social dimensions of the local congregation – even in mixed churches, black women are not likely to attend the WMU – is rare. Many hundreds of SB churches run their own school systems, and few have any black pupils; the Christian school movement carefully does not collect such figures.

Wagner himself explicitly denies fostering exclusivity, saying that "in no case should . . . doors be closed to those of other homogeneous units, either for worship or for membership. This kind of exclusion, in my opinion, is clearly a form a racism and must be rejected on Christian ethical grounds" (1981: 153). But in 1985 the National Convocation on Evangelizing Ethnic America was held at an SB church in Houston, with Wagner on the platform next to the SB chairman, and black groups conspicuously absent.

Southern Baptists, and other southerners, are thus using the homogeneous principle to rationalize the maintenance of black-white segregation because they feel that these two groups, in a very powerful and special way because of the long weight of southern history, should be endogamous castes, just as if they lived in Kerala, India.

The extent of "integration" within churches can only be guessed, since the denomination's voluntary statistical reports do not ask for those data. However, the Foreign Mission Board estimated in 1983 that there were 3,500 to 4,000 churches, or roughly 10 percent of the total, the largest of them near military bases, with some black members. This is a long way from 1958, when J. M. Dawson reported that there were fourteen in the whole Convention. Some of the "integration" has to be seen as token, a dozen people among 5,000 at the First Baptist Church in Jackson, Mississippi, seventeen at the 25,000-plus First Baptist Church, Dallas, nine years after the doors were opened to them in 1968. In few places would blacks actually be turned away from the door of a church today, but there are, of course, many other ways of making them feel alien and unwelcome. In some areas, there has been re-segregation. Southern Baptists *need* a few blacks in order to counter allegations of discrimination. If there start to be more than a few, help will be forthcoming to start a new black SB church. The old attitudes remain: a 1981 Ed.D. thesis at Southern, entitled "Developing a Model of Religious Education for Black SB Churches," raises questions about how different such education might be, and why.

There are about 700 black churches ("predominantly black" is the language used) in the SBC, according to the 1983 estimate by the Home Mission

Board. Much less paternalistic attitudes and rhetoric have been developed, replacing "work *for*" with "work *with*" since the late 1950s. The reasons why black churches wanted to be affiliated with the SBC are no doubt complex (Gibson Winter [1961: 116] says "as a buffer against the lower-class Negro community"), but certainly the wealth of resources available and the strength to be derived from the links with an organization of such size and power are among them. There are, then, separate black churches, token integration in others, a handful of black officials at the association and state levels, and a few nationally – all working with blacks.

Under the veneer of fellowship and cooperation, there is still sometimes rudeness and condescension. At the Pittsburgh meeting in 1983, a young man who had walked across America told about staying with a black family who called him "Al, for Albino" [howls of laughter from the thousands] ". . . I borrowed the son's suit . . . it was Dayglow Green [more howls]." An insulting story at the 1987 meeting led to a proposed resolution against "demeaning language," but the proposal was swiftly disposed of by President Rogers. Southern Baptists, however, are not unique in retreating from the full implications of change. Most Protestant denominations are not facing continued "racial" issues directly; church leaders in North Carolina commented that "inactivity is widespread." Many churches in other denominations are no more integrated than most SB ones, although they are certainly more willing to be.

Privatized Families in Homogeneous Churches

The continuing need to avoid black-white mixing is an important part of the reason for the bustling activity and the reinforcement of the local congregation as a total institution and a primary group. The link is in the current emphasis on families, the crucial and complex reciprocal relationship between family stability, continuity, and growth with that of the local church.

A primary group is small, long-term, informal, and multipurpose. Its members meet and mingle in intimate face-to-face contact, and develop strong reciprocal loyalties to each other and toward the group. Primary groups go with endogamy – that is, the circumscription of the group within which marriage choices are acceptable. Clubs (those that include both sexes) define approved mating potential, and indeed that is one of their reasons for being, as it is for some resorts, many small colleges (one that has students of a single sex is frequently paired with one for the opposite sex),

"Family Night," First Baptist Church, Meridian, Mississippi, c. 1960. (Photograph courtesy of the Southern Baptist Historical Library and Archives.)

or sorority/fraternity pairs within the coeducational schools, and some recreational activities. Churches also may serve that function.

Gibson Winter's *Suburban Captivity of the Churches* reported on the effect of "suburbanization" – the development of largely class-homogeneous residential communities – on the character of the local churches. He was critical: "The separation of residence from place of work has given an artificial, almost hothouse character to the middle-class neighborhood . . . The church is one of the plants that grows profusely in this hothouse atmosphere. Religious fellowship becomes association by likeness . . . The residential area is now a private sphere in which families try to achieve emotional stability and secure their position on the ladder of achievement" (1961: 81).

The churches try to create fellowship without any common base in long-standing association and familiarity. All this "pop koinonia," as Joseph Hough aptly termed it, has a very specific history in the connections between the surge of church building of the 1950s, suburbanization, the mechanization of the home, the Baby Boom, and "white flight." Eleven and a half million people, mostly male, came home from the war with a backlog of psychological, social, educational, and vocational needs. The American economy needed time to adjust, and the GI Bill, in addition to its general social virtues, was an ideal way to stretch out their reentry into the job market.

Before that particular war, the U.S. had hovered on the edge of a revolution in the spread of small machinery, the mechanization of the home, and the advent of television. The democratization of automobile ownership was a possibility; the adoption of the federal highway building program and the resultant "urban renewal" and eventual ruin of mass transportation made it a necessary reality. All these forces pushed the housing industry into a huge expansion of the single-family dwelling. And the new houses needed everything—not just the old-fashioned staples but the newly felt necessities, the Bendix and the Mixmaster and the gasoline lawn mower.

Although there was talk of "piety along the Potomac" and even of a "Third Great Awakening," what looked like a great growth in religious devotion was actually a function of the demography—the great increase in the number of young families—and the need of all these new communities for basic institutions. It now looks as if a lot of this migration was an escape from complexity and diversity—white flight from the war-swollen cities—and into class-based segregation. What was the "development" or "subdivision" all about, if not to make sure that neighborhood incomes varied within a known and narrow range?

This was an era of "togetherness." Amateur craftsmanship went along with homeownership and domestic mechanization. "My hobby is woodworking—look at my power tools," the man would say. "I make our daughter's clothes," the woman would say, "and here is my new machine with all the attachments. As a family we like to fish in our power boat and camp in our trailer and watch TV, one set per age group." All of this was very good for business, as was the increasingly fragmented household. Grandma, not to be dependent on her children, was established in her own little place, and she needed her own full complement of machinery.

The Southern Baptists lived this story: it was this great, one-time transition that lifted the center of gravity of their denomination into the middle class. Their experience was intensified by the peculiar retarded nature of urbanization/suburbanization in the South and reinforced by the upheavals of the sixties. The self-sufficiency and inwardness which became characteristic of both family life and church life, and the fears of diversity, continue to feed on each other. And it is hardly necessary to point out that the leading ideologues of the SBC today, the senior bureaucrats and peak pastors, had their ideas, their dreams, and their sense of normalcy forged during this period.

Sociologist Richard Sennett has suggested that this model not only may be damaging to larger social goals, but is also dreadfully stressful to family members. "Destructive *Gemeinschaft*," he calls it. In Sennett's opinion:

The average teenager will often defend himself against what he sees as the anxious burden of adulthood by trying to define and control his future life before he has begun to experience it, when he is still vague about its possibilities. As a result, he often becomes a self-fulfilling prophecy . . . Middle class suburban life repeats the pseudo-innocence of the adolescent . . . Under such conditions, the isolated family is forced to absorb all the personal stresses, the displaced intimacy, that would have found expression in the diversity of city life (Broyard 1982: 31).

The possibility that the kind of family life Southern Baptists appear to extol may be harmful to their very family health is real: "Church and family are to be dependent upon each other, with church and state divided; the church is to dominate society," writes Donald Lake in a study based on SB church training materials (1967: 69). The figure linking local church and family is the pastor. As one pastor's wife said, "The church wants a good model for family since it is so family-oriented and the pastor is so powerful." How does a pastor get that way?

The Pastor as Role Model and Rule-Maker

If this pastor is typical, he is male and grew up in a Southern Baptist family in a small town or "suburb" in the South. He was entered on the Cradle Roll and heard endless talk about church doings from parents whose social, intellectual, and, to a large part, political and even emotional life centered around them. He might join the Sunbeams as a preschooler; he would certainly start off in age-graded Sunday School classes. In the fifth grade the classes would also be segregated by sex, although the content of the teaching was ostensibly asexual.

Whatever he, like most Americans, learned about the physical aspects of sexuality would be from his peers; he, of course, started learning about the emotional aspects from the moment he was born. In a southern town he certainly wouldn't get anything in school, and the Sunday School gave him no help. (The Broadman Sex Education series is advertised in whispers, and most Baptist Book Stores will not stock it.) Indeed, from the massive silence on specifics, he is likely to learn only that sex is a great, leaden mystery. One SBC book by a physician talks (to parents) about the need for a happy, loving home, and advises them to share an understanding of bodies and sex-associated feelings. Gender differences are learned, but parents should make sure that the child doesn't get a confused picture.

Between the ages of twelve and fourteen, the minister-to-be might be

Sex-segregated denominational socialization; Sunday School class, First Baptist Church, Talla-hassee, Florida. (Photograph courtesy of the E. C. Dargan Research Library, Sunday School Board, Southern Baptist Convention.)

given a book called *About This Thing Called Dating* by Dan and Barbara Kent (1981). A chapter entitled "What's different for Christians" only mentions "Temptation is sometimes strong" and recommends reading I Corinthians 10:13. The rest of his understanding would pour over him from films, television, and magazines.

At some point along the way he would have what Bill Moyers, with rare vagueness, called "a normal religious experience." All advice proclaims the danger of pushing a child into it—but doesn't suggest shrinking from it, either. Parents, SB bureaucrat Tal D. Bonham writes, are the "logical and scriptural ones to lead their children to Christ," and children "can experience genuine salvation when they have reached the level of maturity at which they recognize their sin" (1980: 6). Since the ability of parents to engender a sense of guilt, if not of sin, in their children is usually unbridled, this advice amounts to a blank check of clout. Former SB Horace Newcomb credits Southern Protestants generally for their "highly charged manipulative techniques" (1976: 96); he remembers getting caught playing catch in the sanctuary with the pastor's son – the ball had to be burned.

As he grew older, the boy would ordinarily join the Royal Ambassadors (Southern Baptistized Boy Scouts) and begin gradual training for adult responsibility. Along the way he might act as camp counselor (for a fraction of the minimum wage) to Baptist children, play on Baptist athletic teams, and "witness," with a mixed-sex but thoroughly chaperoned group, to other youth. He might be one of nearly a million to attend a Christian academy, but if his public schools were integrated, and he and his family chose, his entire out-of-school life would center on the carefully self-selected group of Southern Baptist families and their multifarious activities.

In due time he would go off, probably to a Southern Baptist college. His vocation to the ministry – the timing of the "call" – would be subject to many individual factors: whether there are other pastors in the family (one pastor's wife said of her son, "Well, we finally got him into the ministry"), the strength of his conviction and lack of qualms about it, and no doubt the competing opportunities in other fields and his talents for them. Size and self-confidence are factors. (Of one bass-toned messenger President Draper exclaimed, "That a layman should have a voice like that!") During college he might meet his life partner, preferably one who could play the piano.

While he was in college, if at a Baptist institution, the future pastor's religious life would be rich with regular services on campus, active social church-centered groups, and many opportunities for service and for "witnessing." If he was at one of the great southern universities, he might attend a Southern Baptist church, downtown, just off the campus. (At the one in Chapel Hill, the pastor sermonized that "many people have thought that the church is for women – of both sexes", rather than, as he emphasized, for people "redblooded masculine and feminine in the full sense.") There would also be a chapter of the Baptist Student Union, with its own building and a full schedule of organizational activities.

The vocational decision made, he would go off to seminary for a marvelously inexpensive graduate degree. His attitude and activities would become increasingly pre-professional and he would be expected to have a wife before the time to seek his first full-time pastorate. (One female student at Southeastern said "the women come here [to get coupled] deliberately, the men accidentally." She was from Maryland and thought that "southern society was rather strange.")

Here are two male students, both married before, talking over an off-campus lunch in Wake Forest. One has been worrying about how to live on $15,000 a year. The other is selling himself on a career as a military chaplain:

—I can preach . . . associate with other chaplains . . . move every few years and start all over again . . . there's the uniform and the prestige . . . it's a ministry that's wide open . . . the greatest danger is the sameness . . . the importance of a positive attitude . . . I don't think I'd get bored.

—I wouldn't be happy at UNC Memorial Hospital . . .

—Yeah, they're not even Christians . . .

—They told me I was not vulnerable enough to get in and really share feelings with those patients . . . I really believe that God is showing me what to do . . . I consider myself fortunate. Your thing . . . sounds like Naval chaplains are different . . .

—Yeah, they're more conservative. What about this industrial thing? You need to get a regular stable job, get out of debt, get a new car, get married within a year, get really involved with a church, do alcoholic rehabilitation work or something . . .

—There is a girl, has a good job, nice house, can transfer any time she wants . . .

—Other good qualities? Good homemaker?

—Yeah, very clean, good cook . . .

—That's important, man . . .

—Very intelligent, good family background . . . very dependable, very predictable, doesn't have a lot of spontaneity, solid as a rock . . . I tend to get a little bored . . .

—Well, I'm dating this 40-year-old . . . I like her maturity, her age. I like her spiritualness . . . But I feel if I hold out I can get a really nice girl . . .

—I couldn't get what I wanted . . . had to accept a substitute . . . I was pressured into it . . .

—There's one woman God meant for you . . . Pray, and God will bring her to you. On the other hand, whoever you marry is God's choice for you . . . Marriage is total commitment . . .

Somehow they manage to marry, and get ordained, and hope to find a pastorate. For a time the wife may continue with her job, all the while doing her "work" at the church, the bulk of the house "work," her husband's errands, and some typing or bookkeeping. Their evenings are filled with the church: choir practice, committees, Wednesday prayer. She works a five-day week and cleans and shops on Saturdays. His week peaks on Sunday, and she has to appear to peak with him. He can eschew the telephone on Mondays and play golf Tuesday afternoons and know it's good for his health. She has no such chance.

Then the babies—usually not more than two—arrive, and she stays home for maybe seven years. These years seem to be ones of stress for the young couple. They don't look happy with themselves or with each other. Finances are tight; life is a series of balancing acts, even for those of goodwill.

With their children on tagalong occasions—at the annual meetings, at the seminary, at church services—seldom does a mother or father play with a child, or look proud or pleased (or anything but grim and put-upon). In the Pittsburgh soccer arena a two-and-a-half-year-old in yellow organdy whimpered during the interminable sermons; her father, thirtyish, smiled and put his finger to his pursed lips. She whimpered again; he frowned and made a giant meaty fist. She had to be still but she could not understand. Does some of the disassociation from the meaning of words come from this early experience where one has to be quiet, has to listen, but words go on and on and past?

A couple with wedding rings walks across the seminary campus. Their joined hands swing sharply, awkwardly, to the rhythm of his step—not hers. She skips and stumbles to keep the beat. All the while they talk of how he feels about his work and what they can do about it. On a crowded bus in a New Orleans rush hour the air-conditioning fails. A young pastor takes off his coat and lays it carefully across his and his wife's laps. If I'm going to be uncomfortable, so are you, he seems to say.

At Southeastern there is a special shelf for "Seminary Wives"—books on family, marriage, faith, parenting, dying, diet, health, confident entertaining, "I Married a Minister," and works of spirituality. One of the favorites, published by Broadman, C. W. Scudder's *The Family in Christian Perspective*, states that the husband is the head of house, but not autocratic: "Living in subjection, in the biblical sense, meets the wife's basic need. She was created for just such a life" (1982: 95). As Andrea Dworkin describes such wives, "Their desperation is quiet; they hide their bruises of body and heart; they dress carefully and have good manners; they suffer, they love God, they follow the rules" (1983: 69). Of Rosalynn Carter, perhaps the most famous example, her late mother-in-law said, "I have never seen her let her hair down, never heard her tell a joke" (Drew 1978: 310).

Among middle-aged couples there is a striking amount of public affection, touching, grooming. At a conference in a Raleigh church basement, two stiff days in wooden pews, one lumpy couple were tender, the pastor husband reaching behind to massage his wife's neck, she turning to pat down an invisible cowlick. Couples of all ages hold hands, at the annual meetings anyway, as do the Carters, and the Reagans.

The annual invitation sermon one year, by one Rev. James Pleitz of Park Cities Baptist Church, Dallas, was on love and widely reprinted. At one point he departed far from the text, dominating his presentation with this excursus:

My wife knocked on the study door . . . she knows she isn't supposed to do that . . . I knew it was an emergency . . . Maybe she saw the garbage truck going down the street and the cans hadn't been taken out yet . . . Maybe she wanted me to pin up a skirt . . . How many of you have done that? . . . [Several hundred hands] . . . Well, it isn't the most degrading thing a Baptist preacher is asked to do . . . No, this time it was help for the final phase of a home permanent, putting on the solOOtion . . . [laughter] . . . You know, pastors don't have much money, but one of the best uses for the little money they have is to send their wives down to the beauty salOOOn . . . [much laughter] . . . Well . . . [pulling himself back down to earth] . . . she's a precious little girl.

Did anyone in the cavern find that embarrassing? The following year, one of the "moderate" leaders described to the expected laughter naive mistakes of his bride a generation ago as she tried to make cornbread the way he liked it—humiliating her from his pulpit sanctuary. But southern women would say with a little grimness, "We are trained not to cringe."

A pastor's wife, asked when he had graduated from the seminary, replied,"We finished in 1969." At the North Carolina Evangelism Conference the chair read the names of those churches which had baptized more than a hundred the previous year. The pastors with their wives, unbidden, stood to take the applause.

This is much like Lady Bird Johnson's saying on public television, "When we were in the House." And that authentic Southern Baptist, Rosalynn Carter, when asked to explain herself, made it clear that she still resented "misunderstandings" concerning her attendance at Cabinet meetings and her considerable influence in shaping her husband's administration.

What such critics didn't understand was that "Jimmy and I were always partners. After a few weeks in the peanut business," she said, reading back to the days when her husband left the Navy and they returned to Plains, "I knew as much about the business as he did. I did the books. I talked over everything with him. We campaigned as a team. We were a team in the White House. We sat in the rocking chairs on the Truman Balcony, just as we did at the governer's mansion at 4:30 every afternoon, and we talked." Asked if she thought first ladies should be paid, she said she wan't sure. "I was on the stage as much as Jimmy was," she said. "The President was paid $200,000 a year. I felt this was ours" (Curtis 1983: c9).

Yes, they are a team. But the prestige, the respect, the psychic rewards, the economic autonomy seem differentially bestowed. The wives' payoffs are so grudging, their dependent and secondary roles made so explicit, even if everyone knows of their contribution. There is also the view "that problems in relationships . . . can be dealt with by enlarging the individual's capacity to cope with, or accept, feelings of conflict" (Greenhouse 1986: 63). Wives are expected to make the greater part of this effort.

Some of these fragile arrangements are starting to crack. There is now a new type of pastoral counseling – that is, counseling of pastors. One specialist sketched the following picture of his typical patient couple:

The husband peaked at 45. [The parabola of a pastoral career is often reflected in the size of the congregation he serves.] Now, age 50, he is in a smaller church, with a sense of downhill movement. They own nothing – their housing allowances have gone over the years to build equity in the property of the various churches they have served. She is "highly educated" but without skills, or never given credit for having any. She is angry, without clearly knowing why. In the rural areas the picture window in the parsonage often faces the cemetery. The husband is also angry and doesn't understand where his or his wife's anger is coming from. He is impotent fiscally, emotionally, sexually. They scraped to put their son through a Baptist college or the state university. Right out of college, with the right degree, he makes more money than his father.

The increased threat of arbitrary pastoral termination is another source of insecurity and stress. And there are divorces in pastoral marriages, a most grievous double betrayal because of the personal disruption and the pastoral family's failure as role model. Such difficulties, especially those that have to be publicized, wrench at the foundation of their conception of what culture is and what life should be like.

A Southern Baptist woman, in middle life, listed the most important taboos she was given as a child in rural Virginia, in exactly this order: divorce is a moral wrong, God is a judge, don't marry a Catholic, don't acknowledge blacks as friends, and keep strict Sunday observance (don't ever be seen in a store on Sunday even if guests arrive and you've run out of milk).

Southern Baptist ideas of the history of proper family behavior, as might be expected, float free of moorings to specific economic circumstances and systems. There is a fixed notion of what family life and reproductive and sexual behavior should be like, and all else—even scriptural material—is explained away. For example, the doyen of SB seminary social ethicists, T. B. Maston of Southwestern, dismisses Old Testament "polygamy which represented a dramatic departure from God's original plan for marriage" (1983: 46).

Despite the historical and theological fuzziness, the core of SB values can be easily abstracted. The ideal family is caught in that freeze frame of time when the father goes out to work, the mother mothers, and there are dependent children in the home. The parents have a good deal of responsibility and authority over the children, and this is seen as a rather grim challenge. In the father's absence the mother takes over, but when he is there he is head of the house. Sexual behavior is hetero-only and only within marriage. In fact, the whole attitude toward sexuality is what the late psychologist Eric Berne called the "Sex is a Giant Squid" complex, in which the threatening beast is constrained only if it is kept chained under the marriage bed.

Divorce is a dreadful breach of contract, for together—one man and one woman joined together as husband and wife for life—is the way people are supposed to live. Remarriage should follow widowhood. One 61-year-old widow overheard a comment about herself: "It's been two years now; isn't she dating yet?" Singleness is failure and disruption to the pattern. With his target abundantly clear, Maston states that "a Christian should not choose to live single for ascetic reasons, to escape marital responsibilities, or with the opinion that singleness is superior to marriage" (1983: 120). Singles are thought to suffer from sexual tension; they should marry and discipline each other.

The puzzled and token quality of recognition for women is patent. One pastor said at the 1982 Evangelism Conference in North Carolina: "Jesus came to raise sons to God—not to elevate womanhood, although He did." In the Christian Life Commission's brochure about itself, photographs and modest biographies of the bookkeeper and secretaries, all female, were given alongside those of the professionals (all but one male), as if they had equal status and responsibilities. The steady marginalization of the handful of women pastors is an important result of fundamentalist pressure. "Brother," as a term both of address and reference, is often used, a nice bit of democracy or phony bonhomie, but "sister" scarcely at all. A former WMU president visited one church as its first female speaker—she was called "Brother Dorothy."

One senior pastor, when asked why, despite his principled and consistent progressive political positions, he stayed in the denomination, replied, "Never for one instant have I contemplated leaving the Southern Baptist Convention, my marital union, or the Democratic Party." Without acknowledging how insulting that was to his wife, he went on to talk, remarkably, of sonnets and the joys of writing poetry (and by extension, living) within tight rules. He feels that way about the SBC; many SBs may feel that way about the family system they promote and defend. Structured inequality, deference, authority patterns—to some they are a clear denial of autonomy, adulthood and, they might say, "authentic personhood." To others they are security and a freedom from awkward choices and responsibilities, an authoritarian bargain perhaps more tenable in two-person, one-career couples.

Finally, the age-old value for white southerners of black families as "negative reference groups" needs to be emphasized. Part of the traditionalism, then, is an effort to stress SB conformity and stability, to themselves at least, in contrast to black aberration and flux (and higher birth rate). Television personality (and former SB pastor and presidential candidate) Pat Robertson argues that "the home . . . is the basic unit of the church . . . you have to have some unit, and the home/family has been it so far. Now when this goes you have the corollary problems . . . you have the flotsam and jetsam of the ghetto where young people don't know who their parents are" (Michaelson 1979: 20).

Family Ministry and Church Discipline

Southern Baptists are not alone in finding "family" an attractive focus for pastoral concern and denominational activity, but also Evangelicals and mainstream Protestants and, especially, Roman Catholics in the United States. In fact, there is a kind of convergence taking place between Catholic and SB family styles. Why the similarity? Although Catholic prudery, fil-

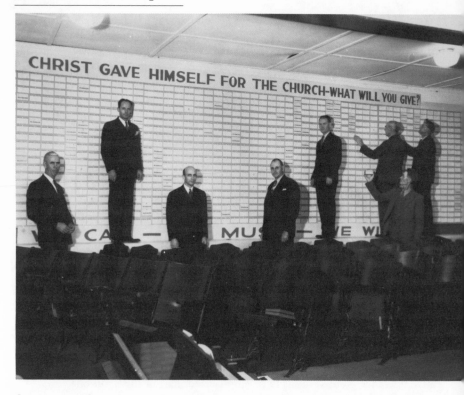

Sex-segregated fundraising, University Baptist Church, Abilene, Texas. (Photograph courtesy of the E. C. Dargan Research Library, Sunday School Board, Southern Baptist Convention.)

tered through an Irish-dominated church, has one set of roots, and SB prudery is WASP- and class-based, leaders in both churches realize that lack of sexual satisfaction (or "compatibility" as it used to be called) had something to do with the incidence of divorce. In the background, dim and unacknowledged, were Freud and Havelock Ellis and Kinsey with messages that humans were sexual beings. Both Catholics and SBs have come to the point at which they acknowledge that sexuality in marriage is good stuff. Priest-sociologist Andrew Greeley's *Sexual Intimacy* is very close to Marabel Morgan's *Total Woman*, and there are evangelical versions of the genre, conspicuously the work of the LaHayes.

In the early days the focus was on "moral purity" or education in "spiritual values," but current materials give more recognition to diversity of family style, more compassion and forgiveness. There is more insight from the social sciences and a very heavy underpinning of pop psychology, the bootstrap approach to mental health. Southern Baptists, like many other Americans, love checklists: five steps to . . . . , three stages of . . . . , seven types of . . . . A key figure in the whole picture is the pastor, with his narrow education, his shallow psychological understanding, and his very male and very American crippling heritage of emotional numbness about his inability, as one wise bureaucrat put it, to apply the Golden Rule within his own family. The same bureaucrat pointed out that "pastoral care" is a way for the pastors to cope with their own feelings. Because of their awkwardness in doing this, they tend to overemphasize the rote approach and wind up with the checklists — put a label on it and it will go away. This process enables them to try to climb back to their own absolutism. In more than one southern city the headings "Clergy" and "Marriage and Family Counselors" are cross-referenced in the Yellow Pages. The responsibility that goes with this identification, however, may become weighed more carefully with the potential of lawsuits for clergy malpractice.

Another bureaucrat pointed out that the very rarity of divorce in the social worlds of some of these people made it more suspicious. He, in his midthirties, had parents who had never known a divorced person in all the years he was growing up. But the incidence of *pastoral* divorce has increased pastoral awareness, if not their ability to empathize, and a surprising number of middle-aged pastors have mentioned their *own* parents' divorces.

Intermixed with all these confused feelings is a pervasive ambivalence about affluence, or "materialism," as they like to call it. This often translates into a message that wives are working for "trinkets" or out of greed, rather than to provide special care for an elderly parent or to help their kids get to college. The link between poverty and lots of children is known but again unacknowledged, as is the inverse one between lots of children and divorce. Southern Baptists "represented broken homes almost entirely as products of individual moral failure," Eighmy writes (1972: 120). The pressure to do so and thus to deny the connections between family life and macro-events like wars and depressions is to compromise their ability to help people except in the most superficial way.

In the background is past and continuing sexual repression and prudery, the emphasis on interiority and sin, the "virtual equation of Christian holiness with abstinence from personal vices," as Samuel Hill called it (1972: 21), an equation which puts SBs again together with U.S. Catholics up to the last decade. The uproar over the time an editor of *Hustler*, albeit born-again, spoke at Wake Forest, or the *Playboy* philosophy was targeted immediately to be shot down at a Christian Life Commission seminar, or Jimmy Carter was interviewed in the latter magazine indicate the frantic fear of association with that slice of American life. Sexual behavior is, of course, one of the most crucial ways in which class insecurities are expressed—some behaviors "look cheap," while "modest" goes with "well-bred" or well-mannered. One pastor attributed the fixation on sexuality (as shown by the degree of its repression) as a striving for power: "One's own body", he said, "is the only area where the individual has control."

The complex of "family" issues is the focus of much current SB argument over church-state relationships. Southern Baptists wish to strengthen "the family" as an institution against the threat of state power and social diversity; in trying to achieve this, they must ask the state to finance certain activities which will serve to strengthen family and parental control. One state WMU director said, "Let's find a way to do Christian ministry and get the government to pay for it" (Petty 1979: 49). Now the fundamentalist insistence on school prayer (an extension of family/church authority into the institution they cannot all afford to duplicate) challenges historic SB commitments and intrudes on cooperation with Roman Catholics and Jews.

Finally, the emphasis on "family" leads to another great denial of difference in class interests in which Southern Baptists have such long experience. A metaphor was proffered to half a dozen pastors (hearing that it was culinary, they looked patient): "It's like making a cake that breaks when you take it out of the pan, but if you smear enough frosting on it the cracks won't show." They liked it, relieved because it was brief and they understood it, and pleased with the image of slathering all that thick, gooey, sweet frosting—all that LOVE—over broken cakes and broken hearts and concealing the fissures within. Family life and family problems link, emotionally and sentimentally, human beings across class and cultural breaches. Keep the focus on the common experience of individual pain; the differences in social experience which may be its cause, and in resources to cope with the result, will recede.

Historically, as SBs are aware, for all their vaunted concern with "family," families were immediately splintered by sex and age when they entered the church building. Now the age-grading becomes more intricate as pre-schoolers are divided into three groups and junior- and senior-high boys separated, all in the pursuit of greater control. And the sex segregation potentiates the role separation and its lifelong reinforcement. Perhaps, it is obviously presumed, Bible study groups have different latent functions for men and for women – who leads them, how democratic or participatory the meeting is, who comes and why, and whether any extracurricular matters are discussed. In the long run, the issues are how the power structure of the sub-group relates to the one in the church and how both relate to the one in the community.

Today there is much more emphasis on couples, but most often the couples and the singles (modern demography predicts most of the singles will be women) are kept apart. The above questions may again be applied. The weekly bulletin of a big church in Montgomery (June 1982) shows that the definition of "family" has sometimes not really been expanded:

FAMILY LIFE CONFERENCE – It's just around the corner! The Family Life Enrichment Conference will be June 25–June 27 here at Ridgecrest. Led by the internationally known husband-wife team . . . the conference will begin on Friday . . . at 7:00 p.m. with a Family Banquet. The weekend of studies, discussions and biblical teachings will conclude with the evening worship on Sunday. Every member of every family will be enriched by this conference . . . SINGLES BYW [Baptist Young Women] – There will be a brief meeting of this group immediately following the service this morning to discuss and vote on a project for the summer months.

The Minister of Counseling at the Falls Church, Virginia, parish who was mentioned at the beginning of this chapter describes the recruitment of his staff:

We expand by the use of interns as well as volunteers from the professional mental health field. But we are also able to broaden our ministries through a program of peer-counseling training . . . Out of these groups there emerged several people who seemed to possess unique gifts as well as basic caring for hurting people. Some of these individuals are lay leaders of growth groups formally organized within the counseling ministry. More importantly, the influence of this training has encouraged individuals to reach out with greater boldness and assurance that they can indeed be bearers of good cold water in Christ's name (Keeton 1982: 41).

No one would claim that these people do no good. There are large groups of Americans who can be helped just by having some attention paid to them – people who have lost any ability to tell the difference between friends and a support group. But the amateur "counselors" are given no clear limits on their abilities to help, no clear warnings of authentic serious illness to watch out for, or much (if any) clear guidance in overcoming their own prejudices. Much good may be done, some harm surely is; there is little indication that Southern Baptists in general might be aware of the difference.

"The entire fellowship served as an effective espionage system to rid the church of moral impurity. One's peers were one's guardians of the conscience; both public and private behavior were under scrutiny from fellow members," writes Milton C. Sernett of nineteenth-century Baptist church discipline (1975: 27). Cortland Victor Smith's study of North Carolina churches in the same period—"closely-knit bodies which exercised strict supervision over the life and conduct of their members" (1967: 133)—corroborates this. "In a way, church discipline was an early form of group counseling," says the historian Boles (1976: 131) about early nineteenth-century Kentucky. Church discipline was a brilliant solution to the challenge of providing a rough social order on a fluid and frightening frontier, of creating a cultural oasis that could be controlled. At the end of the twentieth century the homogeneity, the minute segmentation by age and marital status within that sameness, the proliferation of lay "leadership roles," the dangerous blend of prejudice, piety, and mental hygiene, the overwhelming bustling activity, and the obsession with sexual conformity attempt to accomplish the same ends.

Ideology: Theological, Social, and Aesthetic Dimensions

> What the Church needed, Erasmus argued, was a theology
> reduced to the absolute minimum. Christianity must be
> based on peace and unanimity, "but these can scarcely
> stand unless we define as little as possible." On many
> points "everyone should be left to follow his own judge-
> ment, because there is great obscurity in these matters."
>
> — Paul Johnson (1977: 275)

"Theology" and Ecclesiology

Of the many statements of the Southern Baptist "belief system," one of the most succinct and clearest is by Lynn May, Executive Director of the SB Historical Commission (1979):

> Distinctive Baptist beliefs and practices are: (1) the authority and sufficiency of
> the Scriptures; (2) the priesthood of the believer; (3) salvation as God's gift of
> divine grace received by man through repentance and faith in Jesus Christ; (4)
> a regenerated church membership; (5) baptism, by immersion, of believers only;
> (6) two ordinances, baptism and the Lord's Supper, viewed primarily as symbols
> and reminders; (7) each church as an independent, self-governing body, the
> members possessing equal rights and privileges; (8) religious liberty for all; and
> (9) separation of church and state.

May melds "beliefs and practices," combining ritual, membership requirements, ecclesiology, and politics with aspects of the belief system.
Even Southern Baptist experts thus show some elasticity in their understanding of the boundaries of theology.

Authority of the Bible. Every great tradition has (1) a body of sacred writing, and (2) an approved group of commentaries and emendations upon it. In Hinduism, there are the *sriti* and the *smriti*, in Judaism the Torah and the Talmud, for Moslems the Koran and the *hadith*. For Roman Catholics, there are the Bible and the "teachings of the church"; for many Protestants, the Bible and the Westminster or Augsburg Confessions or the Book of Common Prayer. Southern Baptists, holding fast to their ideal of non-creedalism, have until now lacked this kind of historically sanctioned touchstone, and could look, beyond the Bible, only to the dream of evangelization, the labyrinthine reality of denominational organization, and the shifting and fuzzy statements of belief.

Every great tradition must have a constitution, and a constitutional amendment process because (1) the world changes, bringing new challenges unforeseeable at the time of the original prophecy; (2) that prophecy may be inadequate for the changing position of the religious institution, since many religions have been born in a desperate egalitarianism which does not survive institutionalization, and (3) not least, language itself changes. The King James Version, "Authorized" five years before the death of Shakespeare, recedes from us, as his plays do, with each generation.

In the absence of a creed, or a set of interpretive rules by which new challenges might be evaluated, Southern Baptists can hold together only with a core belief structure of extraordinary generality and ambiguity. The Bible fills the need; it becomes a projective test, a protean Rorschach. As the code words have become "Biblical inerrancy," the Bible itself is less read than preached, less interpreted than brandished. Increasingly, pastors may drape a limply bound Book over the edges of the pulpit as they depart from it. Members of the congregation carry Bibles to church services; the pastor announces a long passage text for his sermon and waits for people to find it, then reads only the first verse of it before he takes off. The Book has become a talisman.

Devotion to Scripture has been a peculiarly Protestant trait. In the effort to challenge the non-biblical accretions of the Roman Catholic Church, the Bible had to become the supreme authority for the Reformers. And it served its purpose well, democratizing the nascent churches and providing the authority for not only liturgical and ecclesiological but also political movements of crucial importance to a modern market economy. Protestants absorbed the Galilean challenge, since the effort to defeat it had made the Roman Catholic Church look ridiculous. The Enlightenment only reinforced the role of reason and hostility towards every form of tyranny over people's minds. And the whole orientation stood as an inexhaustible source of religious creativity until something happened on the way to the twentieth century.

The nineteenth-century florescence (mostly Germanic) in the natural and physical sciences, and extension of the scientific method into the more sensitive fields of archaeology, philology, and theoretical linguistics, eventually found irresistible application to the Bible and its history. That some of the biblical miracles were thus challenged was less important than the fact that the results seemed to show that the Bible itself was the work of human beings – many, fallible human beings writing at different times with their own personal agendas.

How could organized, traditional Christianity respond? One possibility was acceptance of science and its findings, moving theological discussion to metaphor and ethics, the so-called liberal or modernist strain. Theologically, Social Gospel activity was partly grounded in postmillennialism, the proposition that Jesus will return only after humans have created a just world (the Kingdom of God) here. There were a few Southern Baptists involved – B. H. Carroll, the founder of Southwestern Seminary, and William Poteat, president of Wake Forest College, who told students to look beyond the Bible for truth.

A second major category of response might be called mystificatory, a declaration that historical truth and scientific accuracy are simply irrelevant to faith. It is easy to parody this position: "Believe *because* it is impossible," it seems to say. The most popular non-SB theologians referred to by SB moderates are Karl Barth and Emil Brunner, both of whom, despite vast differences on some questions, belong in this category. And Rudolf Bultmann, the demythologizer who ended as a remythologizer, with "an empirically nonfalsifiable stance very similar to Barth's," Peter Berger says (1979: 110). Barth and Brunner are usually called "neo-orthodox," and their approaches permit a return to a self-contained Bible which operates without reference to the external world, independently of its validation.

The third possible response to nineteenth-century science was a reactionary one, and it neatly appeared as Fundamentalism in the years before the United States entered World War I. The term comes from a series of pamphlets published between 1910 and 1915, to which SB theologians E. Y. Mullins of Southern Seminary and J. J. Reeve and Charles B. Williams of Southwestern contributed essays. One version of the famous Five Points included an infallible Bible, the Virgin Birth, the Atonement, the Resurrection, and the Second Coming. Most Southern Baptists had no quarrel with these principles. (Those tempted by modernism quietly moved to another denomination.) Thus SBs did not at this time suffer the public defections that tortured much of American Protestantism in the '20s. Some observers believe that it is now, sixty years later, that SBs are undergoing these same trials.

An analysis of the more recent theological controversies which have troubled Southern Baptists reveals an interesting pattern. Almost all of the nineteenth-century ones—the Campbellites, the Landmark movement, and the Whitsitt episode (which was really a riposte to the Landmarkers)—were primarily concerned with ecclesiology, matters of supra-church organization.

The major controversies of this century, however, all have to do with the book of Genesis. Of course, it is "the beginning," and the *Grundgesetz* for what follows. But there are two additional, and related, reasons. The basic Christian myth, as given in the second, earlier version in Genesis, runs like this: Adam and Eve, the first people, lived innocent and free. The serpent tempted Eve, and she persuaded Adam to follow her into sin, to be shared by all their descendants. Such sin would have ended in eternal hellfire and damnation, but that Jesus, the Son of God, chose martyrdom in order that the rest of humanity might be redeemed. As historian Ferenc Szasz puts it, "Without a Fall, what purpose did a Reconciler serve?" (1982: 2).

Elizabeth Cady Stanton emphasized another link to contemporary controversy. The role of Eve in the story, she suggested, is central to the need for salvation, and thus for the Savior. Without Eve and Adam (and by extension, the whole of Genesis), "the bottom falls out of the whole Christian theology. Here is the reason why in all the Biblical researches and higher criticisms, the scholars never touch the position of women" (Kraditor 1970: n.81). That this aspect of the myth is still operative for SBs may be demonstrated by the reproduction of the resolution against women's ordination passed at the 1984 annual meeting and distributed by the First Baptist Church in Dallas, a week later. The church emphasized the relevant passage thus: "WHEREAS, While Paul commends women and men alike in other roles of ministry and service (Titus 2: 1–10), he excludes women from pastoral leadership (I Tim. 2: 12) to preserve a submission God requires *because man was first in creation and the woman was first in the Edenic fall* (I Tim. 2: 13ff.)."

The grandest public battle yet over the Bible was the series of debates on how to teach creation, or evolution, of the 1920s, culminating in the famous Scopes trial. This, too, was a controversy centering on Genesis, substituting a Rise for a Fall, sketching a theory of the development of ever-more-complex organisms and, by implication, denying any Purpose but adaptation and survival.

The timing was curious. *The Origin of Species* was published in 1859. Controversy was immediate and continuous in England, and American scientists and theologians participated in the discussion, most of the latter adopting the position of "theistic evolutionists." Southern Baptist scientist William Poteat saw evolution as "only the method of God's operation" (Hinson 1984: 19). These leaders accepted evolution as a process but claimed that God had designed it and pushed the starting button. Depreciating the Fall, they were left with the same problems; James J. Thompson, Jr. summarizes their difficulty: "With God's sovereignty diminished man would fashion a new moral code in the perverse depth of his mind . . . With the concept of sin banished there would be no guilt, and without a sense of wrongdoing man would run wild" (1982: 108). Society needed super-naturalistic religion and biblical literalism in order to respect and follow authority. Certainly, for Southern Baptists, biblical reinforcement for hierarchical social relationships – white/black and man/woman being the crucial ones – could not be weakened.

The issue was a very long time coming to a head. Poteat, then president of Wake Forest and one of the few SBs with scientific training, spoke at Southern Seminary in 1900 on evolution without noticeable negative reaction, and wrote of it acceptingly as late as 1915. Some of the energies that might have gone into this struggle were absorbed by the War and then by the final push to ratify the Prohibition amendment. It was William Jennings Bryan who made evolution the central issue of modernism and linked them both to the German defeat and to the demands of American labor. In 1923 he claimed that "Darwin was undermining the Christian faith . . . and had become the basis of the world's most brutal war . . . and . . . the basis of the discord in industry" (Szasz 1982: 109). Bryan was aided in the anti-evolution controversy by Mississippi SB evangelist T. T. Martin.

The central phase can be seen as a classic church-state issue. The legal battles took place over school textbooks, only in the South, and not in every state. J. W. Porter, editor of the state SB newspaper, *The Western Recorder*, from 1905 to 1919, started the campaign against evolution in Kentucky; it was continued when Victor Masters took over, mobilizing some Baptists through the newspaper against other Baptists directed from Southern Seminary in Louisville. In Tennessee a small SB lobby pushed the anti-evolution bill through the legislature; here high school teacher Scopes was encouraged to challenge the law and was tried in 1925, with H. L. Mencken looking on.

North Carolina was the site of the most bitter struggle. T. T. Martin, who had won in Mississippi, was invited to lead the anti-evolutionists. Poteat, whose commitment to science and academic freedom was genuine, started writing columns supporting evolution in *The Biblical Recorder* in 1922. Gatewood writes, "He found it difficult to believe that anti-evolutionists could really be serious in their attempt to stamp out the theory of evolution, since it would be virtually impossible to 'disentangle and expurge' a conception so thoroughly embedded in the intellectual life of the day" (1966: 67–68). Livingston Johnson, then editor of the *Recorder*, refused to carry anti-Poteat writings, among them material by T. T. Martin, even as paid ads. The Baptists were here as elsewhere divided; the dispute raged for several years, but the goals of the anti-evolutionists failed. The bill did not pass, and Poteat did not resign or retire (even under noticeable shrinkage in state Baptist contributions), at least not until it no longer would look as if he had been forced out.

The evolution controversy did a great deal to emphasize southern distinctiveness and expose southern isolation, backwardness, and cultural poverty. The U.S. Census in 1920 gave appalling figures for the percentage of illiteracy: for native-born whites in North Carolina it was 6.8, in Louisiana 11.6, contrasted with 0.3 for Idaho and Utah. Mencken, sitting there in Baltimore, subscribing to all the Baptist and Methodist papers in the South (and lumping the two groups together in his scorn), exposed the gulf and helped to increase sectional feelings—feelings which inevitably became imbued with status anxiety and defensiveness.

The impact of the long controversy on the SB denomination as a whole was mixed. For four years an anti-evolution resolution passed at the annual meetings, culminating in the Houston statement of 1926. This affirmed that the Convention "accepts Genesis as teaching that man was the special creation of God, and rejects every theory, evolution and other, which teaches that man originated in, or came out of, a lower animal ancestry." A further resolution noted with approval that Southwestern Seminary had included this principle in its *Statement of Faith*, and expressed the hope that similar action would follow by other agencies of the Convention. The Education Commission and the Foreign Mission Board, at least, endorsed the statement, which ended with a pious plea that "the great cause of our present unrest and agitation over the Evolution question be effectively and finally removed in the minds of the constituency of this Convention and all others concerned." But other agencies refused.

In 1925 the Convention had adopted its first "faith statement" among outraged cries that Baptists were a non-creedal people. L. R. Scarborough, then president of Southwestern, wrote in the *Alabama Baptist* that year, "We are in great danger of being obsessed by anti-evolution, we must remember that we have other enemies of truth" (Szasz 1982: 31). Southern Seminary president E. Y. Mullins (SBC president also during the most crucial period) warned in the New Mexico paper that "thousands of young people conclude that the ministry and Christians generally are afraid of investigation and by a very short road arrive at the point where it is assumed that science or Christianity must be rejected" (Bernard 1926: 139). There was ambivalence, confusion, and vacillation throughout the Convention. "Dr. Mullins wobbled round a good deal, and on the whole gave encouragement to the anti-evolutionists, editor Virginius Dabney said" (Furniss 1954: n.120). Torn between fear of looking ridiculous and loyalty to the Bible, tortured by the difficulty of developing a synthesis, the SBC ducked and wove and adopted a creed. Typically, the issues were not faced directly, because there could be no solution that way. A lateral move was arranged, the focus for conformity and self-congratulation, but the underlying tensions were never resolved. The Convention did not divide; it capitulated to its commitment to the unity of the lowest common denominator.

There is really a long hiatus until the next theological struggle. Southern Baptist church historian McBeth attributes this gap to "the Depression, dustbowl, and outbreak of World War II" (1982: 86), but the battle over evolution seems to have resulted in more defensiveness and isolationism. Ties to interdenominational groups were unravelled and expressions of interest in social issues withdrawn.

The modern controversies seem to reflect a new wave of experimentation, a hope that more latitude would be available. This has turned out not to be so. One-third of the Southern Seminary faculty were fired in 1958 in order, inter alia, to dispose of one professor who was raising doubts about the biblical canon (i.e., which books should really be included).

In 1961, Ralph Elliott, then on the Midwestern Seminary faculty, arranged for the SBC publishing house to release *The Message of Genesis*, which "advanced mildly progressive viewpoints on the interpretation of some passages" (McBeth 1982: 87). The resultant storm raged in the state papers and reached the annual meeting the following June in San Francisco. The trustees of Midwestern had to respond, there was much fancy footwork and by that fall Elliott was out. McBeth details a typical non-resolution: "One reason the controversy lingered is that Elliott was never convicted of heresy, indeed, was never officially charged. He was dismissed for insubordination, for refusing to obey a request of the president of the seminary (1982: 89).

Those who had pressed to expose the full story were on both sides, either to defend him or to assure his punishment. In the wake of this curiously unsatisfying incident the Convention issued another "faith statement," the *Faith and Message* of 1963, which attempted to clarify and to some extent restate the earlier version. A decade later, Broadman Press issued a new series of volumes of Bible Commentary and the first one, on Genesis again, incorporating much of modern scholarship, started a battle. Once again, everyone, and no one, won—the book was formally withdrawn from sale, but the Convention couldn't bind the Sunday School Board, and the volume continued to be available.

A recent struggle, involving Dale Moody, a professor of theology at Southern Seminary, is of a different sort but illustrates the same pattern of equivocation and evasion. At the 1982 Arkansas State Convention, Moody preached on Hebrews 10:26 and II Peter 2:20, which he stated are the clearest of forty-eight New Testament passages which warn against apostasy or "falling away" ("backsliding" in lay terminology). The problem is that both Southern Baptist *Faith and Message* Statements affirm that this is impossible, a doctrine known as "security of the believer," "perseverance" or even, metathesized, "preservation of the saints."

Perseverance, which goes back at least to Augustine, was played down by medieval scholastics but revived during the Reformation. The subject of furious polemics in Puritan England, it was still one of the most controversial topics in American theology until the Civil War. Why should it continue to be a live issue? Clark Pinnock, then a New Orleans theology professor, wrote:

> Belief in the unconditional perseverance of the saints, or eternal security, is very widely entertained by multitudes of evangelical Christians, even though it belongs generically to . . . a doctrinal system which they do not generally hold in its other dimensions . . . What this . . . will unsettle . . . is a spurious assurance . . . of those who cling to eternal security while deliberately following lives of second or third rate discipleship (1969: 10),

or, as Moody himself put it, who live like the devil. Moody states that it is precisely because of his subservience to *Scripture* that he can challenge theological tradition, including his own. Such purism, and the intellectual and scholarly equipment to support it, are alienating to many who wish to blur the distinction. Some fundamentalists are convinced that Moody was setting a trap and resent him mightily therefor.

The Arkansas Convention voted by an estimated 85 to 90 percent majority a resolution asking the trustees of Southern Seminary to terminate Moody and anyone teaching the same ideas. The trustees, affirming their support for academic freedom, afraid of criticism from both sides, first found Moody a teaching post in Hong Kong (a long-range lateral transfer) but then withdrew the offer, ultimately putting him on paid leave until his imminent retirement. The issue of conflict between Southern Baptist creed and Baptist Bible was not openly discussed on its merits, and the controversy was again transformed into a question of authority, compromising Baptist principles as an uneasy equilibrium was restored, until the next time. Biblical inspiration, then, is questioned. Biblical authority is accepted when it is convenient or doesn't collide with tradition. And the informed and careful discussion necessary to resolve specific issues is bypassed in favor of a blindered chauvinism of the closed Book.

Fourteen million fierce individualists defining their belief system, even with wretchedly limited comparative information and typically American failures of analysis, could only produce an anarchy that would lead to splintering and the failure of the SBC as an institution. On the other hand, the commitment to religious liberty is one of the few aspects of Baptist history that links it to the wider national tradition and gains real support from outside groups of impeccable respectability and the possibility of functional cooperation with them.

The "Priesthood of Believers," Salvation, and the Fellowship of the Regenerate. Nobody argues about salvation, although some may understand it metaphorically and not talk about it. The "priesthood of believers" and "fellowship of the regenerate" are political and tricky, and the precise relationship between them open to question—whether they are coordinate or whether the latter follows from the former, for instance. They both grow, however, out of the very Protestant insistence on a direct line between individuals and God and God's word (the only intermediary, in some versions, to be Jesus) in the context of the Reformation argument against two classes of Christians (clergy and laity). This approach and the social conditions which gave rise to it reinforced political democracy, validating do-it-yourself vocations and lay control of church institutions. All of this was fed by illiteracy and feelings of intellectual inadequacy which themselves nourished attitudes of anti-professionalism and a suspicion of scholarship.

Against this basic democracy are posed the tendencies that come with size, power, and desire for acceptance: the professionalization of the clergy and the inevitable push toward bureaucratization and standardization that comes with wealth and growth. Added to these are certain peculiarly modern American problems, the development of personality cults around media performers (television preachers, star evangelists, or "Astrodome Isaiahs," as Will Campbell calls them), the tendency toward slickness and the commercial models in all forms of communication, and the pressures toward growth, which increase these tendencies. And a special Southern Baptist problem—the handing over of direction of the denomination as a whole to the pastorate and their families, who constitute 70 percent of the attendance at the annual meetings. One ominous trend is in the stated opposition to the ordination of women, for designation of a special status which is taboo to more than half the members automatically results in two classes of Christians again, exactly what Erasmus and Luther aimed to end. Further eroding SB Protestant principles, a 1988 resolution gave authority over individual conscience to local pastors.

Believers' Baptism by Immersion: Two Ordinances. Would anyone today choose martyrdom in order to defend total immersion? Even if that strong a defense is unlikely, the ritual is just different enough from other practices and just easy enough to perform or provide to ensure its continuance. "Believers" means adults, or non-infants, and this poses a more complex question. The individual's self-definition of "the normal religious experience" and the autonomous local church's power to set criteria (if any) both work against any restriction in the form of an age limit—and the constant pressure for numbers, for growth, militates against there being one at all. (Thirty percent of all SB baptisms in 1986 were of children under the age of twelve. If the Southern Baptist Convention wishes to restrict the power of children to guide its destiny, it will have to face these contradictions.) An occasional communion-type service, called the Lord's Supper, completes the minimalistic sacramental life. To say that these rituals are "viewed primarily as symbols and reminders" is to hammer old theological spikes into Catholics and Campbellites alike.

Local Church Autonomy. Here again a time-honored principle fights with political imperatives of growth, cooperation to maximize SB voice and power, and coordination of shared activities. Because relationships among a group of local or regional congregations are much more intimate, and the need for the kind of trust that will make functional cooperation possible so much clearer, the trend is for district associations to want homogeneity – of class, of "theology," of style – and to disfellowship the anomalous.

All this has been going on continuously as each controversy was aired. There is no documentary summary of such activity for the denomination as a whole, but women's ordination is becoming more frequent as the reason. Although some associations and state conventions have taken public stands supporting local autonomy in this matter, and in favor of women's ordination in principle, Bill Leonard of the Southern Seminary faculty pointed out (not in a SB denominational journal but in *The Christian Century*) that "the question of women's ordination may be the catalyst which ultimately brings schism to a diverse and increasingly disoriented denomination" (1984: 55). Fundamentalist pressure for conformity will increase the incidence of these episodes.

Religious Liberty. Baptists were born from the confused and heady matrix of English Protestantism. Those who were called Puritans came to this country to establish religious liberty – for themselves. Baptists, suffering, persecuted, resolved to strive for religious liberty "not only for ourselves but for all men" [*sic*] in the words of recent SB historians Hays and Stealy (1981: 188), who go on to cite the ringing eighteenth-century affirmations of Baptist heroes: Robert Robinson, who said "Liberty to be a Christian implies liberty not to be a Christian," and John Leland, who promised that "no subordination of any one sect or denomination to another shall ever be established by law." It was these Baptist beliefs that found their way into the statutes of Virginia and eventually, in part through Leland's influence on James Madison, into the Bill of Rights in the federal Constitution.

As the years have rolled on, SBs have continued to refer to the tradition despite their doubts about giving what they may define as "cults" full status as religions. In 1986 the SBC resolved that "the suppression of religious expression in American life is destructive of the religious liberty of Baptists" and that its members should "decry denial of the constitutional right of voluntary prayer and Bible reading in the public schools as permitted by the Supreme Court." (Ambiguity about "voluntary" is the crux of the controversy.) Whether this concern for the liberty *of Baptists* represents a shift from the historic commitment is not yet clear.

The two ordinances, from publicity photos of the 1950s: The Lord's Supper. (Photograph courtesy of the E. C. Dargan Research Library, Sunday School Board, Southern Baptist Convention.)

Baptism. (Photograph courtesy of the E. C. Dargan Research Library, Sunday
School Board, Southern Baptist Convention.)

Separation of Church and State. This is one of the true "Baptist distinctives," growing organically out of the commitment to democracy at the individual and local church level, the apprehension about central authority, the traditional fear of dogmatism, and the resultant emphasis on religious liberty. Baptists were denied their rights, imprisoned, and even burned at the stake by governments which tried to tell them what to think. And from their seventeenth-century beginnings in America they have been among the shock troops in church-state battles.

Church-state separation is perceived as a one-sided wall. Church people have every right – perhaps a special obligation – to witness on ethical questions as they affect public policy. Such activity may include sermons, petitions, public educational meetings, resolutions, lobbying, and all other forms of speech guaranteed by the other part of the First Amendment. The church-state questions, strictly defined, arise when the state attempts, from whatever motives, to become involved with the churches, or with religion in general.

The Southern Baptist record leads to a rather stark conclusion that no amount of magnificent rhetoric can hide: after Baptists themselves stopped being the objects of persecution, a great deal of the energy behind their activities has come from two sources, anti–Roman Catholicism and self-interest. Claude W. Sumerlin's analysis of the state papers shows anti-Catholic editorials after the 1870s, when Catholics had become numerous enough to be a threat. In 1915 the annual meeting passed a resolution on church-state separation which referred to "Romish hierarchy, Romish mobs . . . Romish schemes." Then the War Department's policy of pastoral access to the army camps, which seemed to SBs overwhelmingly to favor Roman Catholics, evoked outrage.

By 1924, when Al Smith broke into national politics, an SB resolution opposed the election of any wet candidate, or anyone "about whose Americanism there can be any question." When the Joint Committee established itself in Washington, one Baptist commented that its chief task was "to watch the Catholics"[!] (Reichley 1985: 244). The SBC opposed sending an American (Joseph Kennedy) to the Papal Coronation in 1939 and consistently has fought the appointment of presidential emissaries, let alone ambassadors, to the Vatican right up through Reagan's doing so. Tuition tax credits for private schools have been interpreted as favoring Roman Catholic parents and parochial schools, although there has been more favorable SB comment as "Christian" academies have proliferated in the South.

As the "welfare state" grew and federal and state funds became increasingly available for a wide variety of new purposes, SB sentiment became more divided. In 1936, for example, the annual meeting approved a resolution commending two of the seminaries for refusing student aid from the National Youth Administration. By 1949, however, acceptance of GI Bill funds was common. There was no agreement on federal assistance to schools and hospitals, as some SB hospitals took Hill-Burton construction funds but others were afraid of pressure for integration, nor on the so-called "housing allowance."

Southern Baptists at first opposed the inclusion of ministers and church workers in the Social Security system but then realized that it provided the sort of buffer against geriatric penury for their own people as it did for others. Nonetheless, they protested federal efforts to force them in any way to publicize their finances, "not because the churches wish to hide their financial affairs, but because the First Amendment requires that government not entangle itself in the affairs of the churches," according to Stan Hastey of the Baptist Joint Committee (1979).

The anti–Roman Catholic strain in this agitation scarcely diminished. J. M. Dawson, SB head of the Joint Committee from 1946 to 1953, organized the group known as "Protestants and . . . Other Americans United for Separation of Church and State" (later changed to "Americans United . . ."). In 1947 the annual meeting passed a resolution approving a constitutional amendment forbidding the "use of public monies for private non-tax supported institutions of any kind." The ambiguity of Joe McCarthy and the stunning blow of the Brown decision in 1954 dampened these cries, but then came the threat of a Roman Catholic president. Jack Kennedy's famous Houston meeting in the summer of 1960 was with an audience primarily of Southern Baptist pastors. An SBC resolution that year on "Christian Citizenship" and one the following year on "Religious Liberty and Education" were clearly aimed at reminding him of his stated promise to put patriotism above denominational loyalty. In 1963 the revised Faith and Message Statement underlined SB commitment: "Church and State should be separate. The State owes to every church protection and full freedom in the pursuit of its spiritual ends. In providing for such freedom no ecclesiastical group or denomination should be favored by the State more than any other . . . the Church should not resort to the civil power to carry on its work . . . the State has no right to impose taxes for the support of any religion . . . "

The passage was reaffirmed in 1967, and since "an increasingly complex society constantly raises new questions in application of the separation principle," the Convention asked the U.S. Congress to help clarify the responsibility of the judiciary in interpreting the meaning of the Constitution for separation of Church and State, including the legality of federal funds in church-sponsored programs. As late as 1970 there was a resolution mentioning segregated academies and opposing their support from public funds. The following year opposition was expressed to President Nixon's "unprecedented action" in setting up a commission on non-public schools.

In 1979, however, after a challenge to the Internal Revenue Service ruling that denied tax exemption to private schools discriminating on the basis of color (the so-called "Bob Jones ruling," after the South Carolina university) the Convention saw this action as violating "the constitutional guarantees of separation of church and state and the free exercise of religion." It requested that the Joint Committee, "while being sensitive to our position on racism, work vigorously to maintain the separation of church and state, to protect the free exercise of religion, and to oppose specifically the Internal Revenue Service's proposed intrusions into church owned and operated schools."

But in 1983, after the Supreme Court had ruled against the IRS, the Convention showed itself to be so divided over the issue that a resolution could not be adopted, and the chair (Draper) ruled that consideration would have to be postponed. He remarked that "Southern Baptists have stood solidly on this issue"—solidly, that is, on both sides, as the fundamentalists found their voices.

The Christian Life Commission's reluctance to follow fundamentalist absolutism on the abortion issue has also been framed in anti–Roman Catholic language. "I do not accept the Roman Catholic dogma that a conceptus of 24 hours has equal value with the life of the mother—you do have to use moral judgements with regard to abortion sometimes. I think one does not make blanket judgements . . . on the basis of Roman Catholic dogma or anybody else's dogma," said Foy Valentine (*Recorder*, 18 Jan. 1986: 3).

While the separation principle indeed has deep roots in Baptist history, it has thus increasingly been compromised in practice in recent years. The SBC did not, for example, join the forty religious and civil liberties groups submitting *Amicus* briefs in the Rev. Sun Myung Moon's case before the Supreme Court in 1984. The SBC chooses not to face the contradictions inherent in the military chaplaincy, and there are anomalies like the presence of thirty-two Bible faculty members chosen by Texas Baptists in the University of Texas system until a ruling against them by the state Attorney General in 1985. Since the so-called New Christian Right sees biblical authority and the existence of God as cultural givens (and thus unintrusive by definition) and prayer in schools is one of the items on its political agenda, these questions cannot be expected to go away soon.

Exclusivity and Anti-Ecumenism

Southern Baptists' steadfast reluctance to unite with other Baptist bodies or to join the various interdenominational groups over the years has caused them to be called the problem child of American Protestantism. Many SBs, and some outsiders, attribute this isolationism to Landmark influence. Raymond Ryland, who studied the topic in detail, concluded that this was not the real reason; rather, he says, it is the belief that "as a distinct movement, Southern Baptists' unique mission in the world [is] to bring the gospel truth to the world as no other Christian tradition can. They believe that they have, in other words, a unique stewardship of gospel truth for which they are accountable to God himself . . . This sense of mission has been the strongest single reason, and the basic reason, for Southern Baptist aloofness from ecumenical involvement" (1969: 329–30).

This is not necessarily non-Landmark, but even if the Landmark historical strain is not still active in its original form, the conditions which led to its popularity still exist. The aloofness continues to be adaptive; the sectionalism, the defensiveness, the self-imposed inbreeding and isolation are still there, making comparisons unnecessary. In addition, the Southern Baptists have grown so big (for some of the same reasons) that they don't have to cooperate. Their size and strength result in part from their refusal to compromise with the liberal pressures which ecumenical cooperation would involve.

A review of their relations with other denominations from the closest relatives outwards shows a history of intimate enmity. Southern Baptists belong to the Baptist World Alliance, an organization of Baptist groups from a hundred countries, which meets every five years for discussion of common problems. Southern Baptist annual meeting reports show repetitive complaints about liberal tendencies observed in the BWA. A North American Baptist Fellowship, a loose association of U.S. Baptist groups with Baptists of Canada and Mexico, has even more limited functions. The more activist relationship of the SBs with eight other groups in the Baptist Joint Committee on Public Affairs has already been described. Southern Baptist size and resources and reluctance to compromise inevitably lead to difficulties. Their attitude is like that of the United States toward international bodies at various times – wary of any situation it cannot control. But its very threat of domination leads to resentment that it is incapable of comprehending and reinforces its standoffishness.

American Baptists ("Northern" ones) call themselves an "evangelical, ecumenical, and interracial denomination." On all counts – which may in part be in deliberate differentiation from the southerners – they of course run into difficulties with the SBC. Their mutual evangelicalism, while theoretically unexceptionable, has often brought them into competition. With Western expansion they soon ran into each other, and a long series of agreements not to poach on each other's migrants inevitably broke down, especially after World War II.

The northerners' ecumenism is another source of contention. Because of SB isolationism, the very differences in attitude toward cooperation lead to a failure to engage in it. To the SBs, ecumenism means weakness through compromise and loss of control; to the northerners it means strength through compromise and sharing.

On interracialism it is scarcely necessary to comment. About one-third of the American Baptist Convention (ABC) is made up of minorities, the largest proportion of any of the mainstream denominations, even though there are many homogeneous congregations and underrepresentation at the top. The SBC is not prepared for either those numbers or the commitment they imply. The relationship between southern and northern Baptists highlights the shallowness and irrelevancy of theological components in the American tradition. The differences are social, political, and stylistic – perhaps all the more irreconcilable for that.

There are three ecumenical Protestant groups Southern Baptists might join. The Federal (now National) Council of Churches was started in 1908, in the flush of euphoria about mission cooperation. Southern Baptists were at first interested, but the enthusiasm of the War Department during World War I for lumping all Protestants together chilled SB response and the evolution controversy killed it. The World Council of Churches is a separate and independent group, founded in 1948 in the heyday of international cooperation after the Second World War. The SBC was invited to become a charter member but declined at that time, using the perennial argument of local church autonomy.

In 1941 an American Council of Christian Churches was founded to form a basis for cooperation among denominations to the "right," politically and theologically, of the mainstream. (Members of the Federal Council were explicitly excluded.) In response to this, the National Association of Evangelicals was brought into being the following year, a loose confederation of some thirty-five small denominations also with a distinctly conservative stance. The Southern Baptists belong to neither of these groups, both of which they vastly outnumber. Although there might be less theological compromise at stake in associating with one of them, the latter contains some of those leftist evangelicals (like the *Sojourners* people) whose political positions on, say, peace and disarmament issues (not to mention "race") many SBs would find uncongenial.

The historic anti–Roman Catholic bias of the Southern Baptists has already been stressed. Victor Masters illustrates the tone (as of 1912, to be sure):

> Roman Catholicism, which never changes, will inevitably control our nation and transform all our Protestant ideas, unless we awaken to the danger and arrest her progress . . . As the South is the stronghold of Protestantism in the United States the responsibility is upon us to save the nation from papal control, for there is no doubt in the mind of those who understand the situation that the Vatican has formed a gigantic conspiracy to make itself felt in this country (138–139).

It doesn't stop. At the 1975 annual meeting a man from California, perhaps alarmed by Southern Baptist–Roman Catholic exchanges, made the motion "that all Convention-sponsored witness dialog with Catholics be with the purpose of leading them into a personal faith in Christ Jesus and to serve Christ through a local membership in a Southern Baptist church." These sentiments were repeated in 1987 as fundamentalist dominance was assured.

A generation ago, historical theologian Samuel Hill could compare the SBs and the RCs and find them both dogmatic, authoritarian, and exclusivistic in the regions where they dominate: "highly self-conscious, . . . concerned to conserve dogma, and more important, old forms of old dogmas, . . . isolated from the wider Christian community, . . . ingrown, . . . with little incentive to be self-critical and reformist" (1967: 227–228n.). Today, American Roman Catholics are sparkling with innovations, but the SBs have yet to convene a Vatican II. The RCs, some of them now more introspective, realize what is happening and at least frame the terms of the struggle in ways that are comprehensible to all sides. Southern Baptists, most of them, are light years away from that understanding. They need the old enemy, even as, in some ways, they become more like them.

Southern Baptist relationships with what they call "cults" are even more vexing. The Mormons, the Jehovah's Witnesses, and the Unification Church are all based in part on Christian writings and iconography; the Foreign Mission Board calls them "pseudo-Christian," and all are particularly troublesome since they are active proselytizers. At one service at the First Baptist Church, Dallas, in June 1984, a large group of SBs were given a prayerful send-off—they were going to Utah on a short-term mission. Thinking of retaliation is inevitable as Mormons, in particular, have become more expansive outside their own Empire. Even Joe Edward Barnhart's erudite study (1986) of the current controversy ends with a warning: "The Mormons Are Coming."

Jews present SBs with different dilemmas, ambiguity and ambivalence. There is an intrinsic conflict between the historic nativist anti-Semitism of the SBs and respect for the Bible they share. But American Jews are divided between pleasure at support for Israel and apprehension about intolerance and the old fundamentalist approach to conversion. Reform Rabbi Alexander Schindler expresses these fears: "The deepest reasons for the support given to Israel by the evangelical Fundamentalists are theologically self-serving. As they read Scripture, Jesus cannot return for the Second Coming until all the Jews are in the whole of their Biblical land and then converted to Christianity" (Hill and Owen 1982: 95–96).

After Bailey Smith made his famous remark about Jewish prayers not being heard by God, he visited Israel (not at its expense, he was careful to announce). A CBS-TV documentary on American-Israeli relations showed Smith intoning in typical SB pseudo-intimacy to an Israeli rabbi, "We love you . . . " With a deep bass chuckle the rabbi replied, "We love to be loved." In 1986 a proposed resolution referred to the "Judeo-Christian tradition," whereupon a messenger moved to delete the "Judeo-." Tension between the fundamentalist SBs, with their special vision of a Jewish future, and the Foreign Mission Board, which would love to be loved in Moslem lands as well, and the underlying nativist ambivalence will predictably continue.

Attitudes toward television evangelists are ambiguous and complex. Billy Graham, a member of the First Baptist Church in Dallas, was first cheered by the Convention when he became a national figure in the 1950s. Few are the subsequent years when he failed to address the annual meeting, although sometimes his wife has taken his place. In general the SBC both admires the televangelists' success and is jealous of the competition they provide, not only for members but for financial resources, loyalty, and attention; it is always wary of anything it cannot control. A 1987 resolution, carefully impersonal, deplored financial mismanagement anywhere in Christian ministry.

Despite these difficulties, there are many examples of cooperation among local churches on issues of common concern. And even the SBC as a whole will cooperate on ad hoc functional projects. In 1984, for example, a joint effort of SBs with the National Council of Churches and the National Council of Catholic Bishops produced a packet of materials for Holocaust memorial services.

Social Ethics

The definition of politics, Richard Hofstadter advises, should not be limited to "who gets what when and how, etc" but also "who perceives what public issues, in what way and why?" (1965: ix). The "social gospel" movement did reach the South, and the Southern Baptists. By 1900, Ferenc Szasz writes, SBs were "heavily involved in temperance reform, antigambling crusades, campaigns to eliminate political corruption, the promotion of public morality, care of orphans and the aged, and attacks on child labor" (1982: 62–63). Further, he finds that *The Ethics of Jesus and Social Progress,* by Charles Spurgeon Gardner (1914) was "a major treatment of social Christianity by a Southern Baptist," and E. Y. Mullins (the theologian and president of Southern and the SBC during the evolution controversy) took a "moderate social gospel stance." (The SB *Encyclopedia* says nothing of this side of Mullins' character, and indeed lacks any entry for "social gospel.")

Clearly, such a stance was controversial. Victor Masters treated it with his usual vivid style:

> The irresponsible popular theological twaddle in Sunday supplements, popular magazines, and the books of rationalistic professors of learning in great educational institutions, have not yet made the Christian bodies of the South turn away from the doctrines of the Bible for the modern gospel of salvation through bettering the environment . . . Southern Christianity . . . has not yet been seriously weakened by the new world-gospel of humanitarian service, aside from the Bible and its Christ. With the record of his own teachings that he went after the heart and not the outward man, and that he set up his Kingdom in the midst of far worse social evils than we now know, without instituting a campaign against them, yet the modern partisan of salvation by social improvement boldly seeks to discredit the churches of Christ (1918: 26–27).

Although there were some experiments in social activism, particularly by SB women, these were dampened by the effects of the evolution controversy. Church growth expert Peter Wagner claims that SBs continued to grow (in contrast to Methodists and Presbyterians) precisely because they "prioritized the evangelistic mandate over the cultural mandate . . . they never allowed their social responsibility to take priority over evangelism" (quoted in Stafford 1984: 64). But this is the very reason they're underrepresented in Congress, according to SB former U.S. Representative John Buchanan: "the lack of emphasis in Baptist churches on the important social issues with which governments must deal" (1984: 10).

The issues in which SBs have or have not been involved can be usefully separated into five groups: war, peace and foreign policy; family structure, sexuality and reproductive ethics; other occasions for sin, "vice," and questions of personal "morality"; distributive justice, or economic equity; and "race," which is in part an issue of distributive justice, but also includes "civil rights," political participation, the role of law, and status questions.

War and Peace. C. Welton Gaddy, in his study of the Christian Life Commission, was surprised to find that neither it nor its predecessor made any comment on the morality of World War I or II. Nor did the Convention as a whole, which rather concentrated on the opportunities for evangelism in the camps or the social dislocation leading to a higher divorce rate.

At the North Carolina state meeting in 1967, a resolution against the Vietnam War received exactly seventeen votes from the more than 3,000 messengers. There were, instead, many calls for prayers; Baptists for the most part felt that they either could not or should not take any action designed to bring about peace (Blevins 1980: 238).

The *Christian Century* was struck by the tone of the 1972 meeting: "most of the faithful who gathered in the City of Brotherly Love appeared to have some difficulty distinguishing between Old Glory and the Cross, God and country, four-square patriotism and Christian faith" (1972: 805–6). The Southern Baptist Convention, it went on to comment, was the only major denomination that has refused to criticize the war.

There is, however, a Southern Baptist Peace Movement, growing out of the activities of some professors of Southern Seminary. Its tabloid publication seems well-meaning, sincere, innocuous, and bland. It cites longtime SB support for peace and disarmament, but its programmatic approach is not likely to cause any loss of sleep in the Pentagon.

The beginnings of interest in world hunger exist. The publication *Seeds* comes out of a Southern Baptist church in Georgia, the Foreign Mission program has included direct relief efforts, and there is lay involvement in *Bread for the World.*

Family Issues. The second category of social ethics issues relates to family structure, sexuality, and reproductive behavior. Most of the current so-called "social" issues are really "sexuality" issues. The development of SB attitudes, as these issues became controversial in American law and social policy, has been conservative throughout, with the single and striking exception of contraception, which was quickly but quietly accepted and defined as a non-moral issue.

The SBs were late on higher education for women, but much of this tardiness can be attributed to the paucity of resources. Baylor had a woman graduate in 1855; in general, women had to promise to use their education only at home. Most of the SB women's colleges were started in the 1890s. *Biblical Recorder* editor Gerald Johnson opposed coeducation at Wake Forest College as late as 1930.

As previously noted, the suffrage movement in the South was intertwined first with abolition and then the temperance movement. As abolition was accomplished and SB attention became focused on alcohol, the value of women's votes was seen in a new light. State Baptist newspapers approved even as they remained opposed to allowing women any authority in the church. And a constitutional amendment giving votes only to white women was unthinkable.

As the divorce rate in the United States began to increase in the 1890s its legal and moral issues began to receive widespread attention. As some state laws were liberalized, great disparities arose which were taken advantage of by desperate people. Theodore Roosevelt urged a uniform code in 1905, and there was a general movement during the 1920s for standardized marriage and divorce laws. (Perhaps the triumph of the prohibition amendment encouraged a belief in the further potential of federal legislation.) Southern Baptists found this a congenial approach; at the 1920 meeting the Social Service Commission urged action toward that end. In the following year, however, the Commission had realized that federal legislation might overrule southern state anti-miscegenation laws, and it was more dubious; by 1932 it was sure there would be a federal law.

By now this is a dead issue, since anti-miscegenation laws have been declared unconstitutional. Although overall SB attitudes toward divorce have softened and there is much more emphasis on love and forgiveness, there are still many echoes of the old fears and much ambivalence. As one seminary graduate put it, there is "charity toward those who repent" but still "an unforgiving stance."

The development of contraception as an issue and the curious Southern

Baptist response to it is a complicated history. Margaret Sanger began "birth control" work in the United States in 1913, and her various legal difficulties were subject to much comment in the press. Improvements in vulcanized rubber, and growing medical interest, brought grudging approval from Anglicans in 1931, increasing criticism from Catholic leaders, and expressions of concern from some other Protestants.

Sumerlin (1968), in his analysis of the state papers, reports unanimous censure for birth control between 1901 and 1945. Masters believed in 1931 that the matter should be left to the woman's physician, which, of course, is to define it as a medical rather than a human rights issue. The Social Service Commission's report at the 1934 annual meeting (104), however, used strong language:

> For several years now there has been widespread and persistent agitation by a comparatively small but well organized group to induce Congress to amend the Penal Code of the United States so as to allow the dissemination of information concerning contraceptives and birth control. Of all the proposals for vicious and immoral legislation which have come forward in recent years we believe that nothing is more vicious or immoral than this proposal . . . As it appears to your Commission the whole purpose of the movement demanding such legislation is at base vicious. The proposal is part and parcel of the general breakdown in moral standards and ideals and would encourage the masses of people, insofar as they yielded to its dictates and suggestions, to live their lives on the plane of a course and repulsive animalism.

Southern Baptists explained the Convention's subsequent long silence during the period when "birth control" and "family planning" were burning moral issues for most American Protestant denominations in two ways; first, general sexual repression and prudery, and second, the definition of birth control as an economic issue, not a moral one. Some of the few women executives insisted that they had never given it a thought. Certainly Southern Baptists were as severely affected by the Depression as any other group in American society and their birth rate dropped as the overall one did, in response to the same imperatives. By 1935 the Sears, Roebuck catalog had a whole page of ads for contraceptives—"feminine hygiene products," they were called.

There is another factor in the South. "Before the American Public Health Association's 1959 policy statement, only seven states (Alabama, Florida, Georgia, Mississippi, North Carolina, South Carolina, and Virginia) included family planning as a regular part of their public health services" (Corsa 1966: 265), in striking contrast to the rest of the country, where their distribution was spotty. Soap heir Dr. Clarence Gamble's money provided some of the means, but the motive was clear and ugly. As one 1960 University of North Carolina Medical School graduate said when asked why, when that state was part of the southern bloc against the ERA, it was one of only nine states to continue funding abortions for very poor women, "Well, we don't want too many of them anyway."

Myrdal notes in his mammoth study:

> The South now leads other sections of the country in accepting birth control . . . it is reasonable to assume that the large number of undesired Negroes in the rural districts also has something to do with the lack of opposition on the part of the white South.
> Southerners will never publicly admit that they would like to see the Negro population decrease, but they do point to the poverty that could be avoided . . . Another indication that the presence of the Negroes is a main reason for the lack of opposition . . . is that . . . birth control is taboo as a subject for public or polite conversation even more in the South than in the North (1944: 179).

Southern Baptists would have been thoroughly involved in the planning and funding and carrying out of these programs for "them" and not anxious to talk about it even as they adapted their own behavior.

A few Southern Baptists still have come from very large families of eight or nine children. One said her father had felt it was a moral issue to have as many as God sent. Few young SB parents have only one child by choice, and most are happy with their two. The rule, and the rhetoric, is "responsible parenthood." In 1980 the annual meeting took a stand against the provision of birth control to minors without parental consent as a threat to the rights of the family. The SB bureaucracy is, of course, aware of the implications of smaller families for its evangelistic future and hopes for increased activity with adults to compensate.

On the abortion issue the Convention took a position as early as the 1971 annual meeting, allowing abortion on the basis of "carefully ascertained evidence of the likelihood of damage to the emotional, mental and physical health of the mother," close to a "pro-choice" position. The 1973 Supreme Court decision and the increased focus on the issue since then have involved the SBC in a steady retreat, and at each convention since the fundamentalist recrudescence in 1979 there have been pressures for ever more uncompromising negative stands. A recently founded independent group, Southern Baptists for Life, has forged links with the national anti-abortion groups and successfully pushed synchronization of an annual Right-to-Life Sunday.

A large part of American religion is currently tortured by the issue of homosexuality, particularly the incidence of gays within the seminaries and the religious world. One pole of thought would emphasize forgiveness, love, and an end to judgmental thinking and the division of human behavior into clear-cut categories. This view was represented on one occasion by an ethics professor at Southeastern Seminary. The other—fuzzy, uninformed, full of prejudices, appallingly inadequate in its epistemology, constantly shifting its ground without realizing it—was held by the most vocal of his students. They distanced themselves from their fear and their prurience with extensive quotations from materials a generation or two old and frequent references to the misinformation of friends and relatives. "When I see a couple of guys holding hands I find it hard to love them . . . I'm really scared of them . . ." said one. "Homosexuality, like cancer, has several causes . . . ," said another. They quoted Scripture out of context and criticized others for doing the same. Even the most fervent literalist or inerrantist will exempt Christians from some of the more arcane prescriptions of the Old Testament, or be murky about the ending of the Gospel of Mark, but on this issue even the dubious passages are quoted with full legal force.

One of the basic (and perfectly circular) arguments goes like this: a strong family life with well-marked sex differentiation in roles and authority between the parents is essential to prevent homosexuality in the male children; homosexuality is wrong, or a sin, because it confuses sex role differentiation, which was divinely ordained. Most of the makers of this argument are men.

Southern Baptists would undoubtedly prefer that the issue go away, but the gay rights movement has forced them to react. During the height of Anita Bryant's fame in 1978 (which, some observers feel, may have galvanized conservative Protestants, Catholics and Jews, equally obsessed with sexual orthodoxy, to realize the potential for political coalition around sexual and family issues), she received 3,273 votes for first vice-president of the SBC. The Convention resolved in 1980: "To deplore the proliferation of all homosexual practices, unnatural relations of any character, and sexual perversion . . . and reaffirm the traditional position of Southern Baptists that all such practices are sin and are condemned by The Word of God." (A San Francisco SB pastor said in 1986 on a talk show that the Bible could affirm a faithful and loving gay relationship and pointed out that there must be at least a million SB gays. Golden Gate Seminary took his name off an approved list, and his church lost its state missions support.) Acquired Immune Deficiency Syndrome (AIDS) frightens SBs, and they look for refuge in "Biblical morality." A 1988 resolution, more condemnatory than any adopted before by the SBC or any of the major denominations, overrode current psychological and psychiatric understanding of sexual preference and medical knowledge of AIDS.

There have been resolutions against child abuse—no controversy there—and several on the subject of pornography. In 1986 media reported that SB messengers "commended President Reagan's Commission on Pornography," exactly the impression its supporters wanted. The fundamentalist chairman of the Resolutions Committee had to step aside during the discussion, since he himself had been a member of the Commission.

In 1973, after the newly re-offered Equal Rights Amendment had sailed through Congress and the ratification process was in train, the SBC adopted the resolution:

> The Scriptures bear record to the distinctive roles of men and women in the church and in the home and . . . Christian women have made and are making a significant contribution to the cause of Christ . . . There is a great attack by the members of most women's liberation movements upon scriptural precepts of women's place in society . . . be it Resolved, that we . . . reaffirm God's order of authority for his church and the Christian home: (1) Christ the head of every man; (2) man the head of every woman; (3) children in subjection to their parents—in the Lord . . .
>
> Be it Resolved further, that we . . . reaffirm God's explicit Word that (1) man was not made for the woman, but the woman for the man; (2) that the woman is the glory of man; (3) that as woman would not have existed without man, henceforth, neither would man have existed without the woman, they are dependent one upon the other—to the glory of God.

A 1978 resolution deplored the extension of the time for ERA ratification as an attack upon the Constitution. In 1980 a resolution took a different tone, seeming to come close to approval of women's working outside of the home, urging "fairness for women in compensation, advancement, and opportunities for improvement" but ending, "Resolved, that this Convention, reaffirming the biblical role which stresses the equal worth but not always the sameness of function of women, does not endorse the Equal Rights Amendment." In 1987 full-time homemakers were honored for their commitment "to their families and to the Lord who has ordained the home as a workplace."

Sin and Vice. On the remaining issues of individual morality, sin, or vice (the third category), the SBs have concentrated most of their energy. Minor targets at annual meetings have included gambling, "segregated districts" ("red light," 1917), motion pictures and modern dance (1921), race tracks (1922), obscene literature (1925), "growing and excessive use of tobacco by boys and girls" (1932), and motor vehicles and drunken driving (1934). To this was added any behavior that was likely to expose female bodies – mixed bathing, beauty contests. And, of course, television.

The expressions of outrage against these forms of cultural expression are usually intemperate, but the greatest addiction has been to the temperance, or prohibition, cause. It took a long time for Baptists to get organized. Although the first temperance society in the South was founded by a Baptist minister in 1826, a fear of the association of temperance with abolition, and with the anti-mission movement, kept the South behind. Some Baptist state papers until the middle of the century carried liquor advertising, and an editorial in the Georgia *Christian Index* in 1869 stated that its writer was not sure the *best* liquor was harmful.

After the War the movement spread, and its leaders ventured further into the political arena. As late as the 1888 SBC meeting, when two resolutions were offered on alcohol, they were ruled out of order because they dealt with a "political" issue. Eventually women, Southern Baptists among them, became activist; by 1898 the Women's Christian Temperance Union had 10,000 branches and its membership was nearly half a million, including some children.

The big change came after the turn of the century. As social historian Harold Underwood Faulkner wrote (1931: 227): "The first harvest was in the South where the desire to remove strong drink from the Negroes . . . may have played as prominent a part as moral motives in bringing success." Historian Andrew Sinclair corroborates this viewpoint; the prohibition crusade was different in the South, he said, for it "offered them a moral refuge from their guilty fear of the Negro, as well as a method of controlling one of his means of self-assertion" (1962: 29).

Saloons would provide a means for the forging of cross-caste working class coalitions, and after the "great race settlement" of the 1890s this was taboo. It is this background, of course, which has meant that liquor-by-the-drink was legalized so much later than package stores in much of the South.

The temperance or prohibition issue was allowed to absorb the energies of Southern Baptist social activism for thirty years under the direction of Anti-Saloon League leader A. J. Barton. Some SBs like Edwin Poteat tried to get the Social Service Commission interested in broader concerns, but nothing was done until after Barton's death, for this concentration clearly served mainstream interests as another device for reinforcing solidarity. The issue is still alive and still subject to an annual resolution and lobbying at the state level, despite what some report as changes in SB behavior.

In their crusades against other vices, the SBs lack even a successful if brief noble experiment to savor. They can try to keep their people away from pornographic magazines and X-rated movies, but starting their own television service is an admission of failure to influence what the commercial networks offer. In 1984 in an historic first, the SBC passed a strong resolution against tobacco. The SB leaders in North Carolina, where 42 percent of the nation's crop is grown, promptly took pains to reemphasize that this resolution did not bind the membership because of local church autonomy.

Economic Equity. The fourth category of social issues deals with distributive justice or economic equity, and here Southern Baptist activity is predictably but strikingly absent. Of the three SB social histories, all the authors agree. John Lee Eighmy (1972) notes the omission of labor problems from the Social Gospel in the South. Rufus Spain says that "the social issues over which Baptists were most concerned were those which had some moral or religious implication for the individual or some significance for the denomination . . . [They were] . . . completely apathetic toward political, social, and economic discrimination" (1967: 213). And George Kelsey writes that "the cultural influence is evident in the following of . . . a generally conservative attitude toward existing economic conditions . . . an incredible insensitivity to the great agrarian problems of the South, even during the decades when they were most grievous and most publicized" (1973: 182).

There were a few exceptions. A tiny Chapel Hill, North Carolina, group, Christian Frontiers, in 1946 urged support for a 65-cent minimum wage and black enfranchisement, and opposition to permanent militarization. In general, however, Southern Baptists seemed so afraid of class cleavage that with regard to the labor movement they again took refuge in premillennialism. At the 1947 annual meeting, the Social Service Commission reported:

> we face the imminent possibility of industrial conflict in our area . . . we do not believe that the church can take sides in the struggle. We cannot give aid to the organizing of labor unions; nor can we be identified with the cooperative movements. To do so would be to negate the greater mission of the church. The Kingdom of God cannot be coerced into the narrow confines of labor unions, industrial management or cooperatives. Rather must all these patterns be brought under the judgment of the Kingdom of God.

Southern Baptist "radicals," marching with former U. S. Attorney General Ramsey Clark again
the death penalty, Atlanta, 1977. (Photograph courtesy of the E. C. Dargan Research Library,
Sunday School Board, Southern Baptist Convention.)

As SBs have moved into the middle class, their language on issues of
distributive justice has changed, and they have adopted the code terms
such as "balanced budget"; they pass weak resolutions on hunger and poverty that call for use of mission resources and further education. Even these
changes in emphasis have beeen concealed because they took place during
a period of general economic growth and tremendous social upheaval, the
focus of the last category of social ethics issues.

"Race". Southern Baptists have been in the mainstream of the South on
these "racial" issues, voicing the same range of viewpoints in roughly the
same proportion as the remainder of the mass of people. As might be expected from their place in the class structure, they were heavily involved
in the Ku Klux Klan. In nearly every state, Bernard states, "the general
staff of the Klan includes a large number of former Baptist pastors . . .
Baptist papers [are] unanimously silent on the question of the Ku Klux
Klan . . . the Klan and the Baptist church are in very close communion,
not only in the South, but also in the Middle West . . . when klansmen have

money to give, it always goes to a Methodist or Baptist cause, not a Catholic or Episcopal one . . . When there is a Klan funeral, a Baptist preacher usually officiates" (1926: passim). Involvement didn't stop; in the early 1960s the Imperial Wizard was Robert Lee "Wild Bill" Davidson, director of the Baptist Training Union at a Macon church.

Lillian Smith liked to point out that often it was middle-class religious white women who comforted black families after a lynching or other atrocity—the victims of their own husbands, brothers, and sons. There was much individual kindness, of course, and personal charity. And there were Southern Baptist "liberals" on the color issue. Basil Manly of the Southern faculty said in 1889: "The only way then to deal with a black man whom we find in America is to give him his rights, cordially, frankly, fully" (Potter 1973: 90). Before the turn of the century, J. B. Gambrell, a former president of the SBC, said: "If we hold any part of the negroes down, we will have to stay down with them. If we hold any part of our people down in a ditch, we will have to stand in the ditch with them to do it" (Potter 1973: 87).

The Social Service Commission continued to castigate the Klan in its annual reports, repeating the pathetic and horrible statistics gathered by the lynch-watch center at Tuskegee. In this century the professors of social ethics, particularly Maston at Southwestern and Barnette at Southern, encouraged a whole generation of seminary students to look at the material, social, and legal conditions under which black people of the South lived, and what SBs might do about them. But even the "liberals" could foster only justice and economic opportunity; true social equality was not to be preached.

The mainstream of SB thought, however, was more in tune with the *Alabama Baptist*, which editorialized in 1889 that "the white people of the South mean to rule, and they will rule" (Spain 1967: 83). They expected blacks to continue as farm and domestic labor and vowed that any educational program should be directed by southern whites.

But their own commitments were terribly small. In 1912 the SBC asked only $15,000 for "missions work among blacks," less than one penny from each person. Victor Masters, in his classic, *The Call of the South* (1918), gave voice to all the dominant themes, particularly the romanticization of the slave past:

> No race ever had more passion for liberty than the Anglo-Saxon . . . It was a paradox and a tragedy that such a people should find themselves obsessed with a social order which had gradually built human bondage into its fabric. Nowhere else had slavery ever existed under such humane conditions (52).

Then, resentment against a black leader who wants to guide hs own destiny:

> Boston uplifters . . . have nurtured the radical Negro leader, who from his New England aerie pronounces great swelling words about the rights of his race in the South, . . . DuBois . . . is a gifted man, but shows bitterness of spirit. In his writings he does not seem to be concerned to help the Negroes to be worthy of position, but rather to stir them to demand for themselves their so-called rights, by which he means all that is desirable in the white man's civilization (62).

Yet, a concern for elemental justice:

> Undoubtedly there should be restrictions about the right to vote, but is it ethical or safe to make different restrictions for the different races? . . . A literacy test is perhaps the best practicable safeguard . . . A property requirement might not be bad. But can the dominant whites afford not to apply these tests with fairness to both races? (63) . . . Not a few Southern legal practitioners . . . do not hesitate to say that the blacks for the same offences ordinarily get more punishment in our courts than the whites, and have less than an equal showing before our courts of law. Christian men and women of the South cannot quietly acquiesce in such a situation as this (73).

As national condemnation of the lynchings grew, and the New Deal brought national attention to conditions in the South, Masters voiced fresh resentment of outside interference and the threat of federal intervention. In 1938 he was outraged at the Federal Council, which strove "to ram down the throats of Southerners the theories of Northern liberals concerning race relations in the South, . . . much of the talk emanating from the Federal Council of Churches . . . is tinctured with the virus of Communism" (Valentine 1949: 112). The same year the Baptist World Alliance, meeting in Atlanta, took an anti-segregation position. This prompted Masters to rail against the "counterfeit utopianism . . . being fomented by radicals in relation to practically all indigenous American social and religious outlooks and political institutions" (113).

By 1940 the South was even more on the defensive, and a more analytical tone was heard in the reports of the Social Service Commission. And yet the hedging continued:

> the Negro does not receive the same compensation for the same work as does the White man. We would not be arbitrary nor dogmatic; we would not assert that no differential in wages paid could ever be justified because of difference in social position and living requirements . . . we recognize the fact that absolute equality in the distribution of public funds for education would perhaps not be feasible (82).

By 1943 the commission was approving of statements by liberal southern leaders which criticized discrimination in all its myriad ways, although proposals for action were likely to be very timid, featuring missions work and fellowship between white and black pastors, for example. The Supreme Court had ruled that separate facilities for professional education had to be really equal, and in 1944 it outlawed the white primary. Southern Baptist Harry Truman, goaded from the left, used the presidential directive in 1948 to end segregation in the Armed Forces. (Hitler can probably be credited in part with making racism less defensible.)

There were stirrings of change in the SBC. In 1947 the North Carolina State Convention passed a resolution disapproving of segregation in voting rights, education, hospitalization, and in the church. But after protests came in from around the state, the last section was rescinded, 253 to 158. One SB school in Arizona accepted blacks in 1950, and Wayland (Texas) Baptist College was the first private college in the South to take black students on the same basis as other students. This decision in 1951 brought widespread publicity. Southern Baptist church historian Walter Shurden (1979) pointed out that national resolutions were easier than local church action, and that most of the words dealt with prejudice rather than with integration, love instead of justice. The seminaries, however, were also officially desegregated in 1951, with students leading on the issue.

The Brown decision came like a thunderclap in May 1954, and a month later the Convention had to react. Jesse Weatherspoon, then head of the Christian Life Commission, did some impassioned preaching in his report (1954: 404). He carefully pointed out the crippling impact that U.S. legal segregation had upon this country's reputation in new nations and on his denomination's missionary efforts there. He mollified the messengers with the implied promise that a change in the law would not necessarily imply a change in life: "it will be easier for us to understand the issues involved in this whole question of segregation when we look at it in terms of voluntary separation instead of legal segregation. It is not that the Negro objects to being separated from white people. The facts are, it is not interracial commingling which he desires so much as it is the freedom from the legal system of segregation which denies him that freedom."

In anguish the 1954 Convention passed his recommended resolution, the operative clauses of which were "that we recognize the fact that this Supreme Court decision is in harmony with the constitutional guarantee of equal freedom to all citizens, and with the Christian principles of equal justice and love for all men . . . that we commend the Supreme Court for deferring the application of the principles both as to time and procedure until the nation shall have had time to work out methods by which transition from the present practice may be effected" (1954: 404). Almost immediately local resistance began. Court unanimity was only on the surface, the president (Eisenhower) did not support the decision, and states' rights and other segregationist sentiment forced the Court a year later to issue its "deliberate speed" opinion, delaying implementation of the Brown decision. But in December 1955, Rosa Parks refused to move to the back of the bus, and the struggle was further extended beyond the schools.

Southern Baptists were in the thick of it on both the die-hard and moderate sides as they existed in the South. Moderate pastors, known to have voted for even the tepid resolutions proposed by the Christian Life Commission, lost their jobs. Individual churches, like the First Baptist Church in Sumter, South Carolina, threatened to secede. Brooks Hays, then president of the SBC, was defeated in his bid for reelection to Congress from Arkansas by an ultra-segregationist. Scrambling back toward the SB center in 1959, the much vaunted social ethicist at Southwestern, T. B. Maston, could write: "Even Christians may defend racial segregation as the best method of temporarily and immediately handling a perplexing problem without doing great damage to the cause of Christ, so long as they will not use the curse of Canaan and other biblical incidents and teachings to support their positions, and so long as they do not defend segregation as being the full and final expression of the divine will in human relations" (1959: 117). (His book, *The Bible and Race*, was long held up by Broadman, which insisted on many changes. The WMU ordered 50,000 paper copies.)

By 1963 the resolution on the subject was so fuzzy that it seemed as if Southern Baptists had resorted to talking in code. The relevant statement that year was entitled "On Christian Responsibility," and it emphasized that the issues were "essentially spiritual in nature," urging "open communications" and "prayer and personal commitment." The following year a proposed resolution to "approve the positive action taken by hundreds of Southern Baptist churches in affirming an open-door policy for all people regardless of racial origin" and "pledge to support the laws designed to guarantee the legal rights of Negroes in our democracy" was replaced by one which essentially bumped the problem down to the local church level and urged a search for "peaceful Christian solutions."

But the South Carolina SB Convention voted that same year against black admission to their colleges. And in North Carolina, one of the Chapel Hill churches split over allowing Martin Luther King, Jr., to speak in the sanctuary. He did speak at Southern Seminary but there were threats to withhold future funding. The corporate headquarters of the SBC adopted a security program with private guards and provision for tear gas use. At the 1965 SBC meetings, an amendment added by close vote to an otherwise vague statement a clause to "deplore the open and premeditated violation of civil laws, the destruction of property, the shedding of human blood, or the taking of life as a means of influencing legislation of changing the social and cultural patterns." During this period southerners such as Marshall Frady asked, "Whatever became of the moderates? . . . Where was the spirit of Christian brotherhood? Where was the Southern Baptist Convention?" (1967: 37). George Harmon felt that many SB "moderates" went to the Methodists, increasing the philosophical and social differences between the two denominations (1963: 61).

1968 was a crucial year. Martin Luther King, Jr., had been assassinated in April, there were riots in 130 cities, and Robert Kennedy was shot the day the SBC annual meeting opened. Foy Valentine, by then director of the Christian Life Commission, described the Convention's reaction:

> As the statement was originally prepared . . . it contained a remarkably strong confession of guilt which clearly acknowledged the Southern Baptist sins of commission and omission which had helped produce the then current crisis in the nation . . . [after several waves of amendment, behind the scenes and on the floor, there was] . . . a final watering down of that portion related to Southern Baptist moral responsibility for the crisis of the nation. The statement on the crisis in the nation as finally adopted was a less theologically valid document . . . and it was a far less prophetic utterance than was made by many other denominational bodies (1979: 60).

However, motions to delete an entire "We Voice Our Confession" section, to agree "to deplore the infiltration of communism into the racial movement," and to denounce "pressure" on churches and ministers, were defeated. It is no accident that at that same annual meeting W. A. Criswell, the powerful fundamentalist pastor of the Dallas First Baptist Church, was elected president, and a preference poll to change the name of the Convention gave the following results:

Southern Baptist Convention	4,996
Baptist General Convention	702
United Baptist Convention	611
Other	956

The shift from direct confrontation on racial issues to other forms of reaction and identity-confirmation was beginning.

One of the contemporary SB (and southern) techniques for dealing with "racial" issues is to declare them in the past. In 1978, the bureaucrat McClellan could write, for example, "The 1968 statement on crises in the United States helped stabilize Southern Baptist thinking on the racially oriented disturbances in American cities . . . probably clarified and strengthened the Baptist mind in the area of social righteousness" (1978B: 8) and "though we were slow in our responses, we finally came through in racial discrimination" (1978A: 284). The December 1981 issue of the Christian Life Commission magazine, *Light*, described the "Civil Rights Movement" as a "trial that has been endured and 'overcome'" (9). In 1986 at the SBC annual meeting a resolution somehow slipped through, asking SB agencies to encourage "involvement of Blacks and other Minorities." Although the resolution was referred to all agencies, the only ones to reply substantively in 1987 were the Historical and Radio/TV Commissions.

Liturgy and Aesthetics

The oxymoron, *Southern Baptist aesthetic*, involves exactly those parts of American popular culture which are the dreariest. Street clothing styles, the political cartoon, and the topical "folk" song are lively and expressive art forms in the United States in the late 1980s. But small-town architecture (even when built in the city), most public space interior design, ceremonial clothing, and, especially, serious music for public occasions cannot be sources of pride.

Many Southern Baptists are critical of their denomination's performance in this regard. They say SBs "do not take worship seriously," and "worship is too informal—not enough sense of the transcendent—no conscious use of symbolism." From former SB Samuel Hill: "The religious life is more likely to be somewhat sterile and antiseptic. Often missing . . . are beauty, joy, freedom, risk, celebration, and the casual spirit" (1972: 205).

All American religious groups, no matter how exotic their backgrounds, share some of these deficiencies. A great part of the difficulty comes because corporate forms of aesthetic expression are precisely the way that the nuances of class consciousness are expressed in contemporary American culture. Southern Baptists have particular problems in this department because of historic associations with southern black culture which they feel the need to deny. Historian Marcus Hansen's famous remark that the grandson wishes to remember what the father tried to forget holds here; the SBs are still committed to forgetting.

Asthetic forms are an important way that denominational distinctiveness may be marked. But overwhelmingly, for Southern Baptists, they become the vehicle for the expression of social solidarity, or what David Brion Davis calls "the need for people to hear the gospel in their own cultural idiom" (1981: 90). Gerald B. Palmer comments, "People gravitate to a church where they can 'feel at home'; where they have a chance to express their faith in their own type of music, listen to a preacher whose sermon is understandable in their level of education" (1981: 49).

The buildings themselves are mostly bland, homogenized. Hill says that architecture is "regarded as having secondary importance" (1972: 204). Many of the older wooden churches, now known from pictures in the SB *Encyclopedia*, were breathtakingly without pretense, and those photos suggest that the brick Gothic downtown churches of the turn of this century were very good examples of that idiom. Occasionally on a back road there will be a modest church, maybe in concrete block, which was done by honest workmen with good eyes for scale. The most popular current style is "modified" Colonial, or just plain bland; there is next to no really modern experimentation. The interiors show the same general uncertainty, and the chancels tend to be very cluttered. Except for an occasional composition in stained glass, many sanctuaries are close in tone to the average junior high school auditorium; a coke machine just off-stage would not be out of place.

Vestments may be chosen, and worn, with some embarrassment. The choir is usually robed, and there is a strong preference for two-tones, like 1950s American automobiles. Sometimes these colors are related to the interior decor. Some pastors appear in mufti out of convention. A few dare to be more theatrical—one silver-haired pastor chose a silver brocade poncho. Plain black academic gowns are rare. A woman pastor cannot win.

The order of service in all Protestant churches is derived from the development of the Christian mass, and more or less deliberately related to or differentiated from it. Since the Baptist contribution to liturgy is total immersion, and this doesn't happen every week, there is no clear link to history except a dislike of "ritualism."

The early years of Baptist growth in America took place, of course, primarily among illiterates and the democracy of the do-it-yourself vocation and the ritualized weekly revival. In reaction to this emotionalism, and to certain trends within European Catholicism, United States Calvinists went through a phase of liturgical study, rediscovering Bach chorales and reading Luther, Calvin, and John Knox for their historical liturgical contributions. This movement was intellectually uncongenial to most Southern Baptists, and in their sustained growth they found vindication for rejecting it.

In this milieu the sermon can become itself a ritual—no challenge to the listener to think about something new, but reassurance that it isn't necessary. About the listener Hill comments, "What is said in the church service is of small importance to him; he pays a minimum of attention to the entire occasion" (1972: 199). "We hold together in the Spirit, not around words," insists SB bureaucrat McClellan (1978: 291). The sermon often becomes a form of dissociation, since its mixed metaphors, misused words and ritual repetition serve to deny meaning rather than reveal it.

Many churches have problems with the period before worship—before the processional music starts, the pastor enters, or some other sign is given that the show is about to begin. The model is the movie house or theatre, the chatter unstoppable, denying the possibilities that silence offers. The expectation builds. We stand, we sit, we do not kneel. We are about to be entertained.

Finally the sermon begins, the high point. Homiletics courses used to teach "three points and a poem"—now it's three points and a conclusion. Thus, there's a structure, and it's almost always followed even at the expense of sense. The congregation knows this and counts off. The text, the take-off point, is almost always biblical. Alliteration is cherished. (Adrian Rogers in his Annual Sermon in Atlanta dared a tricky double form which almost made sense: "Saving Belief . . . Sovereign Builder . . . Spiritual Battle . . . Singular Business.") There will be humor, long anecdotes—frequently truncated and pointless—or allusions to children or pets. Trendy slang is frequent: "bottom line," "input," "terrain-wise," "parameter" (misused).

Finally, to the music—often the subject of greatest contention; the battleground on which churches may splinter, careers founder, friendships wilt. Its central place is signaled by the position of the choir in most Southern Baptist churches, in the chancel facing the congregation. Sometimes their rows of chairs are banked so sharply that they form a human wall, over which the baptismal pool looms. Americans accept symbolism in music perhaps better than elsewhere—the national anthem, a team's fight song, "Silent Night" across the trenches in Belgium, "Dixie," the song that was playing when a couple first met. And music is age-graded—an important

means by which young people mark off their subculture and old ones remember their youth – and class-graded also. So it is loaded, and controversial, probably because there are so many amateurs. Many who would back
off from decisions on architecture or color schemes, and leave them to the
professionals, will have and voice opinions on the musical arts.

During the Great Revival, singing was recognized for its wide emotional
appeal. Hymns were used for didactic purposes, to teach basic doctrine,
and the famous "lining out" practice was not just an aid to memory but
an aid to memorization. Masters describes its use about 1820:

> Congregational singing without an instrument was prominent and potent in the
> protracted meetings . . . old hymns, such as . . . "Amazing Grace" . . . "raised"
> by a leader, often the preacher himself, and sung with stately and spirited deliber-
> ation by the congregation. Following the reading, or "lining out" of two lines
> of the hymn by the preacher, a great volume of vocal song would respond with
> a plaintive antiphonal effect (1915: 26).

That is the "leader-chorus" pattern, common in West African societies.
For by this time there was a growing number of blacks in the Baptist
churches, and black church music and white church music were one until
the war. As Leonard Ellinwood observes, "It has become apparent that the
Negro spirituals differ but little from the earlier gospel songs. These were
taken up and adapted by the Negro in mid-century, at the very time they
were beginning to go into eclipse in white circles" (1953: 102). Jay Wilkey
puts it more colorfully: "we have absorbed the spirituals and blues as our
very own. As red as our necks may be, we have black souls" (1976: 44).

With the separation of blacks from whites in the churches after the Civil
War, this organic tradition declined. Now, it seems very clear, Southern
Baptists feel a massive ambivalence about the black component of their
musical history. As it becomes so popular, so southern, so American, its
appeal is irresistible, and yet they cannot have it thought that it is their
own. They want to eat their cake but repudiate it too. At the SBC meeting
in New Orleans, the most exciting musical performer was a black gospel
singer – she was real, she was wonderful. All around there were tapping feet
and nervous laughter, scattered applause mixed with jeers. The audience
wanted to enjoy it without in any way being identified. This ambivalence
is not new: Erskine Caldwell remembered one segregationist who felt that
"When the Saints Go Marching In" should not be sung by Negroes but
rather "should be set aside for the exclusive use of the white race" (1968: 198).

Out of the same shared matrix, the Great Revival, came congregational
freedom to respond, with a "Praise be the Lord," "Amen," or even, some-

times, with something perilously close to a Rebel yell. There was a lot of it at a 1981 North Carolina Evangelism Conference, which, although 98 percent white, brought out the more rural Southern Baptists of the state. "Amen," they said, a low refrain almost like a groan, sometimes one or a few voices, sometimes almost unanimous, but always ending in unison, not the competitive individualism of black worship but a sound almost torn, forced from the defiant group as a whole. In the urban and upwardly mobile churches, these expressions are becoming taboo. Gerald B. Palmer of the Home Mission Board staff decribes the "cultural expression" of his own church, presumably in an Atlanta suburb: "If a person says *Amen,* he is recognized as an old-timer, or probably an outsider. If he is not an outsider now, he probably will be" (1981: 52). And thus are derived the mechanisms by which a person feels "comfortable" in one church rather than another.

Many SBs know the words of many hymns, and many sing parts. The melodies are so unmemorable and the harmonic progressions so predictable that it's actually easier than to learn the top line. But there are special problems as well, such as the linguistic sloppiness of rhyming "ferocious" with "know just." Syntactically baffling, such linkage forces people to tune out. Hymns containing such phrases as "drawn from Thy precious bleeding side" have become informally known as "slaughter-house hymns." A sophisticated professional, asked about the gory image, said, "I never pay any attention to the words." Again, the dissociation of words from their meaning serves to deny that words may have any meaning.

Matters of style, and connotation, are even more important. Wary of anything high-toned or "high church" (which conventionally means close to Roman Catholic practice but is here applied to anything that requires knowledge, background, and musical literacy for understanding or appreciation), they must go to innocuousness, safety, sweetness, and artificiality. Most of the music at recent annual meetings has been redolent of the commercial idioms of the last forty years—the Andrews Sisters, Nat King Cole crooning, Olivia Newton-John, even Jeannette MacDonald and Nelson Eddy. In those huge spaces, taped backgrounds were preferred, with every instrument known to Tin Pan Alley available by electronic magic, overwhelming the amplified screams of the singers. These tricks are seldom utilized to enhance the meanings of words, but are so dissociated from the semantic content that again they serve only to deny there is any meaning at all.

Southern Baptists, and many other American Protestants, are hampered by the lack of an elaborate liturgical year. Rejecting the overloaded Catholic calendar, they also lost the sense of placement in history and the passage of the seasons, the refreshing change in vestment colors and the specialness of the prayer cycle. And they can replace these only with secular holidays in the "civil religion" they verbally despise, high focal points as decreed by the denominational bureaucracy, or token special emphases – Race Relations Sundays and Jewish Fellowship Weeks. Christmas and Easter remain, although they may be attenuated: some attention may be given to Lent ("Why, they're getting so high church, they have services on Maundy Thursday," one pastor marvelled). This suspicion of ritual, the negation of the thought and care and love that go into its design, denies the psychological needs that it serves and results in a bleak poverty which can only be filled by commercial-sounding and mindless piety. J. M. Cameron comments that "kitsch presents us with a serious theological problem" by its denial of the authenticity of "what is, for the believer, the deepest reality" (1986: 56–57).

The yearly cycle of rituals is thoroughly integrated with the civil round of "holidays" and inextricably entangled with the calendar of the school year, sports spectacles, the family vacation, business meetings, and long weekends. One year Christmas came on a Sunday; the state papers were full of discussion as to whether it was better to truncate the morning services in deference to "family," or obscene and sacrilegious to do exactly that. For those active in denominational affairs, meetings of district association and state convention periodize the year and become ritualized, as does the annual SBC meeting itself for the small proportion that attends. Revival meetings (usually held in summer) and Vacation Bible Schools – week-long special study celebrations which are harder and harder to staff as more women enter the work force – stud the year. The Homecoming (going back to the church of one's youth for a Sunday service and a midday "dinner-on-the-grounds") is still held in rural areas, the model for the homecoming sports events of colleges and universities. Being a Southern Baptist can, in other words, be a full-time occupation; Will Rogers said once that our country builds roads so Baptists can wear them out going and coming to meetings.

Private ritual is difficult to get at. Southern Baptists say they read the Bible frequently, and denominational leaders act as though that were true. Private prayer is undoubtedly frequent as well, although "pray" is used metaphorically in a very broad sense. Tense committee meetings at Baptist conferences are "bathed in prayer." One young pastor, asked about a sticky point, said, "We shouldn't make the decision today . . . we need to go home and pray about it for a year." Very often it's "pray about" or "pray over" but also it's "pray for," or "pray" with a direct object as "we need to pray

Psalm 51." Of all the potential kinds of prayer, the only one Southern Baptists specify is "intercessory prayer," often for specific material consequences like rain or money. "Prayer partners" are popular; each person will include the other among those prayed for daily. Prayer may be a reflection of intimacy; one woman said of friendship with another: "We have a wonderful, unusual relationship, why, we can pray together," aloud, extempore.

The central message is that Jesus died to save us all and Jesus loves us — in other words, somebody out there in this lonely world cares, no matter how we behave or what we are. In order to make this true, to validate it, it is necessary only to believe it, to have faith. The pastor in one northern city preached a remarkable sermon: When you're down, when everything is going wrong, remember how wonderful it was when you first believed, remember the ecstasy of the discovery of faith. He was suggesting an analogy to a love relationship, to the emotional high that may come when mutual romantic love is first acknowledged and expressed. This similarity is borne out in modern popular religious music. Twirling the dial on the car radio in unfamiliar territory often results in confusion over whether a song concerns love for a lover or love for Jesus, so saccharine is the tone. Sentimentality prevails, wrapped in a rootless idiom.

Southern Baptists have in general rejected their historical roots in the rural South which might lead to identification with the blacks whom they need to repudiate. Bucolic metaphors — such as "we've chased enough rabbits to make the biggest stew," or "more problems than chiggers in a blackberry patch" — are used less frequently as the slickness increases. In Atlanta (1986) one hapless speaker dared to wonder how many bales of hay would fit in the Convention Center; he got not even a ripple of friendly laughter in response.

They also reject the approach through high culture that demands knowledge, experience, sophistication, informed taste, discipline — all of which are likely to be scarce in Baptist colleges, universities, and seminaries. Even if intellectual and cultural qualities were cultivated, the results would be incomprehensible in many of the churches. This leaves the majority of Southern Baptists with nowhere to go but pseudo-serious popular culture at its most self-conscious and pretentious. The models are commercial; the folk music of today is the soft drink jingle, the folk wit the one-liner to canned laughter. The public ceremonies are directed from Los Angeles and New York and beamed at an audience which knows little else but Nashville, rock radio, Saturday Night Live, MTV, and the halftime shows at high school football games. No wonder creativity and authenticity are so scarce. Feeling at home in a comfortable cultural idiom is far more important to group solidarity.

Southern Baptist written language suffers from the same dissociation and imprecision. As Bailey Smith said at an annual meeting, "Each one of these resolutions can be interpreted in a hundred different ways."

The enthusiastic singing without paying attention to the words, the passionate passing of resolutions with scant attention to the precision of the language or the possibility of internal inconsistency or congruence with what has been said before on the same issues—both exhibit a strange and Alice-in-Wonderland attitude toward the power of words and the Word. Language is not the only means of communication human beings possess but it is the most precise one; if this potential is wasted, the whole seriousness of the verbal enterprise comes into question.

Is There a Southern Baptist Mind?
Jimmy Carter as Exemplar

"Southern Baptists are representative of Southern culture, and Jimmy and Rosalynn Carter are typical Southern Baptists," said one pastor. Carter's behavior before and during his White House incumbency was generally baffling to many Americans. The *New York Times* religion editor at that time, Kenneth Briggs, wrote that "for the longest time . . . many reporters reacted to Jimmy Carter's unabashed espousal of 'born again' Christianity with about as much befuddlement as if Mr. Carter had said he had ridden in a flying saucer" (1977: 19). Regeneration wasn't the problem; rather it was the complex mental traits which grow out of Southern Baptist experience. Although Carter has had some distinctive experiences, he is thoroughly congruent with that huge and locally dominant subculture in which he grew up and then came to exemplify and express. One has only to look at press accounts, social histories, and biographies to make the connections.

His approach to knowledge is by rote. David Kucharsky recounted Carter's description, in a television interview, of the teacher who introduced him to classical music: "She would make me do it . . . And she'd make sure that I learned the famous paintings, and the authors, and the artists, and she gave me books to read" (1976: 16). When Bill Moyers asked Carter if he were in effect a "decent but provincial and narrow-minded man from the South," Carter didn't respond to the question but simply went over his biography again (Mazlish and Diamond 1979: 163). Betty Glad talked about

President and Mrs. Jimmy Carter at the National Conference of Baptist Men, Atlanta, June 1978. (Photograph courtesy of the E. C. Dargan Research Library, Sunday School Board, Southern Baptist Convention.

a long-time Carter friend who asked him to explain his favorite Dylan Thomas poem. He didn't even try, but just kept repeating it over and over. Glad continued, "There are other cues that Carter does not deeply understand many of the philosophers and poets he quotes. When asked about their views, he usually elaborates on certain external facts of their lives or how he came to know their work, but does not engage in reflection on the meaning of what they say" (1980: 483).

Garry Wills described asking Carter a question on which he drew a blank: "For a bright and educated modern man, dealing with the thing he says matters most to him, he shows an extraordinarily reined-in curiosity. He suggests a kind of willed narrowness of mastery. He moves quick and certain within a deliberately circumscribed territory. He sticks to his base, his certitudes" (1976: 53–54).

This looks like a typical SB approach to theology, Herschel Hobbs' "anchored but free," the vaunted educational commitment to "biblically-based intellectual inquiry," or "academic freedom in Christ." This approach says, in effect: Behold the cultural world; if you can label it, identify it, pigeonhole it, it will be yours. Don't look below the surface; repeat a fact or an idea as a litany and you will absorb its *mana*; know *about* and you need not know. Such an attitude is not only pretentious but anti-intellectual, anti-cultural.

Carter was remarkable for his waffling and vacillation. His "eagerness to accommodate all sides on all issues resulted in his pleasing no one and being regarded as a weak and wishy-washy president," wrote Clark Mollenhoff (1980: 254). He tried to appeal to the supporters of both George Wallace and Martin Luther King, Jr. – a quixotic enterprise, in Marshall Frady's opinion.

Carter's ambivalence was reflected in his theology. Religious historian Brooks Holifield said that Carter's belief structure encompassed Southern evangelism with roots in the Puritan era, an eighteenth-century variety of religious pluralism, and a sophisticated "Christian realism": "The compound may at first seem incongruous . . . His capacity to hold these strands in harmony may determine . . . his appeal" (1976: 15). Psychohistorians Bruce Mazlish and Edwin Diamond pointed out that the "threads of Niebuhr, evangelism and 'born-again' experience may clash with one another; yet for Carter they make up part of the same cloth of religious belief" (1979: 167).

Nor was Carter more consistent on domestic policy issues. He was simultaneously against abortion, government funding of abortion, and a constitutional amendment banning abortion. Jules Witcover said that "Carter's handling of the abortion issue in Iowa was a signal of things to come. He would display a talent for being on both sides of an issue that both dismayed and frustrated his opponents" (1977: 207). His approach was similar on the subject of private academies, most of them founded to avoid integration. According to Mazlish and Diamond, Carter at first denounced them, then supported private education but opposed its support from public funds: "Carter's staff had advised him originally to stay out of the private school issue; yet he had insisted first on making the earlier statement, and then on trying to hold on it while elaborating a second position, complex and/or hedging, depending on the listener's feelings" (1979: 182).

The division in Carter's approach extended to foreign policy. He hedged his bets by appointing two advisers with radically different approaches and philosophies. "Too inexperienced in foreign affairs to choose between their conflicting recommendations, he tried to ride both horses simultaneously, even when they were galloping in different directions," Ted Sorenson wrote (1986: 35). Ronald Steel said Carter "tried to weave a path between these two men, often with ludicrous results—for example, an important foreign-policy address at Annapolis which was one-half Brzezinski and one-half Vance, each half contradicting the other" (1986: 179).

After he announced his running mate, Carter proclaimed, according to Elizabeth Drew, "I'm not ever going to be constrained by absolute consistency" (1978: 310). Mazlish and Diamond (1979) saw these attitudes as "Carter's fundamental need to fuse contradictions" (221) and "to embrace contradictions" (231). Before he was elected president, his life had been "a successful balancing act" (234) and his character was formed of "controlled opposites" (260). But he, like many other Southern Baptists, fails or refuses to see them as contradictions. Their mental life is a series of balancing acts, freedom of conscience yet confessions of faith, local church autonomy but expulsion for unpopular views, a resolution this year 180 degrees from last year's on the same subject.

Throughout his presidency, Carter mixed an ambivalence toward power and authority with a faith that organizational structure would solve everything. Frady called this "running on the administrative passions, the managerial fervors of salvation through procedure and technique" (1980: 345). Mazlish and Diamond wrote, "Baptists believe in a divinely ordained form of church government in which all power belongs to the people. But . . . leaders emerge with no clearly defined roles . . . Baptists are unwilling to confer authority upon their leaders and are equally unwilling to recognize that these leaders have attained power apart from authority . . . Baptist leadership has a style of its own . . . a certain innocence about power" (1979: 161). This confusion and innocence, the tolerance for divided and countervailing centers of power, sometimes results in the simultaneous faith in pure organization itself: "When an institution does not work well, the explanation may be that the right people are not in charge or that it is not organized efficiently," commented Mazlish and Diamond (162). In Carter's case, this kind of approach affected the abortive rescue effort of the Iranian hostages. Its deficient authority structure showed a failure to recognize that the blurring, the diffusion of decision-making might well seal its doom. The same blindness may have caused part of Carter's reputation for weakness and indecisiveness.

The lack of direction in matters of policy had a counterpart in Carter's synthetic intimacy. Bert Lance was "the associate Carter called his closest friend in the world, although they had known each other only since 1966," wrote Mazlish and Diamond (1979: 201). Carter liked to call world leaders close personal friends after brief meetings. His platform remarks (like "I feel very close to all of you") had, Frady noted, "a peculiar sort of mass, impersonal intimacy (1976: 352). Perhaps it was "some furtive tone of cal-culation to his folksy flourishes, . . . a combination of . . . the sentimental with the deliberation of a mechanical engineer," as Frady described it (352), that made his audiences wary of any of his feelings, distrustful even of his affection toward his wife and of such pieties as wanting government as good as the American people.

Finally, Carter was all too willing to separate ideas and attitudes from their underpinnings. "Malaise" has entered the American language, and many people who never heard of Hegel were heard to remark that Carter failed to consider that there might be real reasons for their unhappiness. This "Christian Science" approach to social problems—expecting to find their causes in people's heads—is, of course, an historic Southern Baptist attitude.

"Carter remains a perplexing figure, self-contained and often unfathom-able . . . He wants to prevail by purity . . . the conviction that fervid good will would carry the day," a *Time* editorial concluded (19 Aug. 1980: 11). This describes so many Southern Baptists—likeable, some even admirable, but somehow unpredictable in their naiveté and their shallow understand-ing of history and their own behavior. Carter's wife Rosalynn rejoiced at his election. For the people, she thought, had found someone "good, hon-est and capable" (1984: 4). And he is, and they are, and the contradictions persist.

6   Southern Baptists, the New Religious Political Right, and the South

> What increasingly engages the Southern novelist . . . are no
> longer Faulkner's Snopeses, or O'Connor's crackers or
> Wright's black underclass but their successful grandchildren
> who are going nuts in Atlanta condominiums.
>
> —Walker Percy (1979: 83)

The Southern Context
of the New Religious Political Right

Most Southern Baptists, in classic fashion, have interpreted the
last decade of denominational churn as if it had little to do with the great
world outside. But their internal controversy—the fundamentalist takeover—
belongs in the context of the current social movement variously termed the
New Right, New Christian Right, or New Religious Political Right (NRPR).
In order to do that, the NRPR has to be placed in the context of the South.
"[It is] no accident that this modern, negative side of American evangelism
originated in the South, or that the leading electronic preachers were Southerners," political writer Johnny Greene says (1981: 120). This regional base
has been masked by the nationwide reach of the television networks and
widespread forgetfulness of the extent to which southerners have spilled
over into southern California and the Ohio Valley. Two of the largest churches
in the same Baptist Bible Fellowship that claims Jerry Falwell are the huge
Temple in Indianapolis, where Greg Dixon is pastor, and one in the San
Diego area where Tim LaHaye, now of an organizing group in Washington,
used to be. All the attitudes, therefore, which make the Southern Baptists
so southern are present—the militarism, chauvinism, sexism and sexual re-

pression, familial authoritarianism, anti-intellectualism, intolerance. Harvey Cox simply terms the NRPR the "Revival of Redneck Religion."

Included in this, of course, is basic racism. Like the SBs, the Rev. Jerry Falwell has put open racism behind him, and there are a few blacks in his Lynchburg congregation. There are a few black pastors at NRPR meetings, too, and the same wonderful black gospel singer, Willa Dorsey, whom SBs jeered in New Orleans, was featured at the Prayer Breakfast after the 1984 Republican Convention. But these are scarcely representative of blacks as a whole or of their interests.

Hill and Owen say that for the NRPR there is "a sense that sacred boundaries have been violated, that things are out of place," and they mention feminism, homosexuality, promiscuity, pornography, sex education (1982: 117–18). But what about desegregation, violation of the South's most sacred boundary? They go on to cite other factors, such as welfare, which "represents a dislocation of proper state power, as does state interference in the educational process in general," as in busing and Head Start, but they never draw the connections. The NRPR was looking for issues that people care about, and Richard Viguerie listed "busing, abortion, pornography, education, traditional biblical moral values, and quotas" (Reichley 1985: 319). Lincoln Caplan describes the Reagan social agenda: "eliminating abortion, affirmative action, school busing, and some established rights of criminal suspects; permitting school prayer; and so on" (1987: 31). In such lists the "race"-related issues are hidden. Allen Hunter points out that "the silent majority cuts across religious as well as regional lines; it excludes blacks, not Catholics . . . the rhetoric of Christianity is a way of saying white without mentioning race" (1981: 126). In fact, this approach has pulled some Catholics in—those most threatened by changes in the hierarchies of color and sex.

There is, however, a New Right which is not necessarily racist. It is usually dated from the first weeks of the Nixon-Kennedy campaign, a meeting in Sharon, Connecticut, at which Bill Buckley (who had founded the *National Review* five years earlier) organized Young Americans for Freedom, with a platform of support for the Constitution and the division of powers, a free market economy, and military superiority (not mere parity) over international communism. The Heritage Foundation was started in 1972 as a deliberate foil for the liberal organizations like the Brookings Institution, and in 1974 it was followed by Paul Weyrich's Committee for Survival of a Free Congress, in opposition to the older liberal National Committee for an Effective Congress. The American Enterprise Institute and many satellites followed. In a separate development, Richard Viguerie started his direct-mail company in 1965, at first working for such conservative causes as Gun Owners and Right-to-Work groups, and was founder-publisher of the *Conservative Digest.*

But even these groups, in their commitment to untrammeled free enterprise, may also have an anti-black bias. There are three principal ways to accomplish this without being open about it. One is to widen the holes in the "safety net," which, because proportionately there are more poor blacks than poor whites, will hurt blacks more. The second is to starve public sector investment. As black political scientist Charles V. Hamilton of Columbia University pointed out, 67 percent of black professionals and managers worked for government, as opposed to 17 percent of the total population (1979 figures), and cutting government at all levels is a most direct way to check black middle-class development. The third is to cut back on programs that help children and young people achieve equal opportunity – housing, parks, infant nutrition, prenatal and child health care, school lunches, Head Start, libraries, college loans. All of these can be and have been abolished or underfunded in the name of fiscal conservatism without ever breathing a word about blacks.

To this economic program can be added a group of constitutional, states' rights, and pro–private sector policies – shrinking the role of government, returning programs such as education and welfare to state and local control, deregulation (implying a loss of worker safety and environmental protection), crippling labor unions – again without mentioning their disproportionate effect on blacks. Finally, the "civil rights" programs in the strict sense can be separated from economic questions, legal action can be restricted to cases of individual discrimination, enforcement agencies can be packed with quislings and withered by lack of funds, and the Justice Department can defend municipalities that are balking at school desegregation, and, in demanding fidelity to "original intent," avoid the implications of the Fourteenth Amendment. All of these policies have been part of what is called the "Southern strategy": "against civil-rights progress and federal intervention; for defense expenditures and private enterprise," as Kirkpatrick Sale characterizes it (1976: 112–13). The "Southern strategy" and the NRPR are closely related since they are both at heart responses to southern desegregation and the "civil rights" and black power movements. They are being played out against a background of events in several different categories of southern culture.

Despite Sunbelt migration and Power Shift, the South continues to experience economic changes which are producing huge human problems.

Pockets of boom exist, like Charlotte and Atlanta, but outside them there is severe hardship. The shrinkage of the manufacturing sector hits low-wage, low-tax small towns hard as those jobs are exported, and the last decade of drought has exacerbated declining farm income and increasing bankruptcy. The crisis in energy production adds to those troubles. All of this takes place against a backdrop of low public sector investment, especially in education, continuing illegal immigration, and new techniques for segregation in school, neighborhood, and church. New Right emphases attempt to justify the part of these changes that have been favorable for whites and distract from the ones harmful to them.

Another element in the larger context is the massive exchange of voters between the two national parties. Between 1955 and 1985 the percentage of Republicans who were white southerners went from 10 to 33. During the same period the percentage of Democrats who were black went from 10 to 20 (*Harper's* Index, April 1985: 11). As Black and Black comment, "The breadth of the Democratic collapse is staggering. It would be difficult to find comparable instances in American political history of such a rapid and comprehensive desertion of an established majority party by an entire region" (1987: 267–68). In this migration of conservative whites from the Democratic to the Republican party – a migration in which "race" has been the principal factor – Ronald Reagan tops the list; John Connally and Philip Gramm of Texas are other well-known names. Among these crossovers, the list of Southern Baptists is notable: Strom Thurmond, Jesse Helms, Thad Cochran, Trent Lott, Newton Gingrich, and Pat Robertson. They have been joined in the past few years by a surprisingly large number of SB pastors, whose attachment to the Republican party rose from 29 to 66 percent between 1980 and 1984, while Democratic affiliation went in the other direction, from 41 to 25 percent. These pastors are precisely the group the NRPR has tried to reach as local cadres.

The population as a whole has followed these trends to the point at which the South has a working two-party system, but the accompanying instability has surely made it easier for people to use religious vehicles for their political ideas. Conversely, religious sociologist John Simpson concludes, "The politics of morality still serves the interest of the Republican party by creating an issue/interest cross-pressure in the minds of many traditionally Democratic downscale Americans. The politics of morality, then, sets the stage for loosening traditional political loyalties" (1984: 9).

Judicial history is also part of the context for the rise of the NRPR. Jerry Falwell, after his speech at a SB Christian Life Commission Conference (Atlanta, March 1982) was asked, The NRPR: Why now? He replied almost as if talking to a child: 1954, the Brown decision; 1962–63, the decisions banning prayer and Bible reading in schools; 1973, abortion. He made the connection: three clangs of a giant bell, three blows to the head, three enormous crimps in the style of the pious white southern male, coming from an institution essentially perceived as hostile and outside. One of them, desegregation, must not be discussed or attacked directly, but rather through devious economic policies and private sector institutional investment. The other two issues, however, are the heart of the NRPR public policy agenda, which now extends to the commitment to change the composition of the Court itself.

Finally, the NRPR has ridden a wave of changes in the most powerful communications medium, television. In the 1970s, stations were allowed to sell time for religious broadcasting. Mainline churches opted out of this transaction, and their places were filled with individual entrepreneurs who aimed at wider audiences. At the same time production costs dropped for a while, and cable TV was at the height of its expansion. From this emerged a group of southern religious leaders, appearing nationally, who had no denominational constituency, no institutional matrix to provide them with a braking history and tradition. They were responsible to no one but the thousands they faced through the lens; they were free to improvise. Hill and Owen point out that the lack of consistent moral principles in the NRPR makes policy positions unpredictable, the leader-follower gap wide, and the followers more dependent. Small wonder that the principal SB pastors who are caught up in the NRPR tend to be the superstars from the megachurches.

The Southern Strategy, the New Religious Political Right, and the Capture of the Southern Baptist Convention

The Southern Baptist Convention has been in large part taken over by a faction intimately involved with the NRPR. It is this effort and its opposition that have so bitterly divided the Convention since 1979.

The Grand Old Man is W. A. Criswell of the First Baptist Church, Dallas. One of the lieutenants is Paige Patterson, head of the Criswell Center for Bible Studies, which is part of the First Baptist Church complex, historically financed in part by various Hunt family members. Criswell and Patterson were joined by Paul Pressler, a judge in Houston. The five men they have elected to the SBC presidency since 1979 are:

Adrian Rogers, pastor of Bellevue Baptist Church, Memphis, the second largest SBC church. He is thought to be the greatest preacher in the denomination.

Bailey Smith, formerly pastor of the First Baptist Church, Del City, Oklahoma. His presidency was the most contentious. He has become an itinerant evangelist, which means he can convert more people, and make more money, than he ever could even in an affluent church.

James Draper of the First Baptist Church, Euless, Texas. Formerly an assistant pastor at Criswell's church, and now in another part of the Metroplex, he is hard-working and genial – some say no one dislikes him.

Charles Stanley of the First Baptist Church, Atlanta, who has been characterized as "a leader in the campaign to get Christians involved in politics" (Liebman and Wuthnow 1983: 59). The star of a long-established regional television ministry, he grew up outside the SBC and graduated from a non-SB seminary.

Jerry Vines, co-pastor of the First Baptist Church, Jacksonville, Florida, which has participated only minimally in SB programs. Vines comes out of rural Georgia, and appears to be an articulate spokesman for the fundamentalist position.

Rogers served only one year the first time, so a list of the ten year-long presidencies goes: Rogers, Smith, Smith, Draper, Draper, Stanley, Stanley, Rogers, Rogers, and Vines elected in 1988.

The story of the southern strategy and the NRPR begins with the national debt to black service in World War II and growing international awareness of the profundity of America's race problem. Gunnar Myrdal's *American Dilemma,* a thousand-page Carnegie-sponsored study of "America's greatest failure," as the author called it, was published (1944: 1041); India and Pakistan became independent in 1947; there was a new recognition of the relationship between color and power. Southern Baptist Harry Truman, pushed by Henry Wallace to his left, asked Congress for some modest civil rights beginnings after he had desegregated the armed forces. Southern Baptist Strom Thurmond struck back with a third party and carried South Carolina, Alabama, Mississippi and Louisiana in the 1948 election, as Truman increasingly appealed to urban black voters. Eisenhower took four different southern states (Virginia, Tennessee, Texas, and Florida) in 1952, added Louisiana in 1956, and the party reshuffle was on its way.

What the nascent New Right needed to shock them into action was the Supreme Court's 1954 decision in *Brown vs. Board of Education.*

Nevertheless, a Republican coalition of southern liberals, the upper middle class, the old Republican mountain counties, and newly enfranchised blacks proved to be not enough for Nixon in 1960. Kennedy's support in the South was complicated, of course, by the Roman Catholic factor. W. A. Criswell publicly repudiated Kennedy's assurances to the Houston ministers.

During Kennedy's administration, the Court provided more issues for the New Right agenda with *Engel v. Vitale*, striking down government-sponsored prayer in schools, and *Abington School District v. Schempp*, prohibiting Bible reading, in 1962 and 1963, respectively.

The Southern strategy surfaced openly in the 1964 campaign. Phyllis Schlafly, head of Republican women in Illinois, earned national attention with her book supporting Goldwater's candidacy, *A Choice, Not an Echo*, and founded her group of conservative women, the Eagle Forum. Goldwater's opposition to civil rights legislation earned him the same pattern of support in the South as Strom Thurmond. Lyndon Johnson redeemed himself from his solid racist history by signing the epochal civil rights legislation.

In 1968 Nixon, heading off defections to Reagan on his right, followed a version of the southern strategy tailored to newly Republican Strom Thurmond's specifications, bowing to Thurmond's vetoes of vice-presidential suggestions and joining his upraised hands with the Senator's as his nomination victory was celebrated. Nixon, and George Wallace (a Methodist) on a third ticket, split 68.9 percent of the southern presidential vote that year as the Democrats pursued the politics of joy.

In the midst of that year of the assassinations of Martin Luther King, Jr., and Robert Kennedy, the police riot at the Democratic convention, the height of student protests over the Vietnam War, and the beginning of feminist organization, the SBC elected W. A. Criswell as president. The following year he published *Why I Preach that the Bible Is Literally True*, provoking an unusual challenge to his eventual reelection and the beginning of the open politicization of the SBC presidency.

Early in Nixon's administration, the NAACP Legal Defense Fund and the U.S. Justice Department were on opposite sides for the first time. Kirkpatrick Sale comments that Nixon, who "made every effort to reduce funds for school desegregation . . . and to block enforcement of integration laws, . . . tried to sabotage the Voting Rights Act" (1976: 244). He appointed William Rehnquist to the Supreme Court. In 1972 he rejoiced in a solid Republican South. The Equal Rights Amendment passed in Congress and was quickly ratified by 28 state legislatures, inspiring the formation of Phyllis Schlafly's "Stop ERA" campaign the following year.

Other groups in the emerging New Right coalition were outraged by the Supreme Court's decision on abortion, *Roe v. Wade*, in 1973.

The early 1970s were also the period of the first SB neo-fundamentalist organization, the Baptist Faith and Message Fellowship, founded in Charles Stanley's newly orthodox First Baptist Church in Atlanta. (His position as senior pastor there was obtained after a split over his aggressive conservatism — the moderates left.) The Fellowship started to publish an independent *Baptist Journal*, edited by William A. (Bill) Powell, Sr., a former Home Mission Board staff member. There was a fuss, Powell left for a while, and his place was taken by Russell Kaemmerling, Paul Pressler's brother-in-law.

In 1974 came what Liebman and Wuthnow characterize as "the first major effort to build a national movement of conservative evangelicals" (1983: 50). Arizona Congressman John Conlan and Campus Crusade for Christ founder Bill Bright joined forces and focused on a publishing house called Third Century. At the SBC annual meeting in 1975, W. A. Criswell and Adrian Rogers gave a special reception for Representative Conlan, whom Billy Graham also supported, and of whom Ed McAteer (who was himself to rise swiftly in the conservative leadership) said, "I was really impressed with his intellect and his desire to see something done in the government and to change it along moral lines" (Wallis and Michaelson 1976: 7). Some Third Century founders went on to the Christian Embassy, a Washington lobby on whose board sat Graham, Criswell, and SB evangelist and sometime *Christianity Today* editor Harold Lindsell, who was beginning to warn of liberalism in SB seminaries.

The theological common ground of "evangelicalism" failed to keep all of them together. Some objected to the emphasis on civil religion, which historian (and evangelical) Richard Pierard credits Senator Mark Hatfield with highlighting in a "memorable" National Prayer Breakfast Speech in 1973. After this time the "left" evangelicals paid more attention to civil rights, poverty, and the environment, and founded journals like *Sojourners*. The factions may still agree on the abortion issue, but they find most other coalitions impossible.

The Watergate denouement in 1974 helped further to weaken party loyalties, and new legal controls on political fund-raising made small contributions important. The New Right fortuitously had its institutions in place; Paul Weyrich's Heritage Foundation and his political mobilization arm, the Committee for the Survival of a Free Congress; Howard Phillips' Conservative Caucus; Richard Viguerie's computerized direct-mail fundraising and for a decade his *Conservative Digest*; and the American Legislative Exchange Council, dreamed up by North Carolina SB Jesse Helms, "the favorite senator of the far-out white supremacy groups" (Crawford 1980: 132). The American Legislative Exchange Council, which aimed at state legislators in the pipeline for higher office, had striking success in crucial congressional elections and showed their power to make dynamic alliances with single-issue groups on gun control, busing, affirmative action, abortion, and the Equal Rights Amendment.

The 1976 presidential election divided the New Right as it did the Southern Baptists, who were just beginning to flirt with it openly. Religion went public that year, but no one was sure whether it was for better or worse. The American Independent Party rejected the bid, perceived as elitist, of Phillips, Weyrich, Viguerie, and William Rusher of the *National Review* to take it over, and instead nominated Southern Baptist Lester Maddox (who, as Bill Buckley once said, would rather hit a black over the head with an ax handle than serve him fried chicken) for his last hurrah.

The Republicans nearly repudiated incumbent President Ford as some on the Right dreamed of a Ronald Reagan/George Wallace ticket, and religious fundamentalists helped this effort, particularly in the critical North Carolina primary. When it failed, the fundamentalists either voted for Carter or not at all. Carter was not one of them, but the understandable inability of the national press to see this at first and Carter's understandable reluctance to differentiate himself obscured the reality—Carter was a Southern Baptist moderate, with all the internal contradictions that implies.

For reasons some of which were beyond his control, Carter became a disappointment to nearly everybody. He was not what Mazlish and Diamond said the world feared he was, "the stereotypical Southern Baptist small-time bigot" (1979: 188). Political analyst Sidney Blumenthal felt that Carter advanced two powerful ideas, first "restoring integrity to government after Watergate, a commitment demonstrated by his religious authenticity; and second, solidifying racial and regional reconciliation, a commitment demonstrated by his being a southerner devoted to civil rights" (1984A: 15). But reconciliation was not what the Right wanted: Pat Robertson endorsed Carter, but Criswell came out for Ford, shocked, he said, by Carter's interview in *Playboy*, and the multitude of SBs were divided too. Kenneth Woodward wrote in *Newsweek* at the time, "In Texas . . . furor over the Carter candidacy has stripped away the last veneer of Southern Baptist claims to political non-partisanship . . . Criswell's endorsement of President Ford is only the most public act in a whirl of political activities that have found some Southern Baptist clergymen moonlighting in the Carter campaign, while others donate their time and money to right-wing Christian causes (1976: 70).

Carter was a letdown to blacks and economic progressives, too. Carter's hero was Martin Luther King, Jr., and Andrew Young was his friend. But at the end of his term, Atlanta black leader Julian Bond commented that Jimmy knew the words to black songs but not the figures on black paychecks. In the *New Republic*, economist Robert Reich (30 Jan. 1984: 32) explained why: "On the core economic issues of how the burdens and benefits were to be distributed, Jimmy Carter proved himself by the end to be the most conservative Democratic President since Grover Cleveland left the White House in 1896." No wonder he was so hard for the South to figure. Even that master comic Roy Blount, whose inference from Carter's election was "trash no more," may have felt betrayed. Carter's presidency failed to do for white southerners what Kennedy's had done for Catholics — make them respectable in national politics. He had to be repudiated in favor of a smoother, more successful individual who would share all their attitudes and pretensions, their racism, sexism, and homophobia, plus a sort of *arriviste* populism that would play well all over the country.

Two important issues came to public attention during the Carter years and are cited often as the bases for New Right mobilization. One was gay rights, spotlighted by a referendum in Dade County, Florida, and dramatized by SB Anita Bryant. She sparked the "first successful coalition of right-wing Baptist fundamentalists with conservative Jews and Catholics," Percy Deane Young claims (1982: 37). Jerry Falwell helped. Edward L. Ericson explains how "traditional Catholics and Protestants (and Orthodox Jews) could agree that homosexuality was an 'abomination in the eyes of the Lord.' . . . [T]he counterattack against the public acceptance of homosexuality began. It was a cause in which Southern fundamentalist Protestants could show unreserved feeling, demonstrating as passionately for 'decency' and 'family protection' as militant Catholics were crusading against 'baby killers' and a prenatal 'holocaust.' Each group of zealots discovered the other" (1982: 48–49). At the SB annual meetings of 1976 and 1977 there were resolutions and the Christian Life Commission issued a publication: the subject was out of the closet.

The other issue was tax exemptions for religious schools that practiced "racial" discrimination on religious grounds, an enormously complicated matter that came to be known as the Bob Jones Controversy. Here again, Southern fundamentalist Protestants could form alliances with formerly unsympathetic mainline groups afraid of intrusion into their finances. The case dragged on and ultimately gave the Reagan Justice Department an outstanding opportunity to join with the NRPR. In the Supreme Court, however, they lost, with Mr. Rehnquist, in lone dissent, siding with them.

"McAteer Key Figure in SBC Swing to New Right Causes," headlined the Baptist Press analysis of this history (Hastey 1982: 8). In 1976, Ed McAteer joined the Christian Freedom Foundation, the quasi-lobbying organization started with Pew (Sun Oil) money, and continued with support from DeVos of Amway and Talcott of Ocean Spray and the leadership of Bill Bright and Representative Conlan. McAteer was a member of the Bellevue Baptist Church in Memphis, pastored by Adrian Rogers. "In the early '70s," he told an interviewer, "the busing legislation went through. I knew that was not only—well it wasn't even practical—it wasn't good" (Lofton 1981: 75).

As a salesman for Colgate-Palmolive, and as a lay evangelist, McAteer had traveled widely and knew hundreds of leaders in different roles. He retired early and in 1977 became national field director for Howard Phillips' Conservative Caucus. Phillips has said, "Ed was the most important person in making the religious right happen . . . He took me around to meet a lot of people" (Blumenthal 1984B: 22). These meetings linked Phillips and Viguerie with Falwell, Pat Robertson, and Texas SB evangelist James Robison. The goal of the religious right was "to defend the free enterprise system, the family, and Bible 'morality,'" although Michael Novak, Resident Scholar in Religion and Public Policy at the American Enterprise Institute, gleefully pronounced at a conference that "the Moral Majority is simply the curse deserved by the Left," a payback for those turned-around collars in the Selma march and the protests against the Vietnam War.

Another (initially independent) organization, Christian Voice, was begun in opposition to a Gay Rights ordinance in California. Its Washington representative was Southern Baptist Gary Jarmin, and its specialty became the targeting of individual congressional candidates in pursuit of NRPR goals. (The Jesuit Father Robert F. Drinan got a zero morality rating.) The 1978 elections brought heartening success in the election of senators like Southern Baptist Thad Cochran of Mississippi and the reelection of Southern Baptist Jesse Helms in North Carolina, in whose behalf Viguerie raised $5.2 million. Anita Bryant received 3,273 votes for first vice-president of the Southern Baptist Convention that year.

In 1979 McAteer founded yet another part of the network, the Religious Roundtable, to work more closely with pastors and mainline religious leadership and "to reach into the Southern Baptist Convention . . . as well as other conservative denominations" (Wald 1987: 189). He sat on its Board of eleven with other Southern Baptists, Paige Patterson, James Robison, Charles Stanley, and Adrian Rogers. On the wider Council of 56 were W. A. Criswell, Jesse Helms, and Bill Powell of the *Baptist Journal*.

Also in 1979 Paige Patterson and Paul Pressler announced their ten-year plan to take over the Convention for the "inerrantists." Scholarship had led to heterodoxy and liberalism, they said; the SBC must return to its roots, beyond biblical authority to biblical literalism. A series of elected funda- mentalists could use the appointive powers of the SBC presidency even- tually to dominate the agency and seminary boards with like-minded trus- tees. (As Garry Wills has remarked, "The Right just will not learn to keep its mouth shut, to work on a strategy without confessing it" [1969: 251].) At the annual meeting that year they succeeded in electing the Rev. Adrian Rogers of Memphis, Ed McAteer's pastor, to the SBC presidency. Criswell, at the preliminary Pastors' Conference, had said, "We will have a great time here if for no other reason than to elect Adrian Rogers" (Hefley 1986: 66).

Reagan had established close ties to fundamentalists in his 1976 try for the Republican nomination. As the 1980 election approached, the NRPR organized around him, Conlan raising money from Christian businessmen and distributing at the March meeting of the National Association of Evan- gelicals a publication, "Ronald Reagan: a Man of Faith." Adrian Rogers became one of the links: "[he] held a conversation with Reagan early in the primary campaign, in which, he said, he found that God was real to the candidate, who had had a personal experience when he invited Christ into his life. From that point on, Rogers was clearly in the Reagan camp and closely identified with other Christian rightists. *Christian Voice* touted Reagan as the alternative for the Christian voter" (Pierard 1983: 1184).

In April, the New Right, Falwell, Bright, Robertson, and other TV evangelists, produced the "Washington for Jesus" rally on the Mall, and Rog- ers was a featured speaker, using as his text the code passage, II Chronicles 7: 14: "If my people, which are called by my name, shall humble them- selves, and pray, and seek my face, and turn from their wicked ways; then will I hear from heaven, and will forgive their sins, and will heal their land." (The Bible Nancy Reagan held at the 1984 Inauguration was open to that very passage.)

McAteer continued to work behind the scenes at the SB annual meet- ings from 1980, nudging the resolutions committees to harder right positions on the ERA, abortion, and creationism. With floor help from preachers whom he had recruited—including Adrian Rogers, Charles Stanley, and James Robison—these resolutions passed.

Rogers, although he was entitled to, suddenly did not run for a second term in 1980. Some say he had personal reasons (he had had major surgery) or temperamentally had no taste for the necessary battle. Others think his withdrawal was deliberate, to allow the well-organized fundamentalists to elect another of their own as the moderates would be unable to mobilize in time. Another fundamentalist, Rev. Bailey Smith of Del City, Oklahoma, took his place in the SBC presidency.

In the late summer and fall of 1980, Ed McAteer, through the Roundtable, ran Public Affairs Briefings nationwide, bringing the New Right message to at least 40,000 religious leaders. The initial meeting in Dallas (local organization by James Robison) featured Candidate Reagan, who "was uneasy enough about the strength of evangelical support to take the risk of attending," as Pierard noted (1983: 1184). (Carter and John Anderson did not.) At a press conference Reagan expressed his doubts about evolution and, Pierard commented, "irrevocably secured the Moral Majority types for the balance of the campaign" (1184). Reagan's statement made it clear enough where he stood: "I know that you can't endorse me, but I want you to know that I endorse you and what you are doing." Falwell, another featured speaker, could not legally endorse Reagan but urged the audience (over ten thousand) to vote for the Reagan of their choice. Philip Crane, Jesse Helms, Adrian Rogers, and TV evangelists Pat Robertson, James Robison, and Falwell were there. Also Senator William Armstrong, John Connally, Phyllis Schlafly, and Bailey Smith, who made his remark about Jewish prayers on this occasion. Later White House aide Morton Blackwell called the Dallas briefing "a major turning point in the history of the United States" (Blumenthal 1984B: 22).

In the 1980 election, Ronald Reagan carried every southern state but Carter's own. Albert Menendez, an expert on church-state relationships, estimated that Southern Baptist support for Carter withered from 58 percent in 1976 to 40 percent in 1980 (Dunn 1984: 84). In an interview, Ed McAteer explained the decrease, pointing out that many SBs were not active in the Reagan campaign: "Mr. Carter was a member of the Southern Baptist Brotherhood before he got elected President. For various reasons, that being part of it, there is a loyalty factor there. A lot of Southern Baptist preachers did not get involved, and I feel part of it was because of a misconception of where Mr. Carter was theologically, and a loyalty factor that he was one of them. However, interestingly, after the November 4 election, I have personally had several calls from key Southern Baptist pastors congratulating me" (Lofton 1981: 77). That interview was printed in January 1981, by which time McAteer was already feeling frustrated. His calls to the White House were not being returned; he couldn't get appointments. The election results had been analyzed, and as strong as NRPR support had been, it had not been crucial. Reagan's appointment to the Supreme Court of Sandra Day O'Connor, believed to be not adequately absolutist on abortion, led to further frustration. Disgruntled conservatives, including Pat Robertson, were invited to lunch in the office of the White House chief of staff (then Jim Baker) to explain their grievances.

In New Orleans at the SBC annual meeting in 1982, McAteer was on the platform much of the time, openly advising the resolutions committee. He pushed through a reversal on abortion and generated unprecedented support for a constitutional amendment permitting school prayer. In this he had the active urging of the White House but faced opposition by the Baptist Joint Committee, the only time in fifty years the Convention and the Joint Committee had divided. McAteer kept Morton Blackwell (a former Viguerie aide) at the White House informed as to the progress of the fundamentalist takeover. Of the school prayer statement, Blackwell said "McAteer told me the convention was going to do that . . . We were delighted" (Blumenthal 1984B: 23).

McAteer's efforts were not all successful. Stan L. Hastey reported that "messengers wisely—and twice—refused to go along with a resolution which would have expressed the denomination's carte-blanche support for anything the state of Israel chooses to do militarily. According to McAteer, that was the one statement he most wanted to see the convention adopt" (1982: 15). The pre-Convention festivities were also significant. Non-SB and extremely suspect Jerry Falwell met with Bailey Smith, Adrian Rogers, Ed McAteer, and Charles Stanley, Hastey reported. The Sunday night before, the featured speaker was Vice-President George Bush, forging his links to the New Right, telling an intimate group of 42,000 in the Superdome that the mobilization of evangelicals was a healthy development, and giving the Moral Majority and other right groups a strong statement of support. There was a great deal of spluttering about his appearance and the national publicity it received. At this meeting, Jimmy Draper was duly elected president (how convenient it was to have the beginning of the SBC president's two one-year terms aligned with national elections when more was at stake). Each fundamentalist president dutifully made similar appointments, and each year the proportion of fundamentalist trustees increased.

During Draper's terms a massive attempt was mounted to use missions as a unifying device. Nobody disagrees about the importance of missions — it's an apple-pie issue — but the effort failed, as what was elaborately being presented as a theological dispute, between faithful inerrantists and traitorous, unreliable liberals, enveloped, convulsed, the Convention.

In 1984 at Kansas City, Rev. Charles Stanley, televangelist and pastor of the First Baptist Church, Atlanta, director of the Religious Roundtable, and founding director of Moral Majority, Inc., a man with past ties to the super-right Amway firm, was elected on the first ballot. Paul Pressler was elected to fill a vacancy on the Executive Committee after campaigning for the "inerrancy" cause in more than twenty cities.

Then, in a press conference (oddly enough at the First Baptist Church, Dallas) an enthusiastic pro-Israeli statement was issued by nine top SB leaders, including Stanley. Also listed as signers were two past presidents of the SBC, Bailey Smith and Jimmy Draper. And Criswell, Paige Patterson, and Zig Ziglar (a lay "motivation speaker" and touter of "Christian hedonism," who had never before been to an annual meeting when he was elected first vice-president of the SBC in 1984) — all of whom are connected to the First Baptist Church, Dallas — and a local rabbi. And Paul Pressler, his brother-in-law, Russell Kaemmerling, then editor of an arch-conservative SB magazine, and Ed McAteer. (The absence of the last member of the junta, Adrian Rogers, was not mentioned.) Unable to get a Convention resolution, McAteer got his pro-Israeli statement in another way. The SB Foreign Mission Board trustees, who happened to be meeting elsewhere at the time of the statement, reacted negatively, afraid for their missionaries in the Arab/Moslem lands. Stanley made the ritual visit to Israel that fall.

Stanley then became involved in a lengthy polemic, invited by the Atlanta *Journal* and *Constitution*, with a young, female SB pastor from Chicago on the subject of the ordination of women. Letters to the editor in response filled pages, while letters to the state Baptist papers criticized Stanley's extensive use of Roman Catholic theological writings to make his side of the case.

Meanwhile, Ronald Reagan had been reinforcing his links with the NRPR, proclaiming 1983 the Year of the Bible, for instance. Reciprocally, the NRPR was "playing off the 1984 Presidential campaign in order to expand its political machine, broaden its base, and prepare for the future," Blumenthal noted (1984B: 24). In 1983 and 1984 Reagan addressed the National Association of Evangelicals and the National Religious Broadcasters with widely reported speeches full of phrases both colorful and controversial. In June 1984 came a White House reception, with Reagan and Vice-President Bush present, for yet another NRPR group, newly formed, the American Coalition for Traditional Values (ACTV). Its chair was Tim LaHaye; its field director, SB Gary Jarmin; and its executive board members Falwell, SBs McAteer, Robison, Robertson, and SB presidents Rogers, Draper and Stanley, among others. Bailey Smith was not on the top list although he did belong to a larger "Board of Governors"; ACTV was replacing the Religious Roundtable, abandoned in part because of the reaction to Smith's remark about God's selective deafness with regard to prayers. The goal was voter registration at churches, and ACTV hoped for two million additions to the rolls.

At the Republican convention in Dallas later that summer, James Robison gave the invocation, and benedictions came from Falwell and the local W. A. Criswell. Falwell also gave the blessing at a giant fund-raising party at Bunker Hunt's estate: Criswell had announced the previous Sunday that he thought Reagan was "the best President we've ever had," and hosted a giant Prayer Breakfast later in the week. Jimmy Draper appeared before the Republican Platform Committee in behalf of ACTV and said he wished Southern Baptists would give him an equal opportunity to take strong positions on issues like school prayer, religious liberty, pornography, and homosexuality. Falwell, James Robison, Jimmy Swaggart and Greg Dixon also testified. Many observers remarked on the similarity of the Republican platform to the NRPR agenda.

The American Coalition for Traditional Values "poured" money into Helms' reelection campaign in North Carolina, but "polarization of more than one million Baptists . . . [was] a side effect of the contest . . . that illustrate[d] the depth of the ideological struggle between the religious right and the traditional Democrats," John Herbers commented in the *New York Times*. A Southern Baptist minister working for an NRPR group obtained access to the SB state leaders' mailing list and made it available to the Senator's campaign. "Our thinking," the mailing said, "was that in Senator Helms we had a fellow Baptist, a strong Baptist who had been very active in causes we believe in. We thought we ought to say something for him" (Herbers 1984A: 7). Many North Carolina Southern Baptists felt used.

Just before the election, Lamarr Mooneyham, national field director for the Moral Majority, said in an interview that the apparent success of the religious right this year and the source of its new confidence is based not on political considerations but on its having won crucial ideological battles in the fundamentalist churches . . . For the most part . . . the new activists were Baptists, not only in the South . . . who had held to "the myth" that fundamentalist Christians should not engage in political activity. Moral Majority and other groups spent much of the past four years seeking to destroy "the myth" within the Southern Baptist Convention . . . In the process, the religious right, marching under the banner of literal interpretation of the Bible, and opposition to the ordination of women, took over the leadership positions of the denomination . . . The Southern Baptist Convention was split in the process (Herbers 1984B: 38).

In the 1984 election, 87 to 88 percent of non-whites voted for Mondale (90 percent in the South); 63 to 66 percent of whites (70 percent in the South) voted for Reagan. "The racial gap . . . was the most pronounced since 1972," wrote Bill Peterson and Dale Russakoff in the *Washington Post National Weekly* (26 Nov. 1984: 14).

In early 1985, former SB presidents Rogers, Smith and Draper appeared on Pat Robertson's "700 Club" and strongly criticized the Southern Baptist seminaries for their liberalism.

The 1985 Southern Baptist Convention, meeting in Dallas, reinforced the strains of hostility and bitterness. Fundamentalists used the creaky machinery of the SBC bylaws, so dependent on unspecified notions of good will and common purpose, to win their cause. Moderates, most unable still to believe in the possibility, had temporized and organized only in the previous year, using the denominational institutions which they still controlled as their headquarters.

The outcome would hinge on attendance. Criswell sent out letters to 36,000 pastors, and the fundamentalists predicted 40,000 and victory. The moderates, fearful they couldn't match this effort, calculated their success if attendance didn't top 30,000. Messengers began arriving in pouring rain two hours before the doors opened at eight; helicopters reported bumper-to-bumper traffic nine miles away by 7:30 a.m. The total registration when Stanley was reelected was over 45,000, twice the previous high. The moderate candidate for president (Winfred Moore) was elected to the first vice-presidency under the mistaken notion that Stanley had asked him in a gesture of conciliation. This comedy of errors created a fog of good feeling that lasted a whole day.

Then the crucial appointment procedure split the meeting wide open. The moderates, frustrated at the fundamentalist-drenched slate, proposed to substitute an entire list of nominees made up of the presidents of state conventions and women's groups. Fundamentalists reacted sharply to this frontal assault on the president's prerogatives, using delays and high-handed parliamentary tactics, and turning the Evangelism Conference on the free afternoon into a rally. One evangelist thundered, "For years, I've been saying we've got to take off the kid gloves. People who don't believe the Bible can be as mean as all hell. In grace and love and kindness, we've got to fight."

The grace and love and kindness exhibited that evening as Stanley pushed through the original slate resulted in a lawsuit, challenging the bylaws and Stanley's mangling of parliamentary procedure. The plaintiffs' request to the SBC Executive Committee for an investigation was answered with a bland defensiveness. Resort to the courts implied real desperation, since there are biblical and traditional bases for avoiding litigation. The SBC won the case, the court declining to become involved in the internal affairs of a religious organization, and the decision has been sustained on appeal.

A Peace Committee was proposed and appointed—six from each side plus six supposed neutrals, Stanley, and (after the notion was cleared with Paige Patterson) Vice-President Moore. Under threat of a floor challenge, the committee added two women, one from each side; members were already divided as to their mission before leaving Dallas. The resolutions process was handled by defining as "controversial" anything not on the NRPR social agenda. The Rev. Jerry Falwell praised Stanley's victory, saying that he would further conservative causes.

During the following year, as the Peace Committee met inconclusively, the two sides continued to snarl at and spy on each other and extend their political organization. Even greater numbers were anticipated for the 1986 meeting in Atlanta, but only 40,000 showed up, in an atmosphere more weary, more resigned, but no less fraught with tension and ugly controversy. Stanley, on his home turf, used his presidential sermon (not released to the press in advance as had been customary) as a blatant and unprecedented endorsement of Adrian Rogers, the fundamentalist candidate: "We need to keep going in the direction God has sent us on . . . We must not change philosophy of leadership at the crucial moment in the life of Southern Baptists." Right after his sermon, his son Andy, youth minister at his father's church, prayed: "Father, give us the courage to listen to what we just heard and to obey." A proposal to forbid politicking in the presidential sermon was ruled out of order by the chair.

Rogers was elected, with 54 percent of the vote, over Winfred Moore in his second try. Immediately after the applause died, Stanley read a letter from President Reagan, commending the SBC's rightward trend and asking for its support on his social agenda, defined once again as abortion and school prayer. Then Rogers launched into the annual superstar sermon, scheduled a year earlier. Many observers saw this as further proof that every move had been carefully programmed. He tried to indicate his attitudes toward academic freedom; "we're not telling professors what they must believe, but those who work for us ought to reflect what the great majority of Baptists believe."

The tone of the meeting was even closer to a Republican convention: the music, blue backdrop, more communications gadgets, diminished number of black messengers, and no woman speaker but the director of the Woman's Missionary Union. The sincerity and historic authenticity which used to temper the slickness were lacking in the drive toward victory and efficiency, and parliamentary fairness was seen as dispensable. The tiny glimpses of the other side—changes in wording to say that pornography was demeaning to men as well as to women and children, prayers for the husbands of pastors as well as for pastors' wives—were striking in their incongruity. Overheard in the corridor: "Why, they've gotten so intimidated over there they called him on the carpet for an error in a Bible Trivia game."

The resolutions produced no surprises except for the baroque attention paid to the pornography issue, made more remarkable since the chair of the Resolutions Committee had been the director of the Meese Commission, whose report was just being praised. A procedural change to enable more floor nominations was defeated, confirming presidential power, and most of the individual challenges were overcome. The Peace Committee made a preliminary report, announcing that it had found "significant theological diversity" in the seminaries, asking for a year of intercessory prayer and an end to frantic regional political meetings, unfairness in appointments, non-objective reporting, and intemperate language.

Newspapers in all the big southern cities covered the Convention as Philadelphia or Chicago press might do a papal visit, with pages and pages of detail and background and human interest. It was striking how the Atlanta *Journal* and *Constitution* felt they had to explain Southern Baptists to their readers, for it can no longer be taken for granted that all southerners know.

The six SB seminary presidents meeting with agency heads and some Peace Committee members at the Glorieta, New Mexico, camp in the fall of 1986 issued a document describing the Bible as "God-breathed, fully inspired and not errant in any area of reality," and promising to enforce compliance of their various confessional statements. Moderates felt this was capitulation, even though the Peace Committee agreed to halt its investigation of several seminary professors in exchange. One prominent moderate resigned from the Peace Committee, fearing constriction of theological education. The presidents issued a clarifying statement that "not errant" and "reality" might be subject to different interpretations. Fundamentalists felt this was betrayal.

During the winter (1986–87) the Foreign Mission Board dropped a requirement that all its missionaries have a year of training at an SB seminary, opening the door to acceptance of graduates of the three SB-dominated but non-affiliated institutions (Mid-America, Criswell, Luther Rice) to which the junta leaders have such close ties. The Home Mission Board was the first agency to have a fundamentalist majority on its board. Immediately embroiled in a search process for a new president, the trustees took to closed sessions, and chose, to administer their $70 million budget, the fundamentalist head of a small Missouri college (budget $3 million) partly because he was young (52). Then they voted not to fund any additional churches that called a woman as pastor.

A complex restructuring of the SB Public Affairs Committee avoided setting up a separate SB presence in Washington. The Committee would be assured of permanent existence, in order to act when SBs might be out of step with the pan-Baptist Joint Committee, which had meanwhile voted an amended structure in order to give SBs a greater voice. At the 1987 meeting the SBC approved the by-law change and voted in nine new fundamentalist members-at-large.

An inerrantist but not sufficiently pro-fundamentalist editor (Patterson said he had been unfair to conservatives) took direction of Baptist Press in an acrimonious meeting. A moderate ethicist, personally against capital punishment and believing that God can call women to the ministry, became head of the Christian Life Commission (CLC) in a 16 to 13 vote. (On the test issue of abortion, this man took what might be called the Falwell position, tolerating additional exceptions for rape, incest, and perhaps severe fetal deformity, rather than the Reagan position, which excepts only the mother's survival.) The CLC established a Washington office of its own to work on this and other aspects of the social agenda. Both of these men faced insecurity in their positions as fundamentalist majorities on those boards started to exercise their power.

An independent missions organization called the Genesis Commission was started in 1987 with some Texas money and some advisement from

Paige Patterson. It would start church planting in Mexico; implicit was an emphasis on soul-winning rather than on social service, and a shunning of the ordained woman missionary.

The moderates put out a "Peace proposal" designed with never-neverland naiveté. They suggested a compromise presidential candidate, open discussion of the issues, and repeated the proposal that President Rogers appoint to the first-stage nominating committee the presidents of the state conventions and the state WMUs. Pressler and Patterson rejected the plan, and Rogers replied that he would follow the "dictates of his heart." He would appoint only the very best Baptists, those who would appoint to the second-stage committee only those who were like-minded. "I don't see that as political. I see that as consistent," he said.

The 1987 annual meeting in St. Louis was full of large predictabilities and small surprises. Women in Ministry treated a black woman pastor as one of their own. The WMU reported proudly on its first black staff member, and its attempt to upgrade its professional salaries, the lowest of any SB agency. A floor suggestion that WMU become a full participating agency in the SBC, which would destroy its independent financial base and thus its autonomy, was met with a gracious promise of investigation and subsequently turned down. The number of women elected to agency boards dropped to much less than tokenism.

A derogatory joke about blacks from the podium was followed by a resolution from the floor against derogatory jokes about blacks, which disappeared the way unwelcome resolutions are wont to do. A derogatory joke about Native Americans in Jerry Vines' Annual Sermon was eventually followed by the election of a Native American as second vice-president. Bailey Smith, at the Evangelists' Conference, repeated his notorious 1980 remark about God not hearing the prayers of a Jew; commenting, "If the Bible says it, it is true and you should tell it," he received a standing ovation. A cappella singing by the multitude was absent; the liturgical scene was dominated by orchestral ensembles in full evening dress, and, always, the tiny live people on the dais and the giant Image/Mag screens next to them defying the audience to recognize reality.

The outrage-of-the-year was the Peace Committee report, two years in the making, promised a month in advance of the June Convention but delivered the first day. It was released at 7 a.m. to be voted upon at 9 p.m., with thirty minutes scheduled for presentation and discussion. Particularly difficult for moderates to accept were ominous generalities about seminary conformity to the SBC 1963 Faith and Message, the confusing and ambiguous Glorieta statement, and their various confessional words, and a commitment to the continued existence of the Peace Committee for up to three years "for the purpose of observing the response of all agencies, officers and other participants to the recommendations." The front page of the Richmond *Times-Dispatch* (18 June 1987: 1) read "Baptist employees face doctrinal test." Pressler said in an interview "that Baptists remain free to believe as they wish about the Bible, 'as long as they are not employees of the denomination. The committee is telling us that the path to peace is getting the seminaries back in line'" (St. Louis *Post-Dispatch*, 17 June 1987: 7A).

President Rogers was reelected, also as expected, and ruled the meeting, down to 25,000 messengers that year, with his usual combination of mastery and manipulation. Many resolutions, like the one mandating the showing of the United States flag at future SBC meetings, passed with dispatch. Rogers pushed through others—the ones on AIDS, abortion, and homosexuality—with no discussion, an unprecedented occurrence. His sermon celebrated "doctrinal unity," and closed with the strident, martial, male-gender-specific language of "Onward, Christian Soldiers."

A particularly critical resolution dealt with the SBC attempt to dissociate itself from the contemporaneous scandals involving Jim Bakker and the PTL ministry, and, by extension, from its fund-raising techniques. There was great ambivalence, distaste, envy, and a desire to benefit, mixed with the active involvement on the PTL board of three prominent SB pastors, including Bailey Smith. Jimmy Draper, Ed McAteer, and Sam Moore (head of the Thomas Nelson religious publishing house) gave a reception for Pat Robertson, who was fortuitously in St. Louis that week.

A neglected but highly significant occurrence in the intervening year was the inaccurate statement in *Christianity Today* (the newsmagazine of the Billy Graham wing of evangelical Protestantism) that Reagan's veto of the Civil Rights Restoration Act was supported by the "Southern Baptist Convention" (22 April 1988: 39). This identification of the reflex New Right position with the Convention, this capture of the SB voice on public policy issues, is exactly what the fundamentalist leadership had tried so hard to achieve. It hadn't been the whole SBC, of course, just the cleverly restructured Public Affairs Committee, carefully separated from the pan-Baptist Joint Committee (and headed by one of Jesse Helms' former assistants). The Public Affairs Committee also supported Reagan's nomination of Robert Bork to the Supreme Court; the Joint Committee promptly issued a statement distinguishing itself from the SB Public Affairs Committee and from that position. The SBC has been reluctant so far to make a public break with the Joint Committee, but continues to cut its funding.

A series of events between the annual meetings of 1987 and 1988 had the general effect of advertising fundamentalist muscle and tightening fundamentalist control. A prominent state newspaper editor was harassed until he resigned; a prominent ordained woman was appointed to a pastorate in President Rogers' own district, where the church was promptly disfellowshipped; the head of the Christian Life Commission moved to a ministerial post before he could be forced out. The biggest explosion was at Southeastern Seminary, where the president and several administrators resigned over faculty hiring under the pressure of new fundamentalist trustees, several of whom had completed their education at high school. These events got the headlines, but fear, intimidation, and insecurity surrounded writers and editors, professors, missionaries, and agency executives as well.

The moderate response seemed unfocused, weak, and unrealistic. In 1987 some of them formed the Southern Baptist Alliance, a caucus imbued with self-satisfaction, dreaming of restoring the SBC to where it was before, and insensitive to its own racism and sexism. Some were exploring the foundation of a new SB seminary, perhaps an extension of one of the SB universities. One floated again a proposal for a compromise presidential candidate, indicating a total lack of comprehension of the possibility of compromise.

The supposed commitment to stop private politicking and abusive or intemperate language was violated by both sides. Usually the fundamentalists would move first, and pretend to be naive; the moderates would imitate them, and be so. The basic difficulty was not discussed: in a quarrel between two factions, one hard-line and narrowly committed, one casual, freewheeling, and tolerant, the former is bound to win.

Several of the most important SB state conventions (North and South Carolina, Georgia, Louisiana, and Texas, for instance) fought their own version of the national denominational war, and fundamentalists were defeated. This decentralization may turn out to be healthy, but the national voice, and institutional control, are what is coveted by insiders and respected by those outside.

Some of the national media, non-specialists in religious affairs, finally started to pay attention to Southern Baptist anguish. There was a poignant essay in *Newsweek* (Smith 1987: 9), an episode on a prime-time soap, both dealing with the problems of SB women, and the *Wall Street Journal* published a comprehensive analysis (Waldman 1988: 1). Then Bill Moyers,

uthern Baptist moderates destroying resolution on "priesthood of the believer" in front of the amo, San Antonio, 1988. (Photograph courtesy of Toby Druin, *Baptist Standard* of Texas.)

Southwestern Seminary graduate and ordained SB pastor, did a documentary on public television entitled "God and Politics," and touched most of the bases. He included the connections of the fundamentalist SB leadership with the New Right, especially the secretive Council for National Policy and the Christian Reconstructionist Movement. Southern Baptists have a long reputation for ignoring external opinion; reactions in state papers to all this attention seemed muted and resistant to its import.

At the San Antonio meeting in June 1988, Jerry Vines of Jacksonville was elected president with a 50.53 percent majority of the 32,727 registered messengers. Less prominent outside his state than some of the past presidents, he seems equally committed to a continuation of the theological "correction" within the denomination. He said that his opponents used the same vocabulary but not the same dictionary; the issue is clearly not one of theology but of loyalty to the fundamentalist political cause and the tactics necessary to further it. The Peace Committee was dissolved, having done its turn as a lightning rod, and implying that the fundamentalist victory feels secure.

The other convention highlights included a blistering statement on homosexuality, one of the most condemnatory of any large denomination, and puzzling affirmations of the power of prayer and the historic Baptist belief in a literal hell. What attracted the most attention, however, was the rejection of "priesthood of the believer," of the equal responsibility of every Christian to interpret the Bible in light of individual conscience, without an intermediary between human and deity, in favor of pastoral authority and creed-like conformity of belief, as if the Reformation had never happened. Since the resolution came from the fundamentalist Resolutions Committee, instead of from the floor as customary, it appeared that theology was here being subordinated to discipline and political mobilization, the formation of a mighty army.

Other large American Protestant groups are trying to sharpen denominational distinctiveness and shore up denominational authority in reaction to New Right activities outside (and very possibly New Right pressures within). Similar struggles took place in reaction to the Campbellites in the 1840s and the evolution, or modernism, controversy in the 1920s. The overall result, in each case, has been a check to scholarship, creativity, and tolerance in theology, and to liberalizing drifts in theopolitical positions.

Internal Implications for the Southern Baptists

The specific areas of theological agreement mentioned in the 1987 Peace Committee report concerned the real nature of Adam and Eve, the authorship of the Biblical books, and the historicity of Biblical miracles and Biblical narratives. The Home Mission Board, under its new fundamentalist president, has now gone beyond these. Prospective employees are "to affirm that Jesus was the virgin-born son of God, that he died on the cross for our sins, that he rose bodily from the dead, that he ascended physically into heaven and that he literally and physically will be coming again" (*Baptist Standard,* 5 Aug. 1987: 20); one pastor wondered why they don't just require the Nicene Creed. The Home Mission Board, practicing church discipline in a SB agency, has also recently put in new policies against employing those who practice or promote glossolalia (speaking in tongues), and who have been divorced, except on biblical grounds. This tendency to go beyond even what was so painfully agreed upon can only open up further disagreement and invite further guidelines, and soon the point may be reached at which even the hard-liners will no longer agree.

When this happens, and fundamentalist factions run two candidates for SBC president, the moderates will have a chance to regain control of the Convention. How this could come about otherwise is difficult to see. Staying away from the annual meeting, as moderates evidently have been doing, seems counterproductive. However, the moderates may have a chance to increase the proportion of their presence at the 1989 annual meeting, scheduled for Las Vegas, Nevada, where many fundamentalists have already indicated they would be acutely uncomfortable.

The whole idea that the "side" that "wins" the presidential election should have wide authority to replace denominational employees has been allowed to hang in the air unchallenged. This is not the North American or British political system where the top executives are political appointees, supervising a neutral professional civil service; if the Home Mission Board is any guide, it is a wholesale restaffing. "HMB Staff Told to Conform or Be Replaced," the Texas *Baptist Standard* headlined on 8 July 1987. There is a real possibility that the pendulum is not going to be allowed to swing back.

There has been a tremendous increase in closed meetings, executive sessions, and secret ballots; and the minutes of the Peace Committee are to be sealed for ten years. With the fundamentalist victory assured—all of the boards of trustees now have fundamentalist majorities—there may be more openness. At any rate, the battle can be expected to spread to the state conventions, where differing bylaws and different mixes of culture and class will produce a variety of outcomes.

Relations with blacks will return to the ten-foot pole type. In a letter to the editor of *Missions/USA*, Chan C. Garrett wrote, "Many black pastors have expressed the fear that the current controversy, and the ultraconservative swing could result in lost ground for race relations . . . black Americans perceive there has been a lessening of attention to civil rights under the current administration. Black Southern Baptists have some fear that the same may be true in the Convention as leadership is selected from persons, who, they suspect, are more closely aligned with the national political mood" (Nov.–Dec. 1986: 72).

The received wisdom is that the SBC will not schism, although there was a real chance that the fundamentalists would have walked out if they had lost. "Fragment" or "shatter" are better words, for surely some moderates will depart. As individuals in church situations where they feel increasingly alien and isolated, and at a time when identification with the new SBC authoritarianism becomes increasingly distasteful, they will leave for other denominations. Many would find themselves at home in American ("Northern") Baptist congregations, especially those with a strong evangelical (i.e., missions) emphasis. Some might choose the Methodists, historically so strong in the South. Those SBs who long for a sense of history and more color and drama in their liturgy are likely to move the Episcopalian way, and several prominent pastors have done exactly that. Doctrine, it seems, is again dispensable.

Where there are entire moderate churches, usually in university towns or metropolitan areas, they can simply continue on, running their own missions, doing their own politicking, cooperating with other churches on peace marches and other kinds of local ecumenical social action. They can be "dually aligned" with the American Baptists and the SBC (as some are now), or they can largely ignore the national organizations but continue in the Convention with only minimal contributions. They will do their grief work, mourning the huge parental structure that abandoned them, and maybe wait for its possible return. The state conventions may become more important to such churches, and there could be new regional coalitions if geography is as important as SBs seem to think.

The rallying cry, "missions," has already acquired a fresh ambiguity between its mentalist and materialist connotations. To the fundamentalists "missions" means saving souls: to the moderates "missions" may occasionally involve feeding hungry people and caring for sick ones, and even thinking about changes in social structures that contribute to hunger and sickness. As these differences become explicit, the historic unifying goal will become cause for new species of divisiveness.

The seminaries will be the chief pressure points, especially vexed since the question of academic freedom in religious institutions is totally unclear. Whatever sort of "Accuracy in Southern Baptist Academia" network exists will undoubtedly be expanded and receive more outside support. There will be fundamentalist student groups, disgruntled and disruptive as such groups always are, in the more liberal seminaries. Professors will be further intimidated; the broader-minded ones will hope to leave, and some have obtained second, secular Ph.D.s and published in non-SB journals in order to make that easier. They fear that the better students will choose to go elsewhere, not only for more breadth but for an absence of the distracting acrimony. E. Y. Mullins worried about this in 1926, too.

The fates of the Cooperative Program, the billions of dollars of real estate, and the stewardship habits of millions of lifetimes are unclear. A grim joke circulated among pastors—go with the side that gets the Annuity Board—but it's hard to believe that anyone would be moved by those pittance pensions. Nancy Ammerman's research suggests that the fundamentalists have lower educational backgrounds and lower-prestige jobs, both presumably associated with lower incomes, which might cut donations. But their fewer resources might be made up by additional zeal, and there are those wealthy mega-churches, and what is left of Bunker Hunt. However, moderates can withhold donations, too, or send them directly to agencies like the Joint Committee.

There is some evidence of a painful amount of reciprocal cultural prejudice between the two groups that will impede eventual reconciliation. One of the seminal events in the development of the controversy was the aftermath of the 1969 publication of Criswell's book. Partly in response to the earlier Elliott controversy, Broadman Press gave it wide promotion. *Newsweek* (5 May 1969: 97) cited one of its critics, Robert Alley, SB author of a classic biography of James Madison: "the time is now or maybe never for Southern Baptists to enter the mainstream of theological discussion . . . Our greatest concern is the image of the ministry cast by preachers like Criswell . . . As for Jonah's ride in the whale . . . if the author of that story were to step into the world of today and discover that anybody was accepting him word for word, I have a feeling he'd just collapse from laughter."

Jimmy Draper, however, has known this laughter, and resented it. "All we want," he said, "is to be heard and not to be ridiculed . . . What I want is true freedom . . . the liberty to believe and preach and teach without being ridiculed" (Hastings 1983: 9). His word, *ridicule*, turned up as one of a bizarre pair in a 1986 resolution on religious liberty: "Be it finally RESOLVED, That we call upon Southern Baptists to pray for all those who are suffering persecution and ridicule for their commitment to the Lord."

Richard Marius (SB biographer of Thomas More) tells this story: "One of the moderates, pastor of a large comfortable church, told me privately that the real trouble with Bailey Smith was that he served a one-class 'blue-collar' congregation and that he had never been a member of a downtown Rotary Club. It gave me pause to realize that a moderate (who happened to be a former president of the denomination) prized the Rotary Club as a civilizing influence and as a standard for proper behavior" (1984: 160). Such cattiness and cultural prejudice bode ill for denominational reconciliation. The politics that result from status anxiety, without facing the class issues that are at its essence, become sick and ugly because that anxiety can only be assuaged at the expense of others.

All of the fundamentalists, and some of the moderates, claim the battle is theological, and by now they all have to acknowledge that the power struggle has had its own dynamic and its own second-order consequences. The possibility of achieving theological agreement is nil; the possibility of open discussion is close to that. Barnhart, a moderate who fights on fundamentalist turf, feels that the inerrantists must foster such discussion in order to prove their good faith, but this is as unlikely as the Sri Lankans opening the sacred casket to find out whether the Tooth of Buddha is really inside. In both cases their assurance is too sensitive to the air. Another of Barnhart's solutions is to welcome the three quasi-SB seminaries into the fold, let them be inerrantist as they will wish, but keep four of the six historic ones as islands of academic freedom (1986: 246–48). The inerrantists would have the majority but would have to practice tolerance. If, as some claim, the argument is in part over the power to define what it means to be a Southern Baptist, and over the locus of authority to decide, and for several other reasons, these suggestions are decidedly naive.

There are two women teaching theology at SB seminaries. One, with a Duke Ph.D., was approved for the Southeastern faculty in early 1987 by a 14 to 13 vote. One of the opposing trustees explained, "She is not an inerrantist. And I do object to a woman teaching theology. I don't think it is biblical." If theology is a game only men can play, insisting that the denominational controversy is theological in nature strikes another blow for a male monopoly of authority. The next logical question: Can blacks teach theology?

Some observers consider the theological explanation incredible since both sides are so conservative. One Peace Committee member explained, "If you take the broad definition of inerrancy—that is Scripture is 'truth without any mixture of error'—it includes 90 percent of Southern Baptists or more." He sees "no discrepancy between the Peace Committee's plea for balance and fairness in the appointment of committees by the SBC president and President Rogers' vow to appoint only mainstream Southern Baptists who are inerrantists" (Thompson 1987: 12). The ability of some SBs to deny contradiction has already been noted.

Stan Hastey, Washington bureau chief for the Baptist Press, feels that with fundamentalist victory assured their challenge is now organizational: "The greatest danger they face is that they may try to do too much too quickly. If they get greedy and start firing people, that's the one thing that could turn the denomination back into moderate hands" (Schaeffer 1987: 6D). Lynn Clayton, editor of the Louisiana SB paper, sees the pendulum swinging back in two or three years, after President Reagan and Pat Robertson have gone from the scene. And former SB president Herschel Hobbs, who chaired the committee that wrote the 1963 Faith and Message Statement, thinks the convention will locate just to the right of center due to the political nature of the controversy, but will return to center within five years.

These moderates and neutrals are hopeless optimists, and fail to recognize (or are in positions where they cannot do so openly) the totalitarian nature of the fundamentalist tactics. They have been like the German Jews in 1933, unable to believe that anyone could write *Mein Kampf* and mean it. The New Right is like the Old Left; tolerance and democracy are not on their agenda. The ruthlessness, the brutality of the tactics, the winner-take-all approach, are all familiar to students of the Radical Right. As Richard Hofstadter's classic essay, "Pseudo-Conservatism Revisited," points out, "The extreme right wing . . . simply cannot arrive at a psychological modus vivendi with authority, cannot reconcile itself to that combination of acceptance and criticism which the democratic process requires . . . The right wing tolerates no compromises, accepts no half measures, understands no defeats" (1962: 102).

There are two parts to the fundamentalists, the leaders and the led. Everything known (from Nancy Ammerman's largely unpublished work at Emory University, and James Guth's research which has appeared in several different journals) indicates that the mass supporters of the fundamentalist takeover are more rural, less well educated, less affluent, than the SB moderates. To them the pure literalism supplies absolute security, threatened by the so-called "slippery slope" argument. Ed Young of Houston Second described it thus: "[if] historical facts and events are questions, then so are the doctrines they teach. Once Adam and Eve are denied, then the fall of man is questioned. And when the Fall is denied, there is no reason for the cross" (quoted in Frame 1987: 45). Jerry Vines, in the 1987 SBC annual sermon, put it this way: "If I'm not sure what my Bible says about creation, how can I be sure of what it says about salvation?" Ammerman sees emigration to urban diversity and complexity in the background— Percy's people who are going nuts in Atlanta condominiums, cut off from rural order, homogeneity, and security. Fundamentalism implies a certain distrust of one's own ability, or even right, to develop a personal hermeneutic and apply individual knowledge, experience, and imagination to the

Biblical words. In other words, it's part of an authoritarian bargain, an escape from freedom and responsibility.

The leaders are another matter, those who have held the presidency in the last few years. They are all top evangelists, all with huge congregations, all skillful and experienced users of electronic media, mass manipulators. And they all have strong New Right connections, although they are perceived differently by different observers.

At least a few Southern Baptists have seen the connections, if not always their purposefulness. Southern Seminary church historian Bill Leonard puts the Southern Baptists in perspective: "We have to say we are a part of a much larger movement taking place throughout American culture. That is an effort to create a new religious establishment, and to bring to bear into the public arena certain evangelical Christian political agendas that then define the nature of religion in America . . . Efforts to bring the SBC into that broader coalition illustrate the point" (quoted in Knox 1986: 1). Leonard is even willing to acknowledge the racist element in his list of reasons for the NRPR: "significant frustration over court rulings on prayer and Bible reading in public schools, abortion, and civil rights (The latter is often not addressed publicly but is clearly an issue, particularly for Southerners)" (Bill J. Leonard 1986: 202).

Harvard Divinity School's Harvey Cox interviewed Jerry Falwell regarding the relationship of the Moral Majority with the SBC. Falwell, he found, "cannot even bring in conservative pastors who are still associated with the Southern Baptist Convention, for this would arouse suspicion. That will be the next step, but for now, one small step at a time" (1984: 47). On the other hand, SBs may not yet be welcome. Cox concludes that Falwell's "version of a Baptist fundamentalist ecumene must at present avoid the conservative churches, that, unlike the ones he is now working with, remain within the Southern Baptist Convention (a denomination many Americans regard as itself the archetype of conservatism) because his constituency would regard them as too liberal" (48). Many SBs may have been dubious about the Moral Majority and its more recent umbrella, the Liberty Federation, but there's no reason why that should matter to the NRPR coalition. It's not their membership or their attitude that is important, it is their votes, their money, their potential for organizing around the complex of New Right issues, or for its candidates.

other signature on Pat Robertson's petition; recruiting at the annual meeting, St. Louis, 1987. otograph by Stanley Leary, courtesy of Baptist Press.)

Southern Baptist Identity in the Newest South

The 1988 presidential campaign began with elaborate and wary mating dances among the potential candidatees, the parties and the various strains of the NRPR.

Pat Robertson resigned his Southern Baptist ordination early in his abortive effort but he has close relationships with its fundamentalist junta. He sought advice on his political future from Stanley, Draper, and Houston Second's Ed Young, as well as Bill Bright and Tim LaHaye.

Jerry Falwell originally declared for Episcopalian Vice-President Bush, and the Christian Voice people came out for Jack Kemp, who also gained support from Jesse Helms' Congressional Club. They would unite for this election, and this list shows how firmly the NRPR has attached itself to the Republican party, but from the party's standpoint, what a complex of problems it poses. Finding comfortable positions on class issues is extremely difficult. As Michael Lienesch points out, "Christian conservative strategists have realized that economic interest will tend to draw their potential conservative converts toward liberal economic policies. Thus they have used symbolic issues, not to meet economic ends, but to override them" 1982: 413). And if they move to foreign policy, as Jerry Falwell has tried to do, they find more complications.

The NRPR as a coalition has other potential fault lines, even on "social" issues. The core agenda, as given by countless commentators and highlighted in Reagan's letter to Southern Baptists in Atlanta, is abortion and school prayer. The abortion issue can unite fundamentalists, Catholics, Orthodox Jews, and groups fundamentalists consider marginally or "pseudo-Christian," like Mormons and Moonies. But the school prayer issue instantly fractures that coalition, repelling Jews whose very presence denies the Christianity of the United States, and Catholics who founded their own schools in the nineteenth century exactly to escape the heavy Protestant bias of the public system. Beyond these interdenominational difficulties, the fundamentalists themselves have a long history of falling out on doctrinal matters.

The Democrats have their own problems. As they have lost eight million white southern conservative Christians, they have added an equal number of blacks. But the leadership is increasingly out of touch with the lower-income party members; it wants to be associated with the seemingly dynamic sectors of the economy, it needs campaign contributions from wealthy donors, and its upper-income members have personally benefited from many of Reagan's economic policies. Backing away from its historic economic populism, the party backs off from the poor. Since blacks are disproportionately poor, Democrats back down from that commitment, too. Only three out of ten white males voted Democratic in 1984, although they were 14 out of 15 Democratic candidates that year. White males find it extremely difficult to see why their interests are not identical with the general one, but are only about 45 percent of the electorate. The Democrats might win nationally without them, but for all these reasons, as well as their stake at state and local levels, they have been unwilling to try.

"Evangelicals" are now permanent players in politics. They have discovered anew that participation in this world can be construed as part of their struggle toward the next one. They are overwhelmingly southern, and their "ressentiment" is based overwhelmingly in desegregation and black voting rights, which have denied them the South they expected to inherit. Because mentioning "race" is now taboo inside the fringe — "racism" must be more genteel and its implementation better disguised — the complex issues of sexual and parental authority have become their overt preoccupation, the marker of their identity and solidarity, and a restatement of their

residential solidarity at the annual meeting, St. Louis, 1987, from left: Charles Stanley, 1984– ; James L. Sullivan, 1976–77; Adrian P. Rogers, 1979–80 and 1986–88; W. Wayne Dehoney, 64–66; Jimmy R. Allen, 1977–79; Herschel H. Hobbs, 1961–63; H. Franklin Paschall, 1966– ; Bailey E. Smith, 1980–82; and James T. Draper, 1982–84. (Photograph by Van Payne, cour- y of Baptist Press.)

claim to ownership of the culture. Though their numbers have been exaggerated and their political importance inflated, the capture of the Southern Baptist Convention gives them new strength. They are not going to disappear.

The triumph of the fundamentalist junta in the Southern Baptist Convention is a symbol that the class structure of the South has changed to the point where white solidarity is irrelevant – and impossible. The fundamentalist triumph also represents an acceptance of materialism, "Christian hedonism." (Adrian Rogers' book, published in 1987 by Broadman, is titled *God's Way to Health, Wealth and Wisdom,* although he was eager to add that the best things in life are free.) Probably it implies a new acceptance of economic differences, now subsumed within the denomination by doctrinal unity. There is a new creedalism (for Baptists) and a new imposition of behavioral norms, a new conformity, more like the televangelists SBs have asserted they despise. Falwell and Robertson have been weak in the Deep South precisely because the Southern Baptist Convention was there. But now, with a new identity and purpose for the SBC, the junta leaders will try to align its members with the NRPR. Living with a less sympathetic U.S. president will be the first test.

Southern Baptists branched off from Baptist roots because of the peculiar social role they played in the Solid South. Biblical literalism, exclusivity, and mentalism once worked to draw attention away from the social realities and SBs' somewhat uncomfortable place therein. Now these characteristics are being used as a last-ditch attempt (ideologies are always defensive, Karl Mannheim said) to protect white male authority. The more rural and less well educated are persuaded to see this as continuity and fidelity to tradition. The newly affluent find it a convenient way to celebrate their status. Together they are using, and in turn are being used by, a national political coalition that aims to redesign the entire culture to its liking. The moderates hold to other aspects of the past: the primacy of the individual conscience, local church autonomy, and church-state separation—and, to a certain extent, academic freedom—which made the denomination seem to have moved into the mainstream. (The mainstream, of course, had in part acquired these qualities from the Baptists.)

The late, great, maverick anthropologist Leslie White pointed out that ultimately there is no way to evaluate religions, except that "there is one sense . . . in which one people might be said to be 'more moral' than another . . . the degree to which any people conform in actual practice to the ethical code that it professes to live by" (1959: 223). Southern Baptists find it hard to be both broad-minded and narrowly committed: they have few Jesuits. They have resolved their dilemmas, for a time at least, by dividing their complex and internally contradictory distinctiveness, each "side" in the controversy laying claim to a part. Each affirms ownership of the true Southern Baptist tradition; their identity remains in dispute.

References

Southern Baptist Periodicals Cited

Baptist Program; SBC Executive Committee, Nashville.
Baptist History and Heritage (BH&H); The Historical Commission of the SBC, Nashville.
Book of Reports; issued in time for the annual meeting, containing agency reports and proposed recommendations.
Church Training; Sunday School Board of the SBC, Nashville.
The Home Field [defunct]; Home Mission Board of the SBC, Atlanta.
Home Missions [defunct]; Home Mission Board of the SBC, Atlanta.
Light; Christian Life Commission of the SBC, Nashville.
Missions/USA; Home Mission Board of the SBC, Atlanta.
Quarterly Review; Sunday School Board of the SBC, Nashville.
Recorder, Biblical Recorder; Baptist State Convention of North Carolina, Cary.
Report from the Capital; Baptist Joint Committee on Public Affairs, Washington, D.C.
Review and Expositor; Southern Baptist Theological Seminary, Louisville.
SBC Annual; issued after the annual meeting and containing its official minutes and agency reports as accepted.
Standard, Baptist Standard; Baptist General Convention of Texas, Dallas.
Western Recorder; Kentucky Baptist Convention, Middletown.

AAUP (American Association of University Professors)
    1988   "The Annual Report on the Economic Status of the Profession: 1987–88." *Academe* 74, no. 2 (March–April): 48.
Ahlstrom, Sydney E.
    1972   *A Religious History of the American People*. New Haven: Yale Univ. Press.
Anderton, T. Lee
    1980   *Church Property Building Guidebook*. Church Architecture Department, Sunday School Board, Southern Baptist Convention. Nashville: Convention Press.

Ashmore, Harry S.

1982   *Hearts and Minds.* New York: McGraw-Hill.

Bailey, Kenneth K.

1977   "The Post–Civil War Racial Separations in Southern Protestantism: Another Look." *Church History* 46, no. 4 (Dec.): 453–73.

Baker, James T.

1973   "Southern Baptists in the 70s." *Christian Century,* 25–27 June: 669–703.

Baker, Robert A.

1966A   *A Baptist Source Book.* Nashville: Broadman.

1966B   *The Story of the Sunday School Board.* Nashville: Convention Press.

1974   *The Southern Baptist Convention and Its People, 1607–1972.* Nashville: Broadman.

Baker, Tod A., Robert P. Steed, and Laurence W. Moreland, eds.

1983   *Religion and Politics in the South: Mass and Elite Perspectives.* New York: Praeger.

Barnhart, Joe Edward

1986   *The Southern Baptist Holy War.* Austin: Texas Monthly Press.

Beifuss, Joan Turner

1982   "Catholic Seminaries Open to Other Religious Beliefs." *National Catholic Reporter,* 14 May: 26.

Bellah, Robert

1964   "Religious Evolution." *American Sociological Review* 29: 358–74.

Berger, Peter

1961   *The Noise of Solemn Assemblies.* Garden City, NY: Doubleday.

1979   *The Heretical Imperative.* Garden City, NY: Doubleday Anchor.

Bernard, James D.

1926   "The Baptists." *American Mercury:* 136–46.

Berry, Brian J. L., and John D. Kasarda

1977   *Contemporary Urban Ecology.* New York: Macmillan.

Black, Earl, and Merle Black

1987   *Politics and Society in the South.* Cambridge, MA: Harvard Univ. Press.

Blevins, Kent B.

1980   "Southern Baptist Attitudes toward the Vietnam War in the Years 1965–1970." *Foundations* 23, no. 3: 231–44.

Blumenthal, Sidney

1984A   "Over and Out." *The New Republic,* 13 Feb.: 14–17.

1984B   "The Righteous Empire." *The New Republic,* 22 Oct.: 18–24.

Boles, John B.

1972   *The Great Revival, 1787–1805: The Origins of the Southern Evangelical Mind.* Lexington: Univ. Press of Kentucky.

1976   *Religion in Antebellum Kentucky.* Lexington: Univ. Press of Kentucky.

Bonham, Tal D.
  1980   "Pitfalls of Child Evangelism." *The Baptist Program,* Jan.: 17.
Briggs, Kenneth A.
  1977   "An Evangelical's Rise." *New York Times,* 30 July: 19.
Brownell, Blaine A.
  1975   *The Urban Ethos: the South, 1920–1930.* Baton Rouge: Louisiana State
            Univ. Press.
Broyard, Anatole
  1982   "In Praise of Contact." *New York Times Book Review,* 27 June: 31.
Bruce, Dickson D. Jr.
  1974   *And They All Sang Hallelujah: Plain-Folk Camp-Meeting Religion, 1800–
            1845.* Knoxville: Univ. of Tennessee Press.
Bryant, M. Darrol
  1974   "America as God's Kingdom." In *Religion and Political Society,* ed. Jur-
            gen Moltmann et al., 49–94. New York: Harper Forum.
Buchanan, John
  1984   "A Baptist Witness." *Light,* Feb.: 10.
Burton, Joe Wright
  1977A   *Road to Recovery: Southern Baptist Renewal Following the Civil War.*
            Nashville: Broadman.
  1977B   *Road to Nashville.* Nashville: Broadman.
Caldwell, Erskine
  1968   *Deep South: Memory and Observation.* Rpt., Athens: Univ. of Georgia
            Press, 1980.
Cameron, J. M.
  1986   Letter to the Editor, *New York Review of Books,* 29 May: 56–57.
Campbell, Will D.
  1974   "The World of the Redneck." *Christianity and Crisis,* 27 May: 111–18.
Caplan, Lincoln
  1987   "The Tenth Justice." *The New Yorker,* 10 Aug.: 29–58.
Carter, Rosalynn
  1984   *First Lady from Plains.* Boston: Houghton-Mifflin.
Cash, W. J.
  1941   *The Mind of the South.* New York: Vintage.
Corsa, Leslie
  1966   "The United States." In *Family Planning and Population Programs,* ed.
            B. Berelson. Chicago: Univ. of Chicago Press.
Cox, Harvey, ed.
  1984   *Religion in the Secular City.* New York: Simon and Schuster.
Crawford, Alan
  1980   *Thunder on the Right.* New York: Pantheon.

Curtis, Charlotte
    1983   "Mrs. Carter Speaks Out." *New York Times,* 14 June: C9.

Davis, David Brion
    1984   *Slavery and Human Progress.* New York: Oxford Univ. Press.

Davis, James H.
    1981   "Dilemmas of Racial Transition." In *Churches in Racially Changing Communities.* Atlanta: Home Mission Board, Southern Baptist Convention.

Degler, Carl N.
    1977   *Place Over Time: the Continuity of Southern Distinctiveness.* Baton Rouge: Louisiana State Univ. Press.

Douglas, Ann
    1977   *The Feminization of American Culture.* New York: Avon (Discus).

Drew, Elizabeth
    1978   *American Journal: the Events of 1976.* New York: Vintage.

Driggers, B. Carlisle
    1981   "Witnessing Concepts: Trends and Sensitivity." In *Partners in Ministry,* ed. Chan C. Garrett. Atlanta: Home Mission Board, Southern Baptist Convention.

Dunn, James
    1984   "Wise as Serpents, at Least: the Political and Social Perspectives of the Electronic Church." *Review and Expositor* 81, no. 1 (Winter): 77–92.

Dworkin, Andrea
    1983   *Right-Wing Women.* New York: Perigee Books (Putnam).

Edmonds, Richard H.
    1912   "Southern Wealth and Its Consecration." In *The Home Missions Task,* ed. Victor I. Masters, 97–126. Atlanta: Home Mission Board, Southern Baptist Convention.

Eighmy, John Lee
    1969   "Religious Liberalism in the South during the Progressive Era." *Church History,* Sept.: 359–72.
    1972   *Churches in Cultural Captivity: A History of the Social Attitudes of Southern Baptists.* Knoxville: Univ. of Tennessee Press.

Ellinwood, Leonard
    1953   *The History of American Church Music.* New York: Morehouse-Gorham.

Elliot, Ralph
    1982   *Church Growth That Counts.* Valley Forge, PA: Judson.

Ericson, Edward L.
    1982   *American Freedom and the Radical Right.* New York: Ungar.

Farley, Gary E.
    1987   "The Other Crises in Rural America." *The Baptist Program,* Aug.: 4–5.

Farrell, Michael S.
    1986   "Grace Mojtabai." *National Catholic Reporter,* 1 Aug.: 9–13.

Faulkner, Harold Underwood
 1931   *The Quest for Social Justice, 1898–1914.* Vol. 11 of *An History of American Life,* ed. A. M. Schlesinger and D. R. Fox. New York: Macmillan.
Fitzgerald, Frances
 1987   "Reagan's Band of True Believers." *New York Times Magazine,* 10 May: 36 et seq.
Fleming, Walter Lynwood
 1919   *The Sequel of Appomattox.* New Haven: Yale Univ. Press.
Flynt, J. Wayne
 1969   "Dissent in Zion: Alabama Baptists and Social Issues, 1900–1914." *Journal of Southern History* 35, no. 4 (Nov.): 523–42.
 1977   "Religion in the Urban South: the Divided Religious Mind of Birmingham, 1900–1930." *Alabama Review* 30 (April): 108–34.
 1979   *Dixie's Forgotten People: The South's Poor Whites.* Bloomington: Indiana Univ. Press.
 1981   "One in the Spirit, Many in the Flesh: Southern Evangelicals." In *Varieties of Southern Evangelicalism,* ed. David E. Harrell, 23–44. Macon, GA: Mercer Univ. Press.
Frady, Marshall
 1967   "God and Man in the South." *Atlantic Monthly,* Jan.: 37–42.
 1980   "The Technician from Plains." In *Southerners,* 326–58. New York: New American Library.
Frame, Randy
 1987   "Battle on the Bible." *Christianity Today,* 12 June: 42–46.
Franklin, John Hope
 1967   *From Slavery to Freedom,* 3rd ed. New York: Knopf.
Furniss, Norman
 1954   *The Fundamentalist Controversy.* Rpt., Hamden, CT: Anchor, 1963.
Gaddy, Curtis Welton
 1969   *The Christian Life Commission of the Southern Baptist Convention: a Critical Examination.* Ph.D. diss., Southern Baptist Theological Seminary, Louisville.
Garrett, Chan C.
 1986   "Is racism increasing?" [Letter to the Editor]. *Missions/USA,* Nov.–Dec.: 72.
Gatewood, Willard B., Jr.
 1966   *Preachers, Pedagogues and Politicians: the Evolution Controversy in North Carolina, 1920–1927.* Chapel Hill: Univ. of North Carolina Press.
Genovese, Eugene
 1974   *Roll, Jordan, Roll.* New York: Pantheon.
Gilkey, Langdon
 1963   *How the Church Can Minister to the World Without Losing Itself.* New York: Harper and Row.

Glad, Betty

    1980   *Jimmy Carter: In Search of the Great White House.* New York: Norton.

Goldenberg, Naomi R.

    1979   *Changing of the Gods: Feminism and the End of Traditional Religions.* Boston: Beacon.

Greene, Johnny

    1981   "The Astonishing Wrongs of the New Moral Right." *Playboy,* Jan.: 117 et seq.

Greenhouse, Carol J.

    1986   *Praying for Justice: Faith, Order and Community in an American Town.* Ithaca, NY: Cornell Univ. Press.

Guth, James L

    1983   "Preachers and Politics: Varieties of Activism among Southern Baptist Ministers." In *Religion and Politics in the South,* ed. Tod A. Baker, Robert P. Steed, and Laurence W. Moreland, 161–83.

Gwynn, Frederick L., and Joseph L. Blotner, eds.

    1965   *Faulkner in the University.* New York: Random House.

Harmon, George

    1963   "How to Tell a Baptist from a Methodist in the South." *Harper's,* Feb.: 58–63.

Harrison, Paul M.

    1959   *Authority and Power in a Free Protestant Tradition.* Princeton: Princeton Univ. Press.

Hastey, Stan L.

    1979   *Baptists and Religious Liberty,* The Baptist Heritage Series [pamphlets]. Nashville: The Historical Commission, Southern Baptist Convention.

    1982A   "Bill Moyers: CBS Evening News." *Report from the Capital,* June: 10–11.

    1982B   "McAteer Key Figure in Southern Baptist Convention Swing to New Right Causes." *Biblical Recorder,* 24 July: 8–15.

Hastings, Robert J.

    1983   Baptist Press release. *SBC Today,* June: 9.

Hawkins, Leo

    1964   "Preaching on Race Relations." *Messages from the Third Annual Conference on Human Relations,* St. John's Baptist Church, Charlotte, N.C., 27–28 Feb. (Baptist State Convention of North Carolina, Department of Interracial Cooperation): 57.

Hays, Brooks, and John E. Stealy

    1981   *The Baptist Way of Life,* 2nd ed., rev. Macon, GA: Mercer Univ. Press.

Hefley, James C.

    1986   *The Truth in Crisis: the Controversy in the Southern Baptist Convention.* Dallas: Criterion Publications.

Herbers, John

  1984A "Senate Race in North Carolina Proving a Bitter Mix of Politics and Religion." *New York Times*, 4 Oct.: A7.

  1984B "Moral Majority and Their Allies Expect Harvest of Votes for Conservatives." *New York Times*, 4 Nov.: A38.

Hesselgrave, David J.

  1980 *Planting Churches Cross-Culturally: a Guide for Home and Foreign Missions*. Grand Rapids, MI: Baker Book House.

Hewitt, T. Furman

  1983 Personal communication.

Hill, Samuel S., Jr.

  1967 *Southern Churches in Crisis*. New York; Holt.

  1972 *Religion and the Solid South*. Nashville: Abingdon.

  1980 *The South and the North in American Religion*. Athens: Univ. of Georgia Press.

Hill, Samuel S., Jr., and Dennis E. Owen

  1982 *The New Religious Political Right in America*. Nashville: Abingdon.

Hinson, E. Glenn

  1984 "Southern Baptists and the Liberal Tradition." *Baptist History and Heritage* 19, 3 (July): 16–20.

Historical Commission, Southern Baptist Convention

      Encyclopedia of Southern Baptists. 4 vols. to date, Nashville: Broadman, 1958–   .

Hobbs, Herschel H.

  1978 "The Baptist Faith and Message – Anchored But Free." *Baptist History and Heritage* 13, no. 3 (July): 33–40.

Hofstadter, Richard

  1962 "Pseudo-Conservatism Revisited: a Postscript." In *The Radical Right*, ed. Daniel Bell, 97–104. New York: Doubleday, 1964.

  1965 *The Paranoid Style in American Politics and Other Essays*. New York: Knopf.

  1974 *Anti-Intellectualism in American Life*. New York: Knopf.

Holifield, E. Brooks

  1976 "The Three Strands of Jimmy Carter's Religion." *The New Republic*, 5 June: 15–17.

Hough, Joseph C., Jr.

  1968 *Black Power and White Protestants*, London: Oxford Univ. Press.

Hull, William E.

  1982 "Church-Swapping." *The Baptist Program*, May: 4.

Hunter, Allen

  1981 "In the Wings: New Right Ideology and Organization." *Radical America* 15, no. 1–2 (Spring): 113–38.

Hunter, James Davison

    1983   *American Evangelicalism: Conservative Religion and the Quandary of Modernity.* New Brunswick, NJ: Rutgers Univ. Press.

Hyatt, Irwin T., Jr.

    1976   *Our Ordered Lives Confess.* Cambridge, MA: Harvard Univ. Press.

Johnson, Paul

    1977   *A History of Christianity.* New York: Atheneum.

Jones, Neal T.

    1982   "Strengthening Families through the Church." *Light,* May–June: 3–6.

Keeton, H. Dale

    1982   "Strengthening Families through the Church." In *Strengthening Families* (Conference Proceedings), 39–42. Nashville: Christian Life Commission, Southern Baptist Convention.

Kelsey, George D.

    1973   *Social Ethics among Southern Baptists, 1917–1969.* Metuchen, NJ: Scarecrow.

Knight, Walker

    1987   "Pressler: Politicizing the SBC." *SBC Today,* Feb.: 1.

Knox, Marv

    1986   "Will the SBC Split? Maybe Yes, Maybe No." Baptist Press Advance Background Story, 16 July. Mimeo.

Kraditor, Aileen S., ed.

    1970   *Up from the Pedestal.* Chicago: Quadrangle.

Kruschwitz, William

    1984   "Helping Churches Develop." *The Commission,* June–July: 71.

Kucharsky, David

    1976   *The Man from Plains.* New York: Harper & Row.

Lake, David

    1967   *The Southern Baptist View of the Church.* Ph.D. diss., Univ. of Iowa.

Lapham, Lewis

    1971   "Military Theology." *Harper's,* July: 74–79.

Lee, Richard

    1979   *The !Kung San: Men, Women, and Work in a Foraging Society.* Cambridge: Cambridge Univ. Press.

Leonard, Bill J.

    1986   "Southern Baptists and the Separation of Church and State." *Review and Expositor* 83, no. 2 (Spring): 195–208.

Liebman, Robert C., and Robert Wuthnow

    1983   *The New Christian Right.* Hawthorne, NY: Aldine.

Lienesch, Michael

    1982   "Right-Wing Religion: Christian Conservatism as a Political Movement." *Political Science Quarterly* 97, no. 3 (Fall): 403–25.

Lofton, John D., Jr.
1981   "Roundtable President; Ed McAteer is Music Man of the Religious
          Right." *Conservative Digest*, Jan.: 74–79. (Reprinted in *The New Right:
          Fundamentalists and Financiers*. Oakland: Data Center Press Profile
          no. 4, Fall 1981).
Loveland, Anne C.
1980   *Southern Evangelists and the Social Order, 1800–1860*. Baton Rouge:
          Louisiana State Univ. Press.
Lyles, Jean Caffey
1980   "'Creeping Creedalism' in the Southern Baptist Convention." *Chris-
          tian Century*, 2–9 July: 691–92.
Marius, Richard
1984   "Musings on the Mysteries of the American South." *Daedalus* 113, no.
          3 (Summer): 143–76.
Marty, Martin E.
1974   "M.E.M.O." *Christian Century*, 20 Feb.: 215.
1977   *Religion, Awakening and Revolution*. Wilmington, NC: McGrath.
1982   "Fundamentalism as a Social Phenomenon." *Review and Expositor* 79,
          no. 1 (Winter): 19–29.
Masters, Victor I.
1912   "A Historical Sketch." In *The Home Missions Task*, ed. Victor I. Mas-
          ters, 9–40. Atlanta: Home Mission Board, Southern Baptist Convention.
1915   *Baptist Missions in the South*. Atlanta: Baptist State Mission Boards of
          the South and the Home Mission Board, Southern Baptist Convention.
1916   "Concerning Immigration." *The Home Field*, Feb.: 25.
1917   *Country Church in the South*. 2nd ed. Atlanta: Home Mission Board,
          Southern Baptist Convention.
1918   *The Call of the South*. Atlanta: Home Mission Board, Southern Baptist
          Convention.
Maston, T. B.
1959   *The Bible and Race*. Nashville: Broadman.
Maston, T. B., with William M. Tillman, Jr.
1983   *The Bible and Family Relations*. Nashville: Broadman.
Mathews, Donald G.
1977   *Religion in the Old South*. Chicago: Univ. of Chicago Press.
May, Lynn E.
1979   *The Baptist Story*. Nashville: Historical Commission, Southern Bap-
          tist Convention.
Mazlish, Bruce, and Edwin Diamond
1979   *Jimmy Carter: An Interpretative Biography*. New York: Simon and Schuster.
McBeth, Leon
1977   "The Role of Women in Southern Baptist History." *Baptist History
          and Heritage* 12, no. 1 (Jan.): 3–25.

1982   "Fundamentalism in the Southern Baptist Convention in Recent Years." *Review and Expositor* 79, no. 1 (Winter): 85–104.

McCall, Duke
  1978   "The Cooperative Program: a Critical Review." *The Baptist Program,* April: 16–22.

McClellan, Albert
  1975   "The Origin and Development of the Southern Baptist Convention Co-operative Program." *Baptist History and Heritage* 10, no. 2 (April): 69–78.
  1978A   "Southern Baptist Roots in Practice and Polity." *Review and Expositor* 75, no. 2 (Spring): 279–93.
  1978B   "The Shaping of the Southern Baptist Mind." *Baptist History and Heritage* 13, no. 3 (July): 2–11.

McGavran, Donald A.
  1980   *Understanding Church Growth.* Grand Rapids, MI: Eerdmans.

McGavran, Donald A., and George G. Hunter III
  1980   *Church Growth: Strategies That Work.* Nashville: Abingdon.

Merriam, Edmund F.
  1900   *A History of American Baptist Missions.* Philadelphia: American Baptist Publications Society.

Mollenhoff, Clark
  1980   *The President Who Failed.* New York: Macmillan.

Moore, LeRoy
  1977   "Crazy Quilt: Southern Baptist Patterns of the Church." *Foundations* 20, no. 1 (Jan.): 12–35.

Myrdal, Gunnar
  1944   *An American Dilemma.* Rpt., New York: McGraw-Hill, 1964.

Naipaul, V. S.
  1984   "Among the Republicans," *New York Review of Books* 25 Oct.: 5 et seq.

Newcomb, Horace
  1976   "Being Southern Baptist on the Northern Fringe." In *On Jordan's Stormy Banks: Religion in the South,* ed. Jim Sessions, Sue Thrasher, and Bill Troy. Spec. issue of *Southern Exposure* 4, no. 3: 93–100. Rev. ed., Macon, GA: Mercer Univ. Press, 1983.

Newsweek
  1969   "Battle of the Book." 5 May: 96–97.

Nichol, John W.
  1969   "A Local Church's Struggle for Integrity." Proceedings of the 1969 Christian Life Commission Seminar. Nashville: Christian Life Commission, Southern Baptist Convention.

Niebuhr, H. Richard
  1929   *The Social Sources of Denominationalism.* Rpt., New York: World Publishing, 1972.

O'Brien, David
1982 "The Roman Catholic Experience in the United States." *Review and Expositor* 79, no. 2 (Spring): 199–216.
O'Connor, Flannery
1949 "Wise Blood." In *Three by Flannery O'Connor.* New York: Signet, 1970.
Overdyke, William Darrell
1950 *The Know-Nothing Party in the South.* Baton Rouge: Louisiana State Univ. Press.
Palmer, Gerald B.
1981 "A Homogeneous or a Heterogeneous Church." In *Churches in Racially Changing Communities,* 40–53. Atlanta: Home Mission Board, Southern Baptist Convention.
Parmley, Helen
1985 "Dallas Hour of Power," *Missions/USA,* May–June: 46–52.
Percy, Walker
1979 "Southern Comfort." *Harper's,* Jan.: 79–83.
Peterson, Bill, and Dale Russakoff
1984 "Southern Democrats' Race Fears." *Washington Post National Weekly,* 26 Nov.: 14.
Peterson, Thomas Virgil
1978 *Ham and Japheth: The Mythic World of Whites in the Antebellum South.* American Theological Libraries Association Monograph Series, no. 12. Metuchen, NJ: Scarecrow Press.
Petty, Charles
1979 "Public Policy and the Family." In *Help for Families* (Conference Proceedings). Nashville: Christian Life Commission, Southern Baptist Convention.
Phillips, Kevin P.
1969 *The Emerging Republican Majority.* New Rochelle, NY.: Arlington House.
Pierard, Richard V.
1983 "Reagan and the Evangelicals: the Making of a Love Affair." *Christian Century,* 21–28 Dec.: 1182–85.
Pinnock, Clark
1969 Preface to I. Howard Marshall, *Kept by the Power of God, a Study of Perseverance and Falling Away,* 2nd ed. Minneapolis: Bethany Fellowship, 1974.
Plowman, Edward E.
1980 "Conservative Network Puts Its Stamp on the Southern Baptist Convention." *Christianity Today,* 18 July: 844–45.
Posey, Walter B.
1957 *The Baptist Church in the Lower Mississippi Valley, 1776–1845.* Lexington: Univ. Press of Kentucky.

Potter, C. Burtt, Jr.
   1973   *Baptists: the Passionate People.* Nashville: Broadman.
Putnam, Mary Burnham
   1913   *The Baptists and Slavery, 1840–1845.* Ann Arbor, MI: George Wahr.
Raper, Arthur F.
   1936   *Preface to Peasantry.* New York: Atheneum.
Reavis, Dick J.
   1984   "The Politics of Armageddon." *Texas Monthly*, Oct.. Rpt. in *SBC To-day*, Dec. 1984 and Jan. 1985.
Reed, Roy
   1983   "Mississippi: Twenty Years of Wide Racial Change." *New York Times*, 18 Aug.: B14
Reich, Robert B.
   1984   "The End of Republican Economics." *The New Republic*, 30 Jan: 31–34.
Reichley, A. James
   1985   *Religion in American Public Life.* Washington, D.C.: The Brookings Institution.
Roark, James L.
   1977   *Masters Without Slaves: Southern Planters in the Civil War and Reconstruction.* New York: Norton.
Roof, Wade Clark, and William McKinney
   1987   *American Mainline Religion: Its Changing Shape and Future.* New Brunswick, NJ: Rutgers Univ. Press.
Rose, Larry
   1980   "Perspectives on the Eighties." *Light*, Feb.–March: 6–12.
Sale, Kirkpatrick
   1976   *Power Shift.* New York: Vintage.
Sandeen, Ernest R.
   1970   "Fundamentalism and American Identity." *Annals of the American Academy of Political Science*, vol. 387 (Jan.), 56–65.
Schaeffer, Pamela
   1987   "Baptists: Recent Convention Called Fundamentalist Watershed." *St. Louis Post-Dispatch*, 20 June: 6D.
Schrag, Peter
   1972   "A Hesitant New South: Fragile Promise on the Last Frontier." *Saturday Review*, 12 Feb.: 51–57.
Scudder, C. W.
   1962   *The Family in Christian Perspective.* Nashville: Broadman.
Sernett, Milton C.
   1975   *Black Religion and American Evangelicalism; White Protestants, Plantation Missions and the Flowering of Negro Christianity, 1787–1865.*

American Theological Libraries Association Monograph Series, no. 7. Metuchen, NJ: Scarecrow Press.

Shurden, Walter B.

1978   "The Problem of Authority in the Southern Baptist Convention." *Review and Expositor,* Spring: 220–233.

1979   *Crises in Baptist Life* [pamphlet]. Nashville: Historical Commission, Southern Baptist Convention.

1982   "We are Southern Baptists: Roots and Affirmations." *Church Training,* July: 8–18.

1985   *The Life of Baptists in the Life of the World.* Nashville: Broadman.

Simpson, John H.

1983   "Moral Issues and Status Politics." In *The New Christian Right,* ed. Robert C. Liebman and Robert Wuthnow, 188–206.

1984   "Socio-Moral Issues and the 1980 Presidential Election." Paper presented at the Annual Meeting of the Society for the Scientific Study of Religion, Chicago, 26–28 Oct.

Sinclair, Andrew.

1962   *Era of Excess: A Social History of the Prohibition Movement.* Rpt., New York: Harper Colophon, 1964.

Smith, Cortland Victor

1967   *Church Organization as an Agency of Social Control: Church Discipline in North Carolina, 1800–1860.* Ph.D. diss., University of North Carolina.

Smith, Gaddis

1986   *Morality, Reason and Power: American Diplomacy in the Carter Years.* New York: Hill and Wang.

Smith, Rachel Richardson

1987   "Swordplay in Sunday School." *Newsweek,* 21 Dec.: 9.

Smith, Stephen A.

1985   *Myth, Media, and the Southern Mind.* Fayetteville: Univ. of Arkansas Press.

Soderberg, Kema

1987   "Conservatives Hail Inerrancy Decision." *The News and Observer* [Raleigh, NC], 1 Aug.: 4C.

Sorenson, Theodore

1986   "If You Add Up All Carter's Successes, He Really Wasn't So Good." *Washington Post National Weekly,* 2 June: 35.

Spain, Rufus B.

1967   *At Ease in Zion: Social History of the Southern Baptists, 1865–1900.* Nashville: Vanderbilt Univ. Press.

Stafford, Timothy

1979   "Should the Church Be a Melting Pot? An Interview with C. Peter Wagner and Ray Stedman." *Christianity Today,* 10 Aug.: 11–16.

1984   "Evangelism: the New Wave is a Tidal Wave." *Christianity Today*, 18 May: 42 et seq.

Stampp, Kenneth M.

1969   *The Era of Reconstruction, 1865–1877*. New York: Knopf.

Steel, Ronald

1986   "The Two Carters." Rev. of *Morality, Reason, and Power: American Diplomacy in the Carter Years*, by Gaddis Smith. *Atlantic*, June: 78–80.

Stephenson, Patti

1982   "Journey to Atlanta." *Home Missions*, Sept.–Oct.: 31–38.

Sumerlin, Claude W.

1968   *A History of Southern Baptist State Newspapers*. Ph.D. diss., University of Missouri.

Sunday School Board, Southern Baptist Convention

1986   *Issues Facing Southern Baptists* [Individual Study Guide]. Nashville: Sunday School Board, Southern Baptist Convention.

Sweet, William Warren

1964   *Religion on the American Frontier: The Baptists, 1783–1830*. New York: Cooper Square.

Szasz, Ferenc Morton

1982   *The Divided Mind of Protestant America, 1880–1930*. University: Univ. of Alabama Press.

Tharp, J. Clifford, Jr.

1985   "A Study of the Forced Termination of Southern Baptist Ministries." *Quarterly Review* 46, no. 1 (Oct.–Dec.): 50–56.

Thompson, C. Lacy

1987   "Peace Report Represents Hope for Convention, Sullivan Says." *Biblical Recorder* [NC], 8 Aug.: 12.

Thompson, James J., Jr.

1974   "Southern Baptist City and Country Churches in the Twenties." *Foundations* 17, no. 4 (Oct.–Dec.): 351–363.

1982   *Tried as by Fire—Southern Baptists and the Religious Controversies of the Twenties*. Macon, GA: Mercer Univ. Press.

Tilton, Nelson

1976   "The Homogeneous Unit Principle: a Positive Perspective." In *Churches in Racially Changing Communities*, 71–94. Atlanta: Home Mission Board, Southern Baptist Convention.

Tindall, George Brown

1967   *The Emergence of the New South, 1913–1945*. Vol. 10 of *A History of the South*. Baton Rouge: Louisiana State Univ. Press.

1976   *The Ethnic Southerners*. Baton Rouge: Louisiana State Univ. Press.

Tull, James E.
1960   *A Study of Southern Baptist Landmarkism in the Light of Historical Baptist Ecclesiology*. Ph.D. diss., Columbia University.
1975   "The Landmark Movement: An Historical and Theological Appraisal." *Baptist History and Heritage* 10, no. 1 (Jan.): 3-18.

Underwood, Kenneth
1957   *Protestant and Catholic*. Boston: Beacon.

Valentine, Foy
1949   *A Historical Study of Southern Baptists and Race Relations, 1917-1947*. Thesis, Southwestern Baptist Theological Seminary, 1949. Rpt., New York: Arno, 1980.
1979   "Baptist Polity and Social Pronouncements." *Baptist History and Heritage* 14, no. 3 (July): 52-61.

Vance, Rupert B., and Nicholas J. Demerath, eds.
1954   *The Urban South*. Chapel Hill: Univ. of North Carolina Press.

Vines, William D. D.
1912   "The Place of the South in Religious Life of the Nation." In *The Home Missions Task*, ed. Victor I. Masters, 129-52.

Wagner, C. Peter
1981   *Church Growth and the Whole Gospel*. San Francisco: Harper and Row.

Wald, Kenneth D.
1987   *Religion and Politics in the United States*. New York: St. Martin's.

Waldman, Peter
1988   "Holy War: Fundamentalists Fight to Capture the Soul of Southern Baptists." *Wall Street Journal*, 7 March: 1.

Wall, James
1985   "Jimmy Carter, Religion and Public Service." *Christian Century*, 8 May: 459-60.

Wallace, Anthony F. C.
1966   *Religion: an Anthropological View*, New York: Random House.

Wallis, Jim, and Wes Michaelson
1976   "The Plan to Save America." *Sojourners*, April: 5-12.

Welter, Barbara
1966   "The Cult of True Womanhood, 1820-1860." *American Quarterly* 18, no. 2. pt. 1: 151-74. Rpt. in *The American Family in Social-Historical Perspective*, ed. Michael Gordon. New York: St. Martin's, 1973.

White, Leslie A.
1959   *The Evolution of Culture*. New York: McGraw-Hill.

Wilkey, Jay
1976   "Music and the Making of a Nation, 1620-1776." *Review and Expositor* 23, no. 1 (Winter): 33-45.

Wilkins, Roger

    1984   "Smiling Racism." *The Nation,* 3 Nov.: 437.

Williams, George H.

    1971   "The Chaplaincy in the Armed Forces of the United States of America in Historical and Ecclesiological Perspective." In *Military Chaplains,* ed. Harvey Cox, 11–58. New York: American Report Press.

Wills, Garry

    1969   *Nixon Agonistes.* New York: Signet, 1971.

    1976   "The Plains Truth." *Atlantic,* June: 49–54.

Wilson, Charles Reagan

    1980   *Baptized in Blood: the Religion of the Lost Cause, 1865–1920.* Athens: Univ. of Georgia Press.

Winter, Gibson

    1961   *The Suburban Captivity of the Churches: an Analysis of Protestant Responsibility in the Expanding Metropolis.* Garden City, NY: Doubleday.

Witcover, Jules

    1977   *Marathon: the Pursuit of the Presidency, 1972–1976.* New York: Viking.

Woodward, Kenneth *et al.*

    1976   "Born Again!: the Year of the Evangelicals," *Newsweek* 25 Oct.: 68–78.

Wyatt-Brown, Bertram

    1970   "The Antimission Movement in the Jacksonian South; a Study in Regional Folk Culture." *Journal of Southern History* 36, no. 4 (Nov.): 501–29.

Yance, Norman A.

    1978   *Religion Southern Style: Southern Baptists and Society in Historical Perspective.* Perspectives in Religious Studies, Special Studies Series, no. 4. Danville, VA: Association of Baptist Professors of Religion.

Young, Percy Deane

    1982   *God's Bullies.* New York: Holt, Rinehart, and Winston.

Index

Abington School District v. Schempp, 186

abolition, 155

abortion, 9, 92, 148, 157, 177, 184, 188; as New Right issue, 192, 199, 201, 210, 212

About This Thing Called Dating, 120

"Abstract of Principles." *See* Articles of Faith

Acquired Immune Deficiency Syndrome, 158–59. *See also* AIDS

Adam, 136, 204

affirmative action, 188

Agee, James, 45

agriculture, commercialization of, 27

AIDS, 201

Alabama Baptist, 41, 139, 163

alcohol, 155. *See also* liquor

Alcoholics Anonymous, 108

Alley, Robert, 207

American Baptist Convention, 150. *See also* Northern Baptists

American Coalition for Traditional Values, 195

American Council of Christian Churches, 150

American Enterprise Institute, 181, 190

American Historical Review, 52

American Independent Party, 188

American Legislative Exchange Council, 187, 188

American Protestantism, 136

American Public Health Asociacion, 156

American Revolution, 23, 27; southward migration after, 23

Ammerman, Nancy, 209

Amway, 190, 194

Anabaptism, 21, 34

Anderson, John, 192

Anglicans, 22

Annuity Board, 58, 207

Anti-Saloon League, 160

Anti-Slavery Society, 30–31

Apartheid, South African, 112

Arkansas State Convention, 140, 141

Armed Forces, 165

Armstrong, Annie, 87, 89

Armstrong, William, 192

Articles of Faith, 80, 104

Asociacion Bautista, 113

association, district. *See* district association

Association of Southern Baptist Colleges, 93

Atlanta *Journal* and *Constitution*, 194, 198

Auburn University, 98

baby boom, 109, 117

Bach, Johann Sebastian, 170

Bailey, Josiah, 94
Baker, Jim, 193
Bakker, Jim, 201
baptism: practices of, 21; practices of (illus.), 145
Baptist Adults, III
Baptist Bible Fellowship, 180
Baptist colleges, 69, 71
Baptist Faith and Fellowship, 187
Baptist General Convention of Texas, 15
Baptist History and Heritage, 94
Baptist Joint Committee on Public Affairs, 92, 149, 193, 199
Baptist Journal, 187, 191
"Baptist Lobby," 92
Baptist Press, 59, 208
Baptist Program, 59
Baptist Standard, 15, 205
Baptist Student Union, 121
Baptist Training Union, 102, 163
Baptist University for Women, 26
Baptist World Alliance, 95, 149, 164
Baptist Young People's Union, 45
Baptists: in American Revolution, 23; basic principles of, 23; conservative, 3; early population statistics of, 22–23, 24; first congregation of, 21; first missionary society, 68; lay preaching and, 22; Northern, 3; sermon styles and, 24–25; Southern. *See* Southern Baptists; theological differences in early sects, 22.
Barren Ground, 44–45
Barth, Karl, 135
Barton, A. J., 91, 160
Baylor University, 46, 94, 96, 155
Berne, Eric, 126
Bible Schools, 85
Biblical literalism, 7, 12
Biblical Recorder, 26, 94, 138, 155
Bilbo, Theodore, 2
Bill of Rights, 143
Birch, John, 3
birth control, 156. *See also* contraception

Birth of a Nation, 95
Bisagno, John, 19
Black Codes, 35
Blacks: influence on Southern Baptist music, 171; segregation and, 6; Southern Baptist church growth and, 74; as Southern Baptist missionaries, 69; Southern Baptist seminaries and, 81; treatment in the South, 50; treatment of, by Southern Baptist congregations, 39; voting rights and, 41. *See also* racism
Blackwell, Morton, 192, 193
Blount, Roy, 189
Board of Deacons, 104
Board of Elders, 104
Bob Jones Controversy, 189
Bond, Julian, 189
Bork, Robert, 201
Bread for the World, 154
Bright, Bill, 187, 191, 211
Broadman Press, 76, 140, 166, 207
Broadus, John, 79
Brookings Institution, 181
Brooks, Samuel Palmer, 94
Brotherhood Commission, 89–90
Brown University, 25, 26
Brown v. Board of Education, 8, 47, 49, 147, 165, 166, 184, 185
Brunner, Emil, 135
Bryan, William Jennings, 137
Bryant, Anita, 3, 157, 189
Buckley, William F., 181, 188
Bultmann, Rudolf, 135
Burriss, Bryant, 24
Bush, George, 193, 195, 211
busing, 181, 188
Byrd, Robert, 2

Calvin, John, 170
Calvinism, 21
Campbell, Alexander, 30
Campbell, Thomas, 29
Campbell, Will, 3, 142
Cambellites, 29, 30, 32, 68, 136, 142, 204; defection of Baptists to, 30

Campus Crusade for Christ, 187
Carey, William, 28, 68
Carroll, B. H., 135
Carter, Jimmy, 3, 47, 74, 130, 175–79, 188, 189, 192, 193; as author, 76
Carter, Rosalynn, 123, 124, 175, 179
Catholicism, European, 170
CBS-TV, 83, 152
Charleston, S. C., 25
child abuse, 159
Choice, Not an Echo, A, 186
Christian Century, 143, 154
Christian Embassy, 187
Christian Freedom Foundation, 190
Christian Frontiers, 161
Christian Index, 32, 160
Christian Life Commission, 53, 91–93, 107, 126, 130, 148, 154, 189, 199, 202; and civil rights, 165–68; conference, 184
Christian Reconstruction Movement, 203
Christian Voice, 190, 211
Christianity Today, 187
Church Growth Movement, 109, 111, 113
church-state separation, 146–48, 214
Cincinnati, Ohio, 22
civil rights, 154, 168, 188, 210
Civil Rights Restoration Act, 201
Civil War, 15, 29, 40, 50, 71, 79, 140, 160, 171; Black defection from Southern Baptist churches after, 38; economic impact on Southern Baptists, 38; slaveholders exemption from, 37; Southern Baptist migration to American Southwest after, 38
Clansman, 95
Clayton, Lynn, 209
Cleveland, Grover, 189
Cochran, Thad, 2, 183, 190
Cold War, 48
Collins, Martha Layne, 2
Colson, Chuck, 107
Columbia Baptist Church, 107

Columbia University, 182
Committee for the Survival of a Free Congress, 181, 187
Confederate Army, 36
Congress, U.S., 148, 154
Congressional Club, 211
Conlan, John, 187, 191
Connally, John B., 183, 192
Conservative Baptists, 3
Conservative Caucus, 187
Conservative Digest, 182, 187
Constitution, 143, 148, 159, 181
contraception, 42, 89, 155
Cooperative Program, 56, 57, 108, 207
Couch, William T., 47
Council for National Policy, 203
Cox, Harvey, 3, 180, 210
Crane, Philip, 192
creationism, 192
Creek Indians, 26
Criswell, W. A., 16, 18, 103, 167, 184, 186, 187, 188, 191, 194, 207
Criswell Center for Biblical Studies, 86, 184
Culture in the South, 47.

Dabney, Virginius, 139
Dallas, First Baptist Church of, 16–18, 101, 114, 136, 152, 167, 184, 194
Davidson, Robert Lee, 163
Davis, Jefferson, 36
Dawson, J. M., 114, 147
Democratic Party, 3, 41, 127, 183, 195, 212
Depression, 8, 46, 139, 156
desegregation, 181
Disciples of Christ, 29, 111
Dissenters, 21
district associations, functions of, 99
divorce, 89, 155
Dixon, Greg, 180, 195
Dixon, Thomas, 95
Domestic Mission Board, 28, 31, 36. *See also* Home Mission Board
Dorsey, Willa, 181

Draper, James, 64, 66, 148, 185, 193, 194, 201, 207, 211
Drinan, Robert F., 190

Eagle Forum, 186
Education Commission, 93, 138
Edwards, Jonathan, 22
Eisenhower, Dwight D., 166, 185
Elliott, Ralph, 139, 140
Ellis, Havelock, 128
Emancipation, 35
Emory University, 209
endogamy, 115
Engel v. Vitale, 186
English Reformation, 21
English Revolution, 23
Episcopalians, 2, 14, 57
Equal Employment Opportunity, 92
Equal Rights Amendment, 157, 186, 188, 192
Erasmus, Desiderius, 142
Ethics of Jesus and Social Progress, 153
European Catholicism, 170
Evangelical Protestantism, 25
Evangelicals, participation in politics, 212
Eve, 136, 204
Evolution, theory of, 137, 139, 153, 204

Faith and Message Statement, 140, 147, 209
Falwell, Jerry, 3, 180, 181, 183–84, 189, 191, 192, 193, 197, 199, 210, 211, 212, 214
Faulkner, William, 45
Federal Council of Churches, 90, 150
feminism, 181
Fiddler on the Roof, 111
First Amendment, 23, 146, 147
Flynt, J. Wayne, 98
Ford, Gerald R., 188
Foreign Mission Board, 28, 31, 46, 68, 70–75, 114, 138, 152, 194, 198
Fosdick, Harry Emerson, 3
Fourteenth Amendment, 182

Freud, Sigmund, 128
Fuller Theological Seminary, 110–12
Fundamentalists, 135, 143, 209; defined, 13; geographic centers of, 13
Furman, Richard, 25, 28
Furman University, 79, 96

Gamble, Clarence, 157
gambling, 91
Gambrell, James B., 43, 163
Gardner, Charles Spurgeon, 153
Gay Rights movement, 157, 189, 190
Genesis Commission, 199
Georgetown College, 28
Gephardt, Richard, 2
GI Bill, 47, 117, 147
Gingrich, Newton, 2, 183
Glasgow, Ellen, 45
glossolalia, 204
"God and Politics," 203
God's Way to Health, Wealth and Wisdom, 213
Goffman, Erving, 108
Goldwater, Barry, 186
Gore, Albert, Jr., 2
Graham, Billy, 3, 23, 152, 187, 201
Gramm, Philip, 183
Graves, James R., 32, 34
Great Awakening, 22, 23, 26
Great Race Settlement, 6, 8
Great Revival, 24, 171
Greeley, Andrew, 128
Griffith, D. W., 95
gun control, 188
Guth, James, 209

Habitat for Humanity, 47
Hamilton, Charles V., 182
Hansen, Marcus, 168
Harvard Divinity School, 3, 210
Hastey, Stan, 208
Hatfield, Mark, 3, 187
Hays, Brooks, 2, 66, 166
Head Start, 181, 182
Helms, Jesse, 2, 6, 183, 188, 190, 191, 192, 195, 201, 211

Herberg, Will, 111
Heritage Foundation, 181, 187
High Hills, S. C., 25
Hireling Ministry None of Christ's, A, 78
Historical Commission, 51–52, 94
Hobbs, Herschel, 176, 209
Hodge, Ray, 53
Holman Publishers, 76
Holocaust, 153
Home Mission Board, 15, 37, 46, 70–75, 84, 100, 172, 187, 199, 204–5; on pluralism, 111. *See also* Domestic Mission Board
Home Mission Society, 39
Homogeneous Unit Principle, 111–12
homosexuality, 10, 17, 85, 89, 157, 181, 189, 201, 204
Hough, Joseph, 117
hunger, world, 91
Hunt, Bunker, 195, 207
Hustler, 130

I'll Take My Stand, 47
illiteracy, 138, 141
Inerrancy, 134, 194
Inerrantists, 65, 67, 191, 208
Institute of Church Growth, 110
Institute of Policy Studies, 6
Internal Revenue Service, 52, 148
Interracial Commission, 95

Jackson, Jesse, 3
James, Jesse, 3
Jarmin, Gary, 190, 195
Jehovah's Witnesses, 151
Jent, John, 46
Johnson, Gerald, 155
Johnson, Lady Bird, 124
Johnson, Livingston, 138
Johnson, Lyndon B., 186
Johnson, W. B., 54, 68
Johnston, Bennett, 2
Joint Committee, 207
Jones, M. Ashby, 95
Jordan, Barbara, 3

Jordan, Clarence, 47
Journal of Southern History, 47

Kaemmerling, Russell, 187, 194
Kemp, Jack, 211
Kennedy, John F., 147, 181, 186, 189
Kennedy, Joseph, Sr., 146
Kennedy, Robert F., 167, 186
Kent, Barbara, 120
Kent, Dan, 120
Kerala, India, 109–10, 114
King, Martin Luther, Jr., 6, 166–67, 177, 186, 189
Kinsey, Alfred, 128
Know-Nothings, 32–33
Knox, John, 170
Koinonia Community, 47
Korea, 48
Ku Klux Klan, 96, 162
Kudzu, 3

LaHaye, Tim, 128, 180, 195, 211
Lance, Bert, 178
Landmarkism, 68, 94, 136, 149; appeal of, 34; basic tenets of, 34
Laymen's Missionary Movement, 90
Leland, John, 143
Leonard, Bill, 143
Liberty Federation, 210
Light, 92, 168
Lindsell, Harold, 187
liquor, 42, 47, 91, 160. *See also* alcohol
Long, Gillis, 2
Lott, Trent, 2, 183
Luther, Martin, 142, 170
Luther Rice Seminary, 86
Lutheran Church of America, 57

McAteer, Ed, 187, 190–93, 201
McCarthy, Joseph, 48, 147
McClellan, John, 2
McDaniels, George, 35
McGavran, Donald, 109, 110

McPherson, Aimee Semple, 23
Maddox, Lester, 2, 188
Madison, James, 23, 143, 207
Malcolm, Howard, 28
Manly, Basil, 163
Mannheim, Karl, 214
Marius, Richard, 207
Marlette, Doug, 3
Martin, T. T., 137, 138
Marx, Karl, 17
Masons, 25
Masters, Victor I., 22, 24, 46, 137
Mayflower, 21
Meese Commission on Pornography,
    159, 198
Mencken, H. L., 138
Mercer, Jesse, 26
Mercer University, 26, 96
Meredith, Thomas, 25
Message of Genesis, 139
Methodist Episcopal Church, 30
Methodists, 2, 13, 22, 24, 29, 31;
    slavery and, 28, 206
Mexican War, 15
Mid-American Baptist Theological
    Seminary, 86
Middle Ages, 109
Mission Board: domestic, 28, 31, 36;
    foreign, 28, 31
Mondale, Walter F., 196
Moody, Dale, 140, 141
Moody, Dwight, 23, 71
Moon, Lottie, 54, 89
Moon, Sun Myung, 148
Mooneyham, Lamarr, 195
Moonies, 212
Moore, Sam, 201
Moore, Winfred, 196, 197
Moral Majority, 190, 192, 193, 194,
    195; relationship to Southern Bap-
    tist Convention, 210
More, Thomas, 207
Morgan, Marabel, 128
Mormons, 98, 151, 152, 212
Morris, Orrin, 74
Moyers, Bill, 3, 120, 175, 203

Mullins, E. Y., 135, 139, 153, 206
National Association for the Advance-
    ment of Colored People (NAACP),
    11, 92, 186
National Association of Evangelicals,
    151, 191, 195
National Committee for an Effective
    Congress, 181
National Council of Catholic Bishops,
    153
National Council of Churches, 109,
    150, 153
National Humanities Center, 5
National Prayer Breakfast, 187
National Religious Broadcasters, 195
National Review, 181, 188
National Youth Administration, 147
New (Christian) Right, 92, 93, 148. *See
    also* New Religious Political Right
New Deal, 46, 164
New Religious Political Right
    (NRPR), 5, 9, 10, 181–214
New Testament, 10
New York Review of Books, 17
Newsweek, 15, 82
Nicene Creed, 204
Nixon, Richard M., 148, 181, 186
Norris, Frank, 15
North American Baptist Fellowship,
    149
North Carolina Evangelism Con-
    ference, 124, 126, 172
Northampton, Mass., 22
Northern Baptists, 3, 39, 71, 75, 100,
    206. *See also* American Baptist
    Convention
Novak, Michael, 190

O'Connor, Sandra Day, 193
Odum, Howard, 47
Old Testament, 10, 20
Origin of Species, 137

Papal Coronation, 146
Paris, Ky., 24
Parks, Rosa, 166

Passman, Otto, 2
Patman, Wright, 2
Patterson, Paige, 184, 191, 194, 199, 200
Peace Committee, 197, 198, 199, 200. 204, 205, 208
peace and disarmament, 91
Peale, Norman Vincent, 23
Pendleton, James, 28
People Called Baptists, 35
Pepper, Claude, 2
Perkins, Carl, 2
Phillips, Howard, 187
Pierard, Richard, 187
Playboy, 188
Pleitz, James, Rev., 124
Pope Leo XIII, 95
Populism, 6, 41
pornography, 159, 181, 198
Porter, J. W., 137
Posey, Walter B., 23
Poteat, Edwin McNeill, 47, 160
Poteat, William L., 44, 135, 137, 138
Powell, Jody, 3
Powell, William A. (Bill), Sr., 187, 191
prayer in school, 9, 130, 143, 149, 181, 184, 186, 193, 210, 212
Presbyterians, 14, 24, 29, 31
Pressler, Paul, 184, 187, 191, 194, 200
primary group, 115
Progressive Movement, 41
Prohibition, 137, 161
Prohibition Movement, 42, 43
prostitution, 42
Protestantism, 20–21; American, 136, 149
PTL Ministry, 201
Public Affairs Briefings, 192
Public Affairs Committee, 92, 199, 201
Puritans, 21

Quarterly Review, 57

racism, 5, 185, 212
Radio and Television Commission, 93

Rauschenbusch, Walter, 42
Reagan, Nancy, 191
Reagan, Ronald W., 6, 146, 159, 181, 183, 186, 188, 192–99
Reconstruction, 40
Reeve, J. J., 135
Reformation, 12, 21, 54, 140, 141, 204
Rehnquist, William, 186, 190
Religious Roundtable, 190, 192, 194, 195
Republican Party, 183, 185, 211
Republican Platform Committee, 195
Review and Expositor, 52, 83
Revolution: American, 23, 27; English, 23
Richmond, University of, 96
Right-to-Life movement, 59, 157
Robertson, Pat, 3, 127, 183, 188, 191, 193, 196, 201, 209, 211, 214
Robinson, Robert, 143
Robison, James, 190, 191, 192
Rockefeller, John D., 3
Roe v. Wade, 187
Rogers, Adrian, 66, 67, 170, 184, 185, 187, 191, 192, 193, 197, 198, 208, 213
Rogers, Joyce, 64
Rogers, Will, 173
Roman Catholics, 2, 13, 20, 127, 142, 151
Romo, Oscar, 74
Roosevelt, Theodore, 155
Rotary Club, 207
Royal Ambassadors, 121
Rusher, William, 188

Salem Academy, 26
Sanger, Margaret, 156
Sankey, Ira, 23, 71
Scarborough, L. R., 139
Schindler, Alexander, 152
Schlafly, Phyllis, 186, 192
school prayer. *See* prayer in school
Scopes trial, 136
Second World War. *See* World War II
Secular Humanist Bulletin, 83
Seeds, 154

Segregation, 9, 165
Selma, Ala., 190
separation of church and state. *See*
   church-state separation
"700 Club," 196
Seventh Day Adventists, 57
sexism, 5
Sexual Intimacy, 128
Shakers, 30
Shakespeare, William, 134
sharecropping, 40
Shaw, Bernard, 78
slaves and slavery, 12, 26, 27–28, 30
Smith, Al, 146
Smith, Bailey, 64, 66, 152, 175, 185,
   192, 193, 194, 200, 201, 207
Smith, Lillian, 163
Social Gospel, 42, 89, 91, 135, 153,
   161
Social Security, 46, 58, 92, 147
Social Service Commission, 91, 155,
   156, 160; on the Ku Klux Klan,
   163; on Prohibition, 161; on
   segregation, 164
Social Service and Temperance Com-
   mittee, 91
Sojourners, 151, 187
South: blacks and, 5, 6;
   distinguishing factors of, 5;
   economic development of, after
   Civil War, 44; ideologies of, 5, 6;
   social progress in, 6;
   socioeconomic factors and, 5;
   urbanization in, 48
South Carolina College, 25
South Carolina Convention, 39
Southern Baptist Alliance, 202
Southern Baptist Brotherhood, 192
Southern Baptist churches: changes in
   racial composition, 102; complex
   structure of, 103, 105; integration
   of, 114; role of pastor in, 102–3
Southern Baptist Convention: annual
   meeting described, 60–68; annual
   meeting functions, 62; annual
   meeting sites, 64; black churches

Southern Baptist Convention (*continued*)
   in, 114; black participation in,
   114–15; blacks and, 67; description
   of, 6, 7; Executive Committee of,
   56, 65, 196; fundamentalist
   influence in, 8, 9, 86; goals of, 7;
   messengers, 62–63, 65; moderate
   faction within, 196, 202, 214;
   recent presidents of, 185; Resolutions Committee of, 65, 67, 198; as
   a sociological experience, 59; vice-
   presidents of, 67
Southern Baptist Foundation, 58
Southern Baptist Peace Movement,
   154
Southern Baptist seminaries, 7, 19,
   46, 78–86, 206–8
Southern Baptist Theological
   Seminary, 34, 79
Southern Baptists: anti–Roman
   Catholic sentiment and, 146–48,
   149;2 anti-slavery sentiment and,
   28, 30–31; attitude toward blacks,
   112–13, 205; attitude toward
   divorce, 126; attitude toward evolution; 46; attitude toward Israel,
   112; attitude toward sexuality,
   129–30; centralization, 29; Civil
   War and, 35–36; class conflict and,
   50; class structure and, 1, 14; Confederacy support and, 37; congregational treatment of blacks, 39;
   Denominational Calendar, 59;
   denominational statistics, 1;
   differences from American Baptists, 150; educational achievement
   and, 1; homogeneity among, 111,
   112, 116; ideological dilemmas of,
   7; individual rights and, 52; Landmark influences on, 34–35;
   political party migration and, 183;
   politicians, 2–3; power of, 1;
   prayer and, 173–75; as Protestants,
   20; race and racial identity, 111;
   regional distinctions of the South
   and, 14; response to physical and

Southern Baptists (*continued*)
natural science advances, 135;
socioeconomic status and, 26–27;
split from Baptist roots, 214; split
from northern Baptists, 31; status
anxiety and, 32; urban settings
and, 45; white solidarity and, 1,
14, 40, 42, 213
Southern Baptists for Life, 157
Southwestern Journal of Theology, 84
Southwestern Seminary, Hispanic
branch, 86
Stanley, Charles, 67, 185, 187, 191,
192, 193, 194, 211
Stanton, Elizabeth Cady, 136
State Conventions: basic functions of,
95–98; role in colleges, 96
Statement of Faith, 138
Stewardship Commission, 58
Stone, Barton, 30
Strong, Josiah, 108
Suburban Captivity of the Churches,
116
Suburbanization, effect on churches,
116–19
Successionism, 34
Sumerlin, Claude W., 146
Sunbeams, 119
Sunbelt, 50, 182
Sunday, Billy, 23
Sunday School, 52, 102; sex segrega-
tion in, 119
Sunday School Board, 46, 55, 57, 75,
76, 112, 140; fundamentalist
pressure upon, 77; publications
and publishing, 76
Supreme Court, 8, 48, 143, 148, 157,
165, 187, 193, 201
Swaggart, Jimmy, 195
Syrian Christian Church, 10

Talmadge, Gene, 2
Talmadge, Herman, 2
Teasdale, Thomas C., 75
televangelists, 214
television ministries, 109, 184

Temperance Commission, 91
temperance movement, 155
Tennessee Baptist, 32–33
Texas, University of, 148
Texas Anti-Saloon League, 91
Third Century Publishers, 187
Third World, 70
Thomas, Dylan, 176
Thomas Nelson Publishers, 201
Thompson, Virgil, 3
Thurmond, Strom, 2, 107, 183, 185, 186
Tichenor, Isaac T., 37, 75
Time, 82
tobacco, 160–61
Total Woman, 128
Triennial Convention, 28, 31, 55
Truett, George Washington, 15, 16
Truman, Harry S., 2, 165, 185
tuition tax credits, 146

Unification Church, 151
United Church of Christ, 57
United Nations, 54–55

Vatican, 146, 151
Vietnam War, 154, 186, 190
Viguerie, Richard, 181, 182, 187
Vines, Jerry, 67, 185, 200, 203, 209
voter registration, 195
Voting Rights Act, 186

Wagner, C. Peter, 112
Wake Forest College, 26, 135, 155
Wake Forest University, 96, 130
Wallace, George, 177, 186, 188
Wallace, Henry, 185
War Between the States. *See* Civil War
Watergate, 187, 188
Watson, J. B., 3
Wayland Baptist College, 165
Welty, Eudora, 45
Western Baptist Theological Institute, 78
Western Recorder, 137
Weyrich, Paul, 181, 187
White, Mark, 2
White Citizens Council, 11

"White flight," 49, 117, 118
Whitsitt, William H., 34
Why Not the Best?, 76
Williams, Charles B., 135
Williams, Roger, 78
Wilson, Edward O., 3
Wilson, Woodrow, 95
Winter, Gibson, 116
Woman's Missionary Union, 57, 87–90, 96, 98, 104, 108, 111, 127, 166, 198, 200; blacks in, 114, 200; fund-raising efforts of, 89
Women: in higher education, 155; lay, 86–87; ordination of, 194; as Southern Baptist missionaries, 69; as Southern Baptist pastors, 127; suffrage movement, 41

Women in Ministry, 200
Women's Christian Temperance Union, 160
Women's Suffrage movement, 41, 86, 88–89, 155
World Marxist Review, 83
World War I, 37, 43, 74, 135, 137, 150, 154
World War II, 8, 47, 92, 139, 150, 154, 185

Year of the Bible, 194
Yearbook of American and Canadian Churches, 57
Young, Andrew, 189
Young, Ed, 19, 209, 211
Young Americans for Freedom, 181

The Southern Baptists was designed by Dariel Mayer, composed by Lithocraft, Inc., and printed and bound by Braun-Brumfield, Inc. The book is set in Plantin. Text stock is 60–lb. Glatfelter Natural Smooth.